Aid That Works

Aid That Works

Successful Development in Fragile States

James Manor, Editor

 **THE WORLD BANK**

ISBN-10: 0-8213-6201-1
ISBN-13: 978-0-8213-6201-3
eISBN: 0-8213-6202-X
DOI: 10.1596/978-0-821-6201-3

Cover photo: Paula Bronstein/Getty Images
Cover design: Naylor Design, Inc.

Library of Congress Cataloging-in-Publication Data
Aid that works: successful development in fragile states / James Manor [editor].
    p. cm. – (Directions in development)
Includes bibliographical references and index.
ISBN-13: 978-0-8213-6201-3
ISBN-10: 0-8213-6201-1
    1. Economic development projects—Developing countries—Case studies. I. Manor, James.
II. Series: Directions in development (Washington, DC)

HC59.72.E44A345 2006
338.910117'4—dc22   2006045197

Contents

Boxes

Figures

Tables

Preface

This book is about achieving development success in states that represent some of the most intractable development challenges. Fragile states are those suffering from multiple points of stress—weak institutions and capacity, and vulnerability to conflict. They are home to some of the world's poorest citizens, with twice the income poverty and child mortality rates of other low-income countries. In addition to the poverty of their own citizens, these countries also pose a risk of negative spillovers for their neighbors and the wider global community, through spread of conflict and organized crime, refugee flows, epidemic diseases, and barriers to trade and investment.

While the challenge is clear, the means to resolve the complex web of problems facing fragile states is far from clear. This is partly the result of their other key characteristics: a dearth of institutional capacity with which to deliver basic services such as health care and education, to control corruption, or to inspire confidence among the citizenry in the state. Insecurity in remote regions of fragile states can also obstruct nongovernmental organizations (NGOs) from substituting for this state capacity and can lead to deteriorating human vulnerability in these areas. Furthermore, poorly performing states risk becoming "aid orphans" in a world that rewards good performers. Development policy makers in headquarters do not want to support—or be perceived to support—corrupt states with weak institutions and instability.

All this means that finding a way to support development progress in fragile states is a pressing challenge. This volume is a step, we hope, toward identifying programs that work in fragile states. In it, the authors describe projects from the planning stage, through implementation, to results monitoring in order to be able to identify both what kind of success they had and what factors contributed to that success. In spite of the geographic and sectoral range of the case studies, there are some emerging lessons for practitioners that all the cases support and that builds on the principle for international engagement in fragile states established by the Organisation for Economic Co-operation and Development Development Assistance Committee (OECD DAC) members (see Principle 9).

First, although no criteria were set in advance about the type of project that might work, successful initiatives demonstrate a strong reliance on local institutions. In this, they attempt to balance the two basic objectives that are characteristic of fragile state interventions: capacity building for sustainable development on the one hand, and the delivery of visible and rapid results on the other. Visible results are critical to stabilize fragile transitions. Where national institutions have collapsed or are very weak, local level initiatives may have a comparative advantage in delivering quick, visible results that use and build local capacities. Entry points and modalities

---

Principle 9: OECD DAC Principles for Good International Engagement in Fragile States[a]

Mix and sequence aid instruments to fit the context. Fragile states require a mix of aid instruments, including, in particular for countries in promising but high-risk transitions, support to recurrent financing. Instruments to provide long-term support to health, education and other basic services are needed in countries facing stalled or deteriorating governance—but careful consideration must be given to how service delivery channels are designed to avoid long-term dependence on parallel, unsustainable structures while at the same time providing sufficient scaling up to meet urgent basic and humanitarian needs. A vibrant civil society is important for healthy government and may also play a critical transitional role in providing services, particularly when the government lacks will and/or capacity.

a. OECD DAC members endorsed 12 principles in January 2005. The principles were discussed with leaders of fragile states in March 2005 and are being piloted in some countries.

for local level service delivery are highly country- and context-specific and depend on a sensitive reading of what will work in the local context, so there are no easily generalized principles. However, what is critical is that these cases show that where the effort is made, it *is* feasible to deliver tangible results—and, therefore, to translate the principle quoted in the box into action.

The second part of OECD-DAC's Principle 9 relates to scaling up and the sustainability of institution building. Bypassing central government is not a sustainable approach, especially when international objectives should be to build and support viable sovereign states that have the capacity to deliver services throughout their territories. The cases studied here are notable for the effort taken during planning and implementation to engage with local government institution-building and central government sectoral policy and capacity. They show that while reliance on community-level and nongovernment institutions may be critical to achieve results and ringfence funds from risks of financial abuse, engagement with local, provincial, and central state structures is key for long-term peace building and state building.

Early allocation of a policy, prioritization, or coordinating role to state structures allows the state to take credit for results achieved, even though state treasury systems do not control disbursements in the early stages of project delivery. This approach helps create legitimacy for a state recovering after conflict because it ensures that government is perceived to be delivering positive benefits to the population. In addition, early engagement with state structures creates openings to build public administration capacity, providing a platform for transition from community and nongovernment services to an appropriate long-term role for the state in service delivery. Next, creating links between local state structures, communities, and civil society maximizes the chances for successful scale-up by creating a community of local stakeholders with an interest in—and increasing capacity for—continuing and extending governance and service delivery improvements. Finally, early involvement of state structures can help avoid destructive dynamics of competition between government and nongovernment institutions for resources.

While the cases in this volume do not cover the full range of assistance modality, country type, or intervention sectors, we hope they do in fact move the debate from principles of engagement to program implementation. The cases underline that a variety of approaches, rather than a single model, can work. They present a more hopeful picture of development interventions in fragile states: given careful program design, tangible success not only is achievable but also can itself generate positive externalities, especially in the governance sphere, beyond stated objectives.

Sarah Cliffe, Head
Fragile States Group, World Bank

Contributors

Martin Greeley is a fellow at the Institute of Development Studies, University of Sussex.

Caroline Hughes is a lecturer at the Department of Political Science, University of Birmingham.

Fidelx Pius Kulipossa is a senior researcher for Gabinete de Consultoria e Apoio à Pequena Indústria (Unit for Consultancy and Assistance to Small Industries) in Mozambique.

Sarah Lister is a research fellow at the Institute of Development Studies, University of Sussex.

James Manor is director of the Civil Society and Governance Program at the Institute of Development Studies, University of Sussex.

Mark Robinson is a research fellow at the Institute of Development Studies, University of Sussex.

Andrew Rosser is a fellow at the Institute of Development Studies, University of Sussex.

Abbreviations

AKDN	Aga Khan Development Network
BRAC	Bangladesh Rural Advancement Committee
CAP	Community Action Program
CARERE	Cambodia Area Rehabilitation and Regeneration Project
CBO	community-based organization
CDC	Commune Development Committee
CDRN	Community Development Resource Network
CEFORD	Community Empowerment for Rural Development
CFET	Consolidated Fund for East Timor
CGAP	Consultative Group to Assist the Poor
CPIA	Country Policy and Institutional Assessment
CPMC	Community Project Management Committee
CPP	Cambodian People's Party
DSS	Direct Support to Schools
ESSP	Education Sector Strategic Plan
FUNCINPEC	National Front for an Independent, Peaceful, and Cooperative Cambodia
GTZ	German Agency for Technical Cooperation
HIPC	Heavily Indebted Poor Countries
HSRDP	Health Sector Rehabilitation and Development Project
IDA	International Development Agency/Association

IDPs	internally displaced persons
IFAD	International Fund for Agricultural Development
IHA	Interim Health Authority
ILO	International Labour Organization
INTERFET	International Force for East Timor
LGDP	Local Government Development Program
LICUS	low-income countries under stress
LRA	Lord's Resistance Army
MFI	microfinance institution
MISFA	Microfinance Investment and Support Facility
NADK	National Army of Democratic Kampuchea
NGOs	nongovernmental organizations
NUMU	NUSAF Management Unit
NURP	Northern Uganda Rehabilitation Project
NUSAF	Northern Uganda Social Action Fund
OPM	Office of the Prime Minister
PLG	Partnership for Local Governance
PRGF	Poverty Reduction and Growth Fund
PRSC	Poverty Reduction Support Credit
PRSP	Poverty Reduction Strategy Paper
SIDA	Swedish International Development Cooperation Agency
SNV	Netherlands Development Organisation
TFET	Trust Fund for East Timor
TSP	Transition Support Program
UNCDF	United Nations Capital Development Fund
UNDP	United Nations Development Programme
UNHCR	United Nations High Commissioner for Refugees
UNTAET	United Nations Transitional Administration for East Timor
UPDF	Uganda People's Defense Forces
USAID	United States Agency for International Development
WHO	World Health Organization

All monetary amounts are in U.S. dollars unless otherwise noted.

CHAPTER 1

Introduction: Synthesizing Case Study Findings

How can development be promoted in countries that have recently experienced devastating crises as a result of extreme misgovernment, armed conflict, or both? Their governments are usually beset by severe weaknesses, face daunting challenges, and preside over large numbers of people who are traumatized, displaced, and cynical about government.

How do international development agencies work constructively with governments that exercise limited sovereignty, have little legitimacy, and are severely incapacitated? The main capacity that many governments possess—often as a legacy of armed conflict—is their ability to deploy coercive force. Moreover, they are often grossly overcentralized, because recent conflicts and emergencies have impelled them to concentrate power at the highest levels to survive.

Governments in fragile states—what the World Bank terms low-income countries under stress (LICUS)—must somehow make an excruciatingly difficult transition. They must begin consulting with and responding to ordinary people, many of whom they may distrust. Doing so is essential so that people become willing to engage constructively in and lend their energies to the task of reconstruction.

This chapter was written by James Manor.

Building the developmental capacity of governments—by inculcating new skills and encouraging more open, accountable, and responsive processes—is a matter of urgency. So is the need to change the prevailing habits of mind within those governments. Powerful leaders within regimes that possess only "quasi-statehood" are often deeply insecure about their own authority and legitimacy. They are therefore intensely fearful of change, lest it dilute their grip on society and destabilize delicate situations. They are often especially skeptical of new initiatives that entail power sharing with groups of people whom they may recently have sought to intimidate, who do not share their commitment to ideas that shaped recent struggles, and who do not possess the skills of the technocrats around them. Sharing power in these situations is difficult, but in countries that have been scarred by war, reintegrating former combatants into society and providing them with the means of sustaining their livelihoods is crucial.

Donor agencies that work in these environments also face tough challenges. They often need to adopt emergency measures to ensure the survival of large numbers of people. Because poor governance has often contributed to these crises, they frequently need to create agencies and structures that bypass governments. But this strategy poses a dilemma, because—over the medium term—government institutions must be strengthened and equipped to play a developmental role; agencies that bypass government institutions may undermine what little legitimacy and capacity those institutions retain. In many cases, donors must also make a difficult transition—from relief to development, from substituting for mainstream government institutions to enabling them to perform key tasks. This transition is exceedingly difficult, but donor programs can make substantial headway on this front, in a variety of difficult contexts, as the studies in this volume indicate.

When we began our analyses, we expected that the approaches widely used by donors in countries that are not fragile states would be inappropriate in the extremely difficult environments examined here (see chapter 2 of this volume). That turned out to be true, but only to a limited extent. Many well-accepted principles and strategies have proved their worth in these countries, although they often need some adjustment. In brief, we found that programs can indeed produce constructive results in fragile states if their design is based on an assessment of distinctive conditions and dynamics at and just above the local level in consultation with groups at those levels and if their implementation allows for adjustment on the basis of frequent consultation with stakeholders.

Successful approaches in one sector, government agency, or geographic area often have spillover effects, because some key actors in other sectors, agencies, or areas recognize the utility of those approaches and seize on them. But scaling up initiatives is often a slow and difficult process. As Martin Greeley notes in chapter 2, approaches to this task have been developed in countries in which governments are much stronger than in the fragile states examined here. Nevertheless, when senior government actors perceive that new approaches promote development and enhance their legitimacy, they can become amenable to similar approaches in other spheres.

Two especially important ideas emerge from the findings in this volume. First, at the local level, much greater constructive potential survives conflicts and other complex emergencies than we had expected or than we found at higher levels in most political systems. Second, programs that promote constructive interaction between government actors, civil society organizations (where they can be found), and people at the local level have unusual promise.

Our approach in the case studies is described in chapter 2, which was written before fieldwork began. Therefore, only a few brief comments are offered here by way of summary. In assessing programs, researchers focused on three issues.

First, they identified and sought to explain development results by considering delivered outcomes in general and governance outcomes in particular. Governance outcomes were singled out because improvements in governance were presumed to be (and, in these studies, shown to be) an urgent priority. The case studies reveal that improvements in governance are more feasible than we had anticipated.

The second and third issues examined were design considerations and implementation processes. Analysis of these three topics yielded numerous insights on other important themes.

Chapter Summaries

Eight studies of development initiatives in five developing countries in Asia and Sub-Saharan Africa were conducted in late 2004. Most of these countries qualify as fragile states. The others were either countries in which recent improvements had occurred but in which conditions associated with fragile states persisted to a degree or countries that included regions with severe problems approximating those found in fragile states.

Chapter 3, by Andrew Rosser, is the first of two chapters that consider programs that were macrosystemic in character. It discusses the Transition Support Program in Timor-Leste, an attempt (unique among our cases) to create the structures of a new state and to enable those structures to acquire development capacity. The program provided funding that was essential until expected revenues from oil and gas resources came on stream. Indeed, without this funding the very viability of the state would have been at risk. The program helped improve governance, promote service delivery, and support other development policies that addressed poverty and encouraged the beginnings of economic growth. It was implemented in a flexible, consultative manner that fostered a sense of ownership within the government and—because people's preferences influenced decisions—among ordinary people. (The ethnic conflict which erupted in Timor-Leste in mid-2006, after the completion of this chapter, reminds us that even quite successful programs like this one stop well short of being panaceas, and that the strengthening of state structures may not prevent further outbreaks of strife.)

Chapter 4, by Caroline Hughes, examines Cambodia's Seila Program, which channels funds through provincial governments to small infrastructure projects designed with input from local residents. Crucial to the program's success has been a willingness to proceed incrementally and to make frequent (and cumulatively quite substantial) adjustments in approach as a result of lessons learned from experience. When the program began, provincial governments were in severe disarray. By providing funds and promoting reform and capacity development, the program has enabled them to function adequately. One key type of capacity is collaboration with people at the grassroots. For both donors and the government, this mechanism is favored for delivering resources to rural areas. It has also persuaded a formerly overcentralized government of the utility of decentralization.

Chapter 5, by Andrew Rosser, is the first of two chapters that analyze initiatives focused on single developmental sectors but with systemwide implications. It assesses two successive rehabilitation and development projects in the health sector in Timor-Leste. The first dealt with immediate and urgent basic health needs while developing a new national health policy and an institutional framework to implement it. A pharmaceutical logistics system had to be created, health facilities needed to be rebuilt, and many other basic structures had to be created or revived. The program initially relied heavily (and inevitably) on international nongovernmental organizations (NGOs) for personnel and expertise, but in the interests of long-term government provision, the government coordinated the NGOs' efforts. The second project increasingly drew Timorese (some of whom returned from overseas) and practitioners from other developing countries into roles as managers and health professionals.

Chapter 6, by Fidelx Pius Kulipossa and James Manor, examines the Direct Support to School Program in Mozambique. By decentralizing resources and discretionary powers through government agencies at intermediate and local levels to local schools and communities, this program began to build constructive partnerships between all of these actors, who had exercised little or (at the local level) no power under the previous overcentralized system. The results have been improved governance, greater participation from below, increased enrollments, and more effective education.

Chapter 7, by the same authors as chapter 6, is the first of four chapters that consider programs focused on specific localities and some of which had very wide-ranging impacts. That was clearly the case with the Decentralized District Planning and Finance Program in one Mozambican province. Powers and resources were devolved to the district level, where political and planning processes were made more open and participatory. These changes improved relations between the state and society at this crucial intermediate level and enhanced the developmental capacities of government there. Fearing that this initiative might lead to instability, Mozambique's leaders insisted that it be tried in just a few districts. Once they saw that stability was unaffected and that governance improved, they extended the reform across the entire country.

Chapter 8, by Sarah Lister, analyzes the community forum process in the city of Mazar-e-Sharif, Afghanistan. The forums in question were established through the efforts of UN-Habitat, beginning in 1995. They became arenas in which women (and less often, men) could discuss and then tackle common problems through collaborative efforts. The forums were sustained in the face of appalling difficulties during and after the Taliban era. They produced concrete gains for participants, even enabling women to renegotiate their roles in a hostile, patriarchal society. These results were possible because flexible, consultation-driven processes were used in both design and implementation. The processes were grounded in a sophisticated understanding of local power dynamics, both within communities and between communities and government agencies. Unexpected synergies developed between technical engineering and community processes, between small-scale community development efforts and larger-scale infrastructure processes, and between local authorities and civil society.

Chapter 9, by Martin Greeley, assesses microfinance initiatives in post-Taliban Afghanistan. It demonstrates that microfinance is a valuable tool and a priority for investment in conflict-affected contexts, even though it does not provide the instant resource transfers and service delivery that emergency conditions require. The techniques used in microfinance systems in other countries proved adaptable here, and crucial technical assistance was in some cases provided by foreign specialists who had worked in those systems. Effective coordination among donors ensured that a single, proven set of standards applied. Here, as in many of the other projects studied, efforts to develop congenial, consultative ties among donors, civic associations, and government officials paid dividends. Good results were facilitated by the decision to deliver funds through the national budget, which won the appreciation of officials.

Chapter 10, by Mark Robinson, analyzes the Northern Uganda Social Action Fund (NUSAF) project, a community-driven development initiative in that war-torn region. NUSAF enables local communities to identify, plan and implement local projects to promote livelihood opportunities in ways that ease conflict. The program developed after an earlier top-down initiative proved unsatisfactory. It achieved significant success, because local demand was considerable and because it worked with elected local councils.

Defining Key Terms

Because this book focuses on successful programs in fragile states, explaining what we mean by success is essential. As Greeley explains in chapter 2, *success* is defined as bringing about sustainable change in governance; catalyzing change outside the area, sector, or theme of the original intervention (positive spillover); reducing poverty, improving service delivery, or both; and stemming the negative spillover effects from one country to a neighboring country or the wider region or from one sector, agency, or level to others within a single country.

We also need to clarify the meaning of *local* and *community*. When levels within political systems are discussed, the words *local, intermediate,* and *national* are used. Their meanings may seem obvious, but in some analyses (not in this volume), *local* is used to refer to all levels below the national level. Here the term is used to refer to villages, towns, and cities. Higher subnational levels, such as districts, counties, or provinces, are referred to as *intermediate* levels. This distinction is important because the logic of politics and public affairs at intermediate levels differs in important ways from that of politics at the local level. At intermediate levels, we are dealing with larger and more complex aggregations of interests. Face-to-face relationships have less importance there than in villages and towns. (Note, however, that in cities, large aggregations of interests often exist, and face-to-face relationships tend not to loom as large as in villages and towns.) Transparency and accountability tend to be harder to achieve at intermediate levels and in cities than in villages and towns, where face-to-face relationships facilitate both.

The word *community* does not imply the existence of harmony or solidarity among people living in proximity to one another. In many cases, significant cleavages exist within communities, and powerful minorities dominate decision making and public affairs. Divides within communities are worth stressing because one of the key findings of the cases presented here is that initiatives that engage with local communities are especially promising and that local communities tend to possess substantial constructive potential even when they have suffered serious misgovernment, deprivation, and even brutalization.

Such communities sometimes become more inclusive when democratic or other participatory processes are introduced. But greater inclusion does not necessarily enhance a sense of unity and solidarity. Democratization and broadened participation may intensify competition and division within localities, although they may also lead to accommodations that make competition more moderate and less destructive.

Analyzing Initial Conditions

Attempts to help fragile states rebuild their capacity to spur development, as the case studies show, should reflect understanding of the distinctive conditions in each of these states. Policy makers and donors need to avoid a "one size fits all" approach.

Because conditions in and the recent histories of fragile states vary so much, donor agencies and others involved in development programs must conduct a thorough preliminary analysis before taking action; they must also ensure that subsequent actions are appropriate given the specific conditions. This analysis should be undertaken in partnership with knowledgeable people from those countries. Tailoring a response, which is important in all developing countries, is especially relevant in fragile states, because the severe disruptions caused by armed conflicts and other horrific experiences in such places produce immense changes within very short periods. In such circumstances, catastrophic events may have rendered previous studies of such countries, even those conducted relatively recently, irrelevant.

The following comments may appear unsatisfactory, both because they are very general and because some of them are familiar to many readers. They are nevertheless set out here because our evidence supports them, because they therefore appear well founded, and because some of them may not be entirely obvious.

The aims of a preliminary analysis should be to identify the main and the most urgent problems, the most promising features that might be turned to constructive purposes, and the strategies that might be most appropriate. Power dynamics—at higher and lower levels in each political system, within local communities, and between communities and political actors—require special attention. It usually makes sense for this assessment to be conducted in a participatory manner at the grassroots, so that the views of the people most in need and whose energies are an important resource for recovery can influence the project or program.

Once the key features and problems are identified, possible changes in governance should be prioritized. The case studies suggest that priority should be given to changes that governments are at least half inclined to undertake, even if they are willing to proceed only experimentally and incrementally. Attention must be paid both to the supply side (problems and promise in existing governmental and nongovernmental structures) and the demand side (popular apathy and cynicism on the one hand and strong popular desire for certain change on the other). Evidence from some of the cases, particularly the one described in chapter 7, indicates that preliminary analyses should pay special heed to what, if anything, is already working, because building on and replicating that success may be possible. Special attention also needs to be paid to the local level. Developing initiatives from scratch may not always be necessary.[1]

Ensuring Flexibility and Incorporating Feedback

Once a preliminary analysis has been completed, practitioners need to remain alert to feedback from the field and to be ready to learn from it and adjust their activities accordingly. In Cambodia (chapter 4), for example, the program's objectives changed after key figures sought out potentially useful approaches and adapted their activities to them. The program developed a "learning-by-doing" creed that entailed a willingness to invest funds and energy in experiments, to consider feedback, and to shed goals and adopt new ones in light of new information. The chapter emphasizes that implementation and redesign of initiatives are inter-twined. It argues for an incremental approach, as lessons learned from trials, errors, and unexpected successes suggest adjustments in strategies.

Chapter 5 notes that the health rehabilitation program in Timor-Leste began before all of the details were worked out and that incremental changes were incorporated on the basis of systematically collected feed-back from the field. Chapter 6, on Mozambique's schools, and chapter 10, on Uganda, also conclude that openness to evidence from the field and to experimentation and flexible response resonate with the logic of demand-driven programs. Chapter 8, on Afghanistan, stresses an impor-tant related point: flexibility needs to be underpinned by a clear sense of basic principles.

Ensuring Community-Driven Development

In country after country, constructive potential survived the ordeals of conflict and deprivation common in fragile states. To make the most of that potential, development initiatives must emphasize participatory and consultative processes that give local citizens opportunities to influence program design and implementation.

Chapter 8 illustrates this point. It notes that community-driven processes helped build a sense of consensus within localities on development prob-lems, objectives, and strategies. These processes persuaded program leaders that technical assistance should include not just engineers but people skilled in facilitating community participation. The payoff was substantial. Program staff interacted with both local government authorities and com-munities, helping to draw the two into dialogue. The dialogue yielded equi-table arrangements for providing services and charging citizens for them and made it possible to link processes that extended across municipalities with small-scale initiatives in limited sections of each city.

Chapters 4, 6, 7, and 8 show that use of consultative and participatory mechanisms associated with community-driven development can facili-tate the difficult transition from initial, quick-impact, top-down programs to address dire emergencies to longer-term, bottom-up efforts to promote development and institutional reform. Such mechanisms can enhance government officials and local communities' sense of program ownership. And, as the two chapters on Mozambique indicate, these mechanisms can lead not just to improved infrastructure projects but also to changes in the ways in which both officials and citizens think about governance, state-society relations, and development.

Starting Small Scale or Large Scale

The preceding discussion of the value of experimentation, incremental-ism, and flexible adaptations of strategies might suggest that an initially small-scale approach makes sense, but our findings indicate a more complex picture.

Two of the programs studied—the Transition Support Program in Timor-Leste and the Seila Program in Cambodia—could be described as macrosystemic undertakings. But the Seila Program involved a great deal of experimentation, plus so many learning-based adjustments, that it changed fundamentally over time. A degree of flexibility was also apparent in the Timor-Leste program.

Two other programs—the health programs in Timor-Leste and the schools program in Mozambique—started smaller but ended up introducing major countrywide changes within single sectors. Both of these ambitious single-sector programs were receptive to feedback from citizens and made adjustments accordingly. Thus all four of these initiatives (discussed in chapters 3–6) as well as the other four programs that started small (discussed in chapters 7–10) shared many features. Both the programs that began large and the programs that started small produced successes; neither approach can be seen as inappropriate in fragile states.

In Timor-Leste the choice of a large-scale approach followed a regime change, a new nation's independence. Like most newly independent governments over the last half century, the new regime believed that the magnitude and the dramatic nature of the change called for a makeover of the system and that it enjoyed sufficient popular legitimacy to embark on a makeover. The new rulers were not fearful of change; they were impatient for it. A broad coalition of donors supported the regime's aspirations and was prepared to provide immense resources.

By contrast, the Mozambican authorities had held power for many years and were worried that major changes, taken quickly, might destabilize the political order and threaten their hold on power. They probably also had doubts about their popular legitimacy; they were certainly anxious about the fragility of the prevailing order, as their decision to start small in the district reforms initiative indicates. But they were persuaded to attempt major change in the education sector by the substantial donor support that was available for it and by evidence from other countries that this approach was not destabilizing and could yield significant benefits.

Those who are inclined to urge large-scale approaches should note the two quite different sets of circumstances in which they were adopted in these cases. Contexts clearly matter. They should also heed two key lessons that emerge from the implementation of experiments with large-scale approaches. First, such strategies must create and constantly pursue feedback processes. Second, adopting very simple and clear feedback processes is critical because the magnitude of the undertaking will already present many complexities.

Let us now turn to programs that started small. Such programs are not necessarily destined to have only a limited impact. As Mozambique's district governance program (chapter 7) shows, experiments that start small may eventually inspire sufficient confidence among national leaders to be very widely implemented—and thus to affect entire systems.

Over time, the district governance program in Mozambique had major implications for the entire range of government activities at the district level. The breadth of those implications initially caused national leaders to restrict the program to a few districts in a single province. They feared that if the program went wrong, the damage would be widespread (and far greater than that of the schools program, which affected only a single sector). Once the pilot project showed promise, it was extended to a few districts in other provinces and ultimately to the entire country. The result is an initiative that is transforming most government operations at the key district level across Mozambique. The program involved officials from various line ministries in both multidisciplinary and participatory processes, enhancing their effectiveness. It has thus lent respectability to such processes at higher levels in a broad range of ministries. The program, which began on a small scale, has had macrosystemic implications.

Fostering Constructive Potential at the Local Level

All of the case studies suggested that local communities were better able than governments at higher than local levels to rapidly develop a capacity for constructive action. Nearly all of the successful initiatives involved some sort of engagement with local-level communities or their representatives. (The main exceptions were in Timor-Leste, but because that country has a population of only 800,000, it is akin to districts in some of the other countries examined here.) Many of the initiatives entailed community-driven development arrangements that permitted local preferences to influence the development process, so that the process becomes substantially demand driven. This approach appears to be especially productive in fragile states, where existing institutional capacity is weak and the development challenges are enormous.

Do informal (usually social) institutions and bonds at the grassroots grow stronger during conflicts and crises? Our studies indicate that they do not, that these bonds are always weakened, and that damage to them sometimes leaves barren soil at the local level for certain types of development initiatives. But the unsettled conditions that exist in fragile states may also help constructive groups at the local level challenge and change old hierarchies and patterns of social exclusion, as chapter 8 shows. Although catastrophes may leave local groups worse off absolutely, social and political institutions that sustained inequities often suffer still greater damage. The evidence presented in this volume suggests that when conflicts wreak havoc or state institutions become seriously incapacitated, human and interpersonal resources and bonds often suffer less damage at the local level than at higher levels. As a result, when the time comes to rebuild, it is often easier to make headway at the grassroots than at higher levels.

Examples of this phenomenon include the success of the United Nations Capital Development Fund's (UNCDF's) local development funds in a variety of fragile states and the achievements of President Yoweri Museveni's Movement party in Uganda in creating a state from the bottom up, through local councils, after decades of predatory regimes and devastating wars. People at the local level sometimes develop coping mechanisms amid crises that can be turned to constructive purposes once crises ease. The face-to-face relationships at the local level allow greater scope for establishing trust, accommodation, and a sense of mutuality than do the more anonymous relationships that exist at higher levels. The surviving human resources and bonds at the local level provide a platform on which to mount efforts at reconstruction.

It is important not to overstate this case. First, a distinction must be made between systems in which there is no strong state or ruling party with the capacity to make its influence felt in local arenas and systems in which potent party and state structures exist. In chapter 8 on Afghanistan, Lister argues that the absence of a strong state increases the scope for innovation and that "there may also be more direct access to communities, and people may be more willing to organize, because there is no alternative way of meeting their immediate needs." But even when Leninist parties hold sway, certain experiments—such as Mozambique's cautious attempt at democratic decentralization—can gradually persuade party leaders that their organizations have grown sclerotic and that these new approaches can help bring fresh human resources into the system.

Second, we do not share the views of those who idealize local communities, local knowledge, and localized arrangements for conducting society's business. On the contrary, we remain skeptical of such notions. In many developing countries, local arenas are afflicted by parochialism, factionalism, the danger of elite capture, inequity, and injustice—all factors that can undermine constructive potential. We therefore harbor doubts about claims by Gandhians and others that local communities are often capable of generating a harmonious, all-embracing sense of mutuality.

Nor do we believe that local efforts—on their own—can achieve great things in most circumstances. Local residents need resources, support, and constructive initiatives from agencies (governmental and nongovernmental) at higher levels if they are to make much headway in efforts at development. Nevertheless, our case studies indicate that local communities that have gone through searing experiences as the result of severe conflicts or vile political regimes often retain the capacity to respond to constructive initiatives from outside.

Indeed, it appears that local residents who have lived for extended periods at or close to what Milton called "the utmost edge of hazard" are often strongly inclined to seize on modest opportunities to improve their lives. To say this is not to argue—as Gandhi did—that ordeals burn away impurities and divisions and somehow forge local collectivities into genuine "communities." What we have observed stops short of that.

Adversity does not purify local arenas, but it creates a strong, at times desperate appetite for anything that offers promise. This appetite may minimize the importance of impurities for a time, during which the prospects for constructive policy and political interventions from higher up are good. If such interventions occur, the results can be surprisingly encouraging in these very difficult conditions, partly because the conditions are so difficult and partly in spite of them.

But those interventions must allow local preferences to have an influence and local engagement to yield rewards. If so, constructive patterns of action may be sustained over time.

Linking Constructive Potential to Democratic Decentralization

Another way to ensure sustainability is to encourage the creation of democratic bodies at or just above the local level, thereby institutionalizing processes through which local preferences can influence events. Essential to the effective functioning of such elected bodies or councils are significant resources and mechanisms that ensure government bureaucrats' accountability to elected representatives and representatives' accountability to citizens. Governments are usually reluctant to devolve abundant powers and resources to such institutions, fearing they will get nothing in return. But in practice, governments make major compensatory gains in popularity, legitimacy, and much else[2]—so generosity is in their interests.

Robinson's chapter on Uganda stresses the contribution to sustainability that ensued when decentralized councils were given some significant powers. Even when national authorities were less eager to empower and fund such bodies, as Hughes's study of Cambodia demonstrates, a decentralized system nonetheless contributed to several critically important gains:

- compliance with participatory principles,
- delivery of services and infrastructure,
- cultivation of broad local support for other government initiatives,
- constructive experimentation at the local level—at both the design and implementation stages,
- peace and reconciliation in the aftermath of conflict,
- transition from use of expatriate to use of indigenous personnel,
- capacity building and training within local institutions,
- overall effectiveness of government,
- enhanced participation from below in policy dialogues and other aspects of community-driven development,
- improved state-society relations, and
- poverty reduction.

Elected councils at or just above the local level can also facilitate development programs' exit strategies, because they offer some reassurance that the practices they have introduced have a reasonable chance of survival. This was the case in Uganda.

In countries where formal lower-level elected councils are absent or exceedingly weak, an alternative approach is to encourage variations on the theme of the local development funds created in many countries by UNCDF. These funds may eventually inspire sufficient confidence in decentralized approaches to make establishment of formal elected councils possible. That change can be facilitated by arguing, as Greeley does in his chapter on Afghanistan, that formal decentralization links the central government to a huge number of community-level development committees—in that country, 6,000—which plainly broaden the political base of insecure regimes. By integrating such bodies into formal political structures, governments can more easily ensure that successful experiments from one locality or region are replicated nationally—as Lister suggests in her chapter on Afghanistan.

Democratic decentralization is not a panacea. It seldom serves the needs of people like pastoralists and others who are present within localities only some of the time.[3] Elected local councils may be captured by elites, so that they fail to assist with poverty reduction—although in countries in which a huge proportion of the population is "poor" (which is the case in most of our cases), elites may eventually be compelled to compete for the votes of the poor. But despite its limitations, democratic decentralization has enough virtues (itemized above[4]) to warrant strong support from governments that are fragile.

We need to treat the good news about local-level potential with some caution. If substantial improvements are to occur in fragile states, gains within local arenas must be extended both horizontally to other localities and vertically to higher-level institutions that can integrate localities with one another and with powerful actors in upper reaches of political systems.[5] This latter task is particularly difficult, because constructive mechanisms are often harder to create at higher levels than at lower levels. Nevertheless, rebuilding at lower levels should eventually be linked to government institutions at higher levels.

Enhancing Government Capacity at Higher Levels

Capacity building is essential for fragile-state governments that exercise only tenuous authority over sections of their territory. They need to become capable of delivering goods and services effectively and of enabling people to operate constructively in their own interests[6]—the twin bases on which the initiatives described in this volume are deemed successful. If they accomplish these tasks, their legitimacy in the eyes of citizens increases—and that bolsters the authority of an at least partially developmental state.

Donor agencies and civil society organizations often need to work in concert with governments that have unsavory records to help them accomplish these tasks. Although leaders in such governments are usually open to the argument (which needs to be made) that an increase in their capacity to engage in constructive action is in their interests, they may harbor fears—sometimes wildly unjustified fears (see for example, the studies here of Cambodia and of district-level reform in Mozambique)—about the dangers to their interests and their near-total control of powers and funds that experimentation may pose. Moreover, in fragile states—and especially in postconflict situations—government officials are frequently intensely reluctant to assume the responsibility and risk of introducing initiatives since, if these go awry, they may pay a heavy price. Therefore, international agencies and civil society organizations may need to undertake the initial experiments on their own. Once donor or civil society pilot projects in our case studies produced patent benefits, leaders' anxieties were eased. It then became possible to persuade the leaders that government should take up the projects.

This ability to change attitudes within governments was one of the main virtues of the programs examined here. That often depended on the development of relationships of trust between program managers and key government officials, which could only occur if the former were prepared to work with partially unsavory regimes.

Three further features of these processes deserve comment here. First, political leaders' impatience for the swift delivery of goods and services can impede the slower process of the development of government capacity. That capacity is crucial to the long-term interests of governments and especially to the sustainability of development programs. (We will return to this theme in the discussion of social funds.) A balance needs to be struck between these two imperatives. Second, initiatives should plan for the transition from donor action to government action. (We will return to this point.) Third, this transition usually requires that locals replace expatriates holding key posts in programs. (The two chapters on Afghanistan and the chapter on Cambodia bring home this point.)

Encouraging a Sense of Ownership

The discussion above highlights the importance of fostering a sense of ownership of development projects within governments and of the utility of the programs analyzed here in doing so.

Robinson stresses the importance of pursuing intensive consultations with stakeholders extending from the central government to local communities—including government administrators and elected officials at the local level—at the design stage of a program. In Uganda these consultations yielded a strong sense of government ownership that was sustained in a learning process that entailed (and facilitated) adjustments to the program's approach.

Greeley's study stresses the utility of incorporating microfinance into the formal government budget process (a topic to which we will return). In Afghanistan this strategy gave officials a sense of ownership, which is especially important where state sovereignty is in doubt, as it often is in fragile states. The discussion by Hughes of the increasingly close links between the CARERE 2 program and the Cambodian government—and the greater discretionary power that state actors could exercise over Seila program funds—tells a very similar story. So do both chapters on Timor-Leste.

The chapter on Mozambique's schools notes that provision of training for Mozambican government personnel persuaded leaders that the program was strengthening the machinery of state over which they presided. That enhanced their sense of program ownership. As noted in Lister's chapter on Afghanistan, adequate provision of external funds for programs can be mightily reassuring to governments and can encourage a sense of ownership.

Popular ownership of development programs is also essential. Most of the programs examined in this volume developed strong links with local citizens, which enabled their preferences to influence the development process. This link made popular ownership easier to secure than government ownership.

Engendering Spillovers

Achievements in one sector or geographic area may influence actors in other sectors or areas to adopt the approaches that produced the achievements. (This theme is closely linked to scaling up of initiatives and will be further discussed.) Such spillover can occur within government agencies, donor agencies, and civil society organizations, or can occur within society.

When programs are widely implemented and thus involve officials from several ministries, those officials will absorb the programs' positive lessons. Spillover across sectors follows naturally, as was the case with the district governance program in Mozambique. Officials from various government agencies recognized the utility of more open, participatory governance, and change ensued on a broad front.

Most of the initiatives that we analyzed—and most adopted in fragile states—are on a modest scale, but some have had positive spillovers. When the microfinance program in Afghanistan showed that transparent, participatory processes could deliver vital services in a sustainable manner, it encouraged agencies outside the microfinance sector to pursue similar processes. Our studies show that donor coordination also facilitates spillover among development agencies.

When development programs are demand-driven, as many of those examined here were, spillover into society tends to occur as a matter of course. People in one town learn that people in another town benefited from a development project and seek support for a similar effort. Demand for support from the program that Robinson examined in Uganda was so high that program managers felt compelled to accept more local development proposals than the program budget could fund. Greeley's chapter on Afghanistan stresses the need for donors to provide additional funds to meet escalating demand. In our studies, donors' encouragement of demand from below was inspired in part by a growing awareness that demand-driven processes facilitate spillover.

Scaling Up

In this volume, scaling up refers to "the dissemination of ideas, approaches and methods of work through interactions of people" at different levels in a system and in different spatial areas.[7] It can thus imply the dissemination of ideas and the replication of processes horizontally (at the same level within a system) or vertically (to higher levels within a country or beyond). In our studies, scaling up mainly occurred when authorities at high levels of government were persuaded that an approach adopted at a lower level of government was worthy of replication (horizontally) at the same level or (vertically, upward) at higher levels, when donors drew the same conclusion, or both. We found that efforts at horizontal replication are more promising than attempts at vertical replication—because the logic changes between levels, and because more promising conditions at lower levels offer greater hope of success. Horizontal replication may, however, be more difficult to achieve—unless a system of democratic decentralization provides ready and reasonably effective channels for disseminating information about successful actions among localities.[8]

Even when horizontal replication at the local level is attempted, the institutions of a national government play an essential role. These institutions are needed to extract information on successes in particular arenas, to transmit that information to other arenas, and to lend support to efforts at replication. They deserve support to play this role.

Steps can be taken to assist replication. One is support not just for democratic decentralization, but more specifically for associations of the heads of elected councils at low levels of government. Governments sometimes hesitate to support or even to permit such associations because they might challenge political actors at higher levels. But such associations can help transmit information about successes in isolated areas—both horizontally (to the heads of other councils) and vertically (to the higher reaches of government).

Efforts to scale up some of the initiatives we studied encountered logistical difficulties. In Afghanistan those involved in promoting the impressive work of community forums in the city of Mazar-e-Sharif found the task so onerous that they were unable to keep detailed records of the constructive adjustments that they made in their approach as conditions changed and the capacities of the forums increased over time. The inadequacy of their records impeded their efforts to replicate their success in other Afghan localities. Lister argues that donors need to provide resources for recordkeeping. But as she also notes, such support will not change the fact that scaling up is a difficult task in fragile states.

Developing Parallel Agencies and Bodies

When governments and donors seek to develop constructive institutions at higher-than-local levels to make the most of potential at the local level, they often create special administrative agencies that operate alongside and bypass conventional bureaucratic structures. They also tend to create new committees or bodies at or near the local level to facilitate consultation with local residents. These bodies operate alongside elected councils at or just above the local level.

In emergencies, these parallel agencies and bodies frequently perform tasks that meet urgent human needs and save lives. They can enhance the political legitimacy of governments by showing local residents that the governments can provide at least some services. But if these parallel agencies and bodies are kept separate from mainstream bureaucratic agencies and elected bodies over the long term, they can prevent the latter from developing an administrative and political order that provides, at a minimum, adequate governance.

Social Funds

Several programs we examined are associated with social funds or initiatives closely resembling them.[9] Social funds often entail establishment of parallel agencies to bypass seriously damaged government structures. These agencies are funded separately from mainstream government agencies so that they will not be undermined by government malfeasance or lack of effective fund management capacity. They often enable local residents to identify urgent needs, thanks to their use of techniques that draw grassroots views and preferences into the policy process. They therefore often contribute to the empowerment of ordinary people, make the most of local-level potential, and lead to constructive coproduction arrangements.[10]

These advantages make social fund approaches especially appropriate in the early stages of efforts to address the severe problems encountered in fragile states—when it is a matter of urgency to begin to make good things happen in often dire circumstances. Indeed, social funds were initially intended as emergency measures. But when social funds become a long-term feature of the landscape, as has occurred across much of Asia and especially Africa,[11] they tend to sustain the incapacity of state institutions—both administrative institutions and elected bodies.

If the administrative instruments used to manage social funds remain largely or wholly separate from a government's bureaucratic structures, those structures will not benefit from any efficient approaches developed within the former. And if substantial funds pass through the special agencies associated with social funds while the government's mainstream administration is seriously short of resources, morale within and the capacity of the latter tend to be undermined.

If elected bodies at or just above the local level face severe shortages of funds—as they often do—while social funds have abundant funds available, the former suffer damage. Elected bodies' inability to fulfill their unfunded or underfunded mandates is vividly dramatized to local residents when those bodies stand alongside well-resourced committees associated with social funds. These residents naturally tend to become dismissive of elected local bodies, compounding the problems that such bodies have in acquiring legitimacy and consequently in enhancing the legitimacy of government institutions in general. In such circumstances, social funds undermine not only local bodies, but also the reforming state.

Elected local bodies offer certain other advantages that may be lost if they suffer damage in these ways. First, they can reinforce community-driven development by providing an institutional structure that makes it—more systematically, less randomly—a central feature of local life. Second, in creating local development plans, they can ensure that issues and needs regarded by local residents as priorities receive greater resources and attention than others—in contrast with some social funds that respond to local bids on a first-come-first-served basis. Third, in their coordination of local development projects, multisector elected bodies can help to promote mutual reinforcement among such projects—an advantage not always realized with social funds.

Our studies indicate that when elected local bodies are given significant influence over social funds, constructive results tend to follow.

User Committees and Stakeholder Committees

Single-sector user committees or stakeholder committees (parent-teacher associations, water users' committees, joint forest management committees, and so forth) have proliferated, mainly as a result of donor programs within individual sectors. These committees often fragment collective efforts within localities, making coordination difficult, and they often have a destructive impact similar to that of social funds on elected local bodies. Because user committees are usually well resourced with donor funds that pass through single line ministries, they often undermine the legitimacy of badly underfunded elected bodies that are supposed to deal with multiple sectors.

It thus makes sense to regard committees associated with social funds as structures for providing initial responses to urgent needs but structures that over time should be integrated with mainstream state structures, particularly elected bodies at or just above the local level.[12] Experience from several developing countries has shown that giving elected bodies significant influence or full control over these parallel institutions can produce benefits.[13] Supporting evidence emerges in the chapters on Uganda, Mozambique, Cambodia, and Afghanistan. Linking user committees (which tend to be unelected or "elected" through processes that are less rigorous and genuine than those used to choose local councils) with local councils (which have greater democratic legitimacy) provides community-driven development with solid, unified institutional support. Such support increases the likelihood that community-driven development will be coherent and sustained.

Advantages of Integrating Parallel Bodies and Agencies with Mainstream Government Structures

Integrating parallel bodies and parallel agencies with mainstream government structures can:

- strengthen the legitimacy of mainstream structures and thus erode ordinary people's cynicism about government,
- foster trust in the capacity of local communities to accomplish things by demonstrating that state agencies can lend much needed support, and

- promote citizens' understanding of what is and is not possible from "politics," public action, and state institutions by showing that political accommodations (which necessarily require acceptance of less than total victory) tend not to be zero-sum games.

Determining the Psychological Effect of Improvements in Fragile States

In fragile states, political and policy processes have long been wholly or substantially closed to ordinary people and perhaps even to important interest groups, the state's capacity to perform even basic tasks is quite limited, or both. Even modest improvements in either of these situations can have a dramatically positive psychological effect on ordinary people.

Development practitioners working with a United Nations agency in Vietnam—a closed political system—found that when people were permitted to elect members of local councils (albeit with quite limited powers), the psychological effect was startling. They responded enthusiastically and engaged actively in development projects. The result was similar when China introduced elections to village councils and when the Rawlings regime in Ghana created elected assemblies at the district level in the late 1980s.[14] In Mozambique, creation of elected councils in pilot projects at the local and district levels drew previously apathetic citizens into active engagement with the political and policy processes, as described in chapter 7.

Similar responses have occurred when a government that is largely incapable of performing basic tasks undertakes reforms that enable it to achieve at least modest successes. In her chapter on Cambodia, Hughes notes the highly positive psychological effects of injections of quite modest funds.

A modest change for the better can substantially improve citizens' opinion of the government that brought about the change and increase citizens' willingness to engage with government institutions and in the public sphere more generally, enhancing the likelihood that constructive changes can be sustained and augmented.

Using Donor-Funded Institutions for Partisan Political Purposes

Institutions—parallel and mainstream—are frequently manipulated to enhance the popularity and legitimacy of national-level politicians and ruling parties. This phenomenon occurred in Cambodia, Uganda, and Mozambique, and probably in several other countries featured in this volume.

How concerned should donors be about this? The answer depends on the degree to which ruling elites put delivery of funds, goods, and services to their own narrow, partisan advantage. One extreme case is Zimbabwe, where food supplies provided by donors have been distributed to people who pledge loyalty to the ruling party while others are left to face starvation.

In other cases—including all of those that we studied—the picture is far more complex and less objectionable. Consider government decisions to create parallel agencies to tackle emergencies, or parallel bodies at the local level to facilitate consultations with ordinary people, or elected councils at lower levels to open up previously closed systems. These steps have often been taken in the hope of enhancing the ruling party's popularity and of providing frameworks to facilitate organization building by that party. If such institution building enhances the legitimacy and popularity of ruling elites, we should view this outcome as logical and healthy, because it erodes cynicism about government and opens the door to constructive state-society relations.

The picture becomes more complex when we examine the ways in which such agencies are manipulated for partisan purposes. The extent to which manipulation has occurred in the initiatives we examined varies. The government in Uganda has been accused by some of channeling many of its developmental efforts to areas where people tended to favor the ruling elite—although some evidence indicates that these accusations are unjust. The Cambodian government appears to have carried partisan manipulation further.

At the other end of the spectrum is Mozambique. As one of our case studies explains, after experimenting with open, representative bodies in some districts, the government there has decided to allow these bodies throughout the country. As with its earlier decision to establish elected local councils in roughly one-third of its municipalities, Mozambique was prepared to open up opportunities for the main opposition party to capture power in some arenas for two compensating gains. First, the prospect of new elected posts in these bodies drew talented, resourceful people into what had become a stagnant ruling party organization. Second, the new bodies were widely popular and enhanced the legitimacy of the government and the ruling party.

The partisan use of such institutions is an inevitable feature of democratization in less-developed (and many industrialized) countries. If we want democracy in these countries, we have to be prepared to live with a certain amount of such use. The crucial issue is, how much? Even in small doses, manipulation grates against the liberal sensibilities of many people. But only when it runs to excess are developmental and political gains put at significant risk.

Addressing Needs during or after Armed Conflicts

Many fragile states have experienced or still face armed conflicts within their borders. To ignore the problems that the conflicts create is to risk revival or prolongation of strife. And even when renewed conflict is unlikely, the causes and consequences of recent wars need to be tackled to make development constructive and legitimate governance possible. Our studies uncovered a number of promising approaches to conflict-related problems.

In countries where control of territory is still contested, community-driven initiatives at the local level should be prepared to develop at least tenuous working relationships with whatever armed group controls the region. It makes sense for these relationships to remain tenuous and non-partisan until the conflict ceases and something resembling a "government" comes into being, lest communities be victimized for having close ties with former adversaries. This describes the situation and the approach adopted by the community-level organizations in Afghanistan.

As Lister notes, such community-level initiatives often make valuable contributions amid conflicts. By providing local residents with some livelihood opportunities, basic services, and emergency assistance, they can reduce the number of people immigrating to other areas. This prevents émigrés from having to face dire threats as they move through battle zones, and eases the refugee burden on whatever authorities and humanitarian agencies may be present.

Robinson's chapter on conflict-ridden northern Uganda lists many benefits from the decision to locate the management of the development program that he examined within the region to which the program was targeted. This decision not only reduced travel costs and logistical problems, it sent the message that the program was to be rooted within the region's social and institutional framework. It allowed program staff to be hired from the region—people who would have a direct stake in the program's success and who would accept lower salaries than their counterparts in the capitol. Finally, it made the program transparent and accountable to the region's residents.

Funds from that program go primarily to projects originating from camps inhabited by people displaced by the conflict, including former combatants. These projects usually facilitate income generation within the secure confines of refugee camps. The program enables victims of conflict to adapt program guidelines—which are applied flexibly—to the distinctive conditions in which they must live.

As Lister notes in her chapter on Afghanistan, community-based programs can contribute to "peace-building by providing stability and a model of negotiation and cooperation." The decision in Cambodia to permit former insurgents to participate in dialogues on the direction of the Seila program had the same effect. So did the willingness of the Mozambican government to open posts on municipal and district councils to former insurgents from Renamo, which became an opposition party once the war there ended. Lister's Afghanistan program—like its counterparts in Cambodia, Mozambique, and elsewhere—also provided incentives and means of livelihoods that help people disengage from the conflict-ridden past.

Considering Implications of Case Studies for Donors

Let us consider some of the more important implications of these studies for donor agencies.

A Question of Timing: The Logic Changes When Emergencies Pass

When international development agencies first address fragile states, they often have to grapple with extreme humanitarian emergencies in which many lives are at immediate risk as a result of armed conflict, the collapse of state machinery, or other dire circumstances. As long as extreme emergencies exist, development agencies have a responsibility to adopt whatever measures seem most promising—to deliver food, seeds, medical services and supplies, and so forth to save lives and meet urgent needs. This is true even if those measures do not necessarily lend themselves to sustainable long-term solutions.

However, our analyses also focus on longer-term issues because in nearly all of the cases that we analyzed, extreme emergencies soon—or eventually—subsided sufficiently to impel us to consider those issues. Our emphasis on them should not be read as a condemnation of short-term measures to tackle extreme situations—for a time. But our studies indicate that in most cases time was mercifully rather limited, so that it soon becomes necessary to consider longer-term arrangements that will be sustainable amid somewhat more "normal" circumstances—and to adjust initial strategies accordingly. The adjustments are necessary, because the initial advantages of emergency measures—notably parallel structures—tend strongly to pose long-term dangers to the legitimacy of mainstream government institutions, which become crucial once emergencies ease.

Why Governments Matter

Some development analysts and practitioners in donor agencies and civil society organizations do not accept the following ideas, so they deserve an airing. Governments—in which politicians almost always count for more than technocrats—have an enormous capacity to do both harm and good. They are also an unavoidable feature of the landscape. It is therefore essential that donors engage with them in ways that may persuade and equip them to pursue constructive strategies.

The capacity of governments to do harm is vividly apparent in many fragile states. But their potential as constructive actors is also great. We were surprised at how positive their contributions have been in many of the cases analyzed here.

Governments (at least potentially and usually in practice) have far more comprehensive reach—horizontally across territories and vertically down to the grassroots—than do civil society organizations, the main alternative available to donors. In only four developing countries are claims by pro-poor civil society organizations to have national networks that penetrate into many local arenas accurate—and none of them have fragile regimes.[15] Governments, by contrast, usually achieve this to such reach. Only they are capable of constructing institutional frameworks— administrative structures, somewhat open policy processes, systems of democratic decentralization, or all three—that succeed in encompassing entire territories and all levels within political systems.

Almost all governments, even where regimes are fragile, command far more resources than do the sum total of civil society organizations. And in this era of increasingly open, democratic political systems, many governments offer ordinary people greater opportunities to inject their preferences into policy processes than they used to do and than civil society organizations can do (because the latter lack the reach of governments).

Governments with some legitimacy find it easier to draw people into active engagement in the public sphere and to mobilize local resources (financial and, perhaps more crucially, human) that make constructive development projects more likely to succeed and more sustainable. The acquisition of greater legitimacy (a common theme in our cases) also improves state-society relations and increases the chances that interest groups will see the need in more open political systems to moderate their behavior and to accept political accommodations. Finally, when donors openly acknowledge the importance of governments, they find it easier to persuade them to commit to efforts to promote further reform. This increases donor influence with governments.

Influencing Governments

Donor agencies obviously wish to influence governments in less developed countries. One way (the usual way) of doing so is to offer them substantial funds, but our evidence indicates that other approaches may be promising—indeed, more promising.

One key task is to persuade governments that new initiatives are nonthreatening. Some of the most impressive achievements noted in our case studies occurred when governments concluded that changes initially appearing to imperil them could actually enhance their effectiveness and responsiveness and thus their legitimacy and popularity. Government leaders—especially senior politicians who are almost always the key figures within them—are especially likely to feel threatened when they are asked to part with certain powers. In seeking to persuade them to do so, reliance on experiments within a small number of arenas may be crucial. Empowerment of a few consultative bodies at the district level made the Mozambican authorities nervous at first, but they eventually saw that it served their interests—so they extended the change to the entire country.

Successes of pilot projects can help persuade governments to scale up the projects. But the impact of such successes can be even greater. When reform initiatives produce benefits for different interest groups that regard one another as rivals, it encourages a belief that those initiatives and the political bargains that they often entail are worth trusting—even though no interest group gets everything that it seeks. Political actors inside and outside government are persuaded that reform processes offer something other than zero-sum games. At this point, the groups often become inclined to remain engaged with political and policy processes, making changes in governance and the assets created by development projects sustainable.

And at this point, people develop a realistic understanding of what is and is not possible in the public sphere. This understanding makes them less likely to cling to unrealistic expectations that inevitably lead to disappointment, which can be destabilizing. It also makes them less susceptible to wildly unrealistic promises made by extremists.

One further approach is worth noting. We encountered it in three of the programs we examined: the CARERE/Seila program in Cambodia, the Transition Support program in Timor-Leste, and the district-level program in Mozambique. Despite the diverse contexts of these programs, it worked in all three.

The approach involves donor agencies working closely with government officials over several years. (This long-term engagement may not be possible in some other cases.) In Cambodia, United Nations Development Programme (UNDP) engaged with key government actors, while in Mozambique, UNCDF personnel operated within the Ministry of Finance. The donors listened and responded sympathetically to what they were hearing. Initially in Cambodia, the program sought to achieve change largely by itself. But in 1998, it was altered to reinforce the government's own efforts, and its objectives were changed to conform to the government's preferences. The program's main focus changed from improvement of infrastructure and services to promotion of citizen participation and synergistic state-society relations. In Mozambique, UNCDF demonstrated—by making many small adjustments—a willingness to fine-tune the program in response to suggestions from government officials. In both countries, adjustments were made because donors recognized the importance of their close, congenial relationships with governments in inspiring trust and changing government perceptions in constructive ways.

Donors stressed that adaptations to development programs could empower the governments. As a result of these adaptations, donors were able to persuade powerful government actors that more open, democratic governance (at the local level in Cambodia and at the district level in Mozambique) would serve the political interests of the authorities at higher levels. In Mozambique, the way was opened to extension of open processes beyond a few districts where they had been tried on an experimental basis to the whole of the country.

Donors often had to accept suboptimal decisions, but they did so because they recognized that the best might be the enemy of the good. Pursuing practicable initiatives that will make governance "good enough" is important when ideal solutions are less or not at all practicable (Grindle 2004).

Ambitious Reforms in Difficult Circumstances

Donor agencies tend to favor ambitious reforms, but caution is advisable when dealing with fragile regimes. Some initiatives are ambitious in terms of scale—as when a program in northern Uganda that we analyzed

(NURP-I) sought to bring changes to seven development sectors and became overstretched. (Donors responded sensibly by scaling the program down.)

Other initiatives are ambitious in terms of degree or the magnitude of changes sought. They involve fundamental reforms entailing decisions that challenge formidable interests. Many governments in developing countries hesitate to attempt such initiatives, because they carry serious political risks. They often prefer to undertake more modest, incremental reforms that do not produce macrosystemic change, because their capacity and legitimacy are open to serious doubt, and because they find it more difficult than well-entrenched governments to withstand reactions from potent interests. Our cases indicate that donors did little to press for transformative reforms in these countries. They were preoccupied with changes that would promote limited capacity building and limited improvements, which have powerful psychological effects in dire situations.

This does not mean, however, that ambitious reform is unthinkable in or utterly unworkable in difficult conditions. In the study of the district government program in Mozambique, we witnessed a fundamental governance reform—national leaders were persuaded to pursue more open governance in an entire (and strategically located) tier of government, the district level. This case illustrates what we mean by "ambitious" reforms and how they might be achieved.

The program in Mozambique was ambitious in both scale (the entire country and multiple sectors were eventually affected) and degree (processes at the district level are changing in fundamental ways). It falls under the heading "democratic decentralization," experiments in which have been ambitious in scale (most have created elected bodies at lower levels nationwide or at least in all urban centers or in all rural areas) but not in degree of change (most have not devolved substantial powers and resources to these elected bodies). These experiments have resulted in a large number of decentralized systems that limp along, underempowered and underfunded.

In 1998 Mozambique's government devolved some significant powers and resources to elected councils at the local (municipio) level across roughly one-third of the country. That task was unambitious in terms of scale and only modestly ambitious in terms of degree of change attempted. But our concern is with a subsequent pilot project in which powers and resources were devolved to democratic institutions at the district level in one province. This change was potentially important to elected councils at the municipio level because actors in autocratic structures at the district level had often crippled their efforts. More to the point, if district-level government could be opened up, the character of the Mozambican regime would change in fundamental ways.

National-level leaders agreed to the experiment in only a few districts because they were deeply anxious that democratization at that level might prove destabilizing. So although the exercise was reasonably ambitious in degree of change undertaken, it was decidedly unambitious in scale.

The pilot project gradually demonstrated that opening up the district level could produce significant improvements in development outcomes without causing destabilization. On the contrary, they enhanced the legitimacy of the government and the ruling party that had introduced the change. Nor was there any sign that this initiative would threaten national unity—an implausible worry that had nonetheless troubled some key figures at the national level. It actually enhanced citizens' sense of belonging, and it persuaded many previously alienated and apathetic people to engage proactively with the policy and political processes.

This turn of events persuaded national leaders that the project was worth extending to some other districts and provinces. When the program produced similar outcomes there, it was extended to every district in the country. Thus the project became ambitious in both scale and degree.

The project suggests that prospects for democratic decentralization might improve if the decentralizing process began incrementally through pilot schemes. That approach is unusual. Most governments have decentralized across their entire countries from the start. But that ambition in terms of scale has been accompanied by (and has often inspired) a distinct lack of ambition in the degree to which powers and resources are devolved. In Mozambique, an incremental approach turned out to be more promising.

Such an approach has a psychological effect on both ordinary people (among whom a modest reform may ease alienation and inspire some belief in the legitimacy of the political order) and national leaders (who gradually recognize that reforms serve their interests).

Disbursement Strategies

Our studies contain only limited insights on different approaches to disbursement of aid funds. But two comments on these approaches are in order.

First, on the question of whether broad budget support or a more focused approach is preferable, our studies suggest that the key consideration is not the choice between these alternatives, but rather the arrangements made for fund management. They also suggest that more focused arrangements are usually preferable in fragile states. In a few cases, (for example, Timor-Leste, which is unlike the other countries in our case studies in that it just achieved national independence), budget support appears to have worked tolerably well at an early stage. But it is usually wise to provide budget support only after pilot projects have changed governments' perceptions and operations sufficiently to enable them to make good use of it.

Second, the costs of running special agencies that bypass mainstream government institutions may be so high that a relatively modest proportion of the funds provided actually reaches people in need. It may be necessary to create such agencies where government incapacity is a severe problem. But the high costs of this approach need to be considered carefully.

Balance between Knowledge Transfers and Financial Support
Our studies suggest that in many cases donors should emphasize knowledge transfers over financial assistance—although this is not an "either/or" issue. Sometimes the most valuable knowledge transfers are importation of ideas from other places, but often they entail dissemination of knowledge from one part of a system or country to another (usually horizontally). Special efforts are needed to draw on the promise of local knowledge, including local arrangements for tackling problems (such as the women's forums discussed in Lister's Afghanistan chapter). UNCDF's experience with local development funds provides especially valuable insights on this task.

Dangers of Too Much Emphasis on Single Sectors
Many donors understandably concentrate on programs in single sectors. Our studies indicate certain dangers with this approach. First, donor support for a single sectoral ministry gives that ministry power that it may abuse. In Mozambique, for example, donor-supported ministries felt strong enough to ignore the preferences expressed in multisector plans developed through consultations at lower level of government. People involved in those consultations grew cynical. Donor-supported sectoral ministries in several other countries have also defied government attempts to coordinate development activities. Second, as was noted earlier, single-sector user committees may undermine the legitimacy of elected, multipurpose councils at lower levels. Donors can seek to discourage these trends without abandoning support for single sectors.

Coordinating and Integrating Aid Interventions

Our studies contribute to discussions of the utility (and difficulties) of coordinating the efforts of multiple donor agencies. But they also suggest that this task ought to be considered in a broader context of several other critically important types of integration.

Let us begin on familiar ground, with coordination among donor agencies. It is often useful to have multiple donors involved in development initiatives in fragile states, because they bring with them a diversity of potentially constructive experiences and approaches. But their varied approaches may not resonate with one another. And individual agencies may insist on remaining somewhat aloof from coordinated donor efforts. Difficulties can also arise when there is a rapid turnover of donor staff, as there often is.

Mechanisms to promote coordination among donors can take various forms and can do more than foster constructive ties among donors. They tend to include government actors/agencies and nongovernmental organizations (NGOs) as well, which pay dividends. In at least one of our cases—the women's forums program in Afghanistan—a mechanism that was mainly intended to promote dialogue among nongovernmental groups promoted coordination among donors as well.

Our studies revealed promising examples of donor coordination efforts. Donor agencies with special expertise can be drawn in to provide distinctive contributions in line with an initiative's basic vision, as when the International Labour Organisation (ILO) and United States Agency for International Development (USAID) joined the microfinance program in Afghanistan. In that case, the ILO representative used her extensive contacts in the NGO community to promote resonance between the microfinance program and other NGO undertakings. These organizations—governmental and nongovernmental—borrowed insights and techniques from one another, and all profited as a result.

In Cambodia, periodic workshops conducted at the district level enabled various donors to inject ideas into the decision-making process so that consensus was sustained. Representatives of provincial governments exercised considerable influence there and thus developed a strong sense of ownership of the program. This ownership helped ensure both the long-term sustainability of the program and its influence on government thinking in other spheres.

Two great advantages follow from extending coordination efforts beyond donors to government and NGOs. First, it builds the capacity of the latter two—and government agencies badly need to acquire the capacity to operate openly and responsively. Second, the collegial relations between governments and civil society organizations—which often begin to develop when both are drawn into coordinated activity—may also enhance the capacity of government institutions to collect revenues, so that the state becomes better resourced. Finally, it prepares the ground for the eventual exit of donors from programs. Lister's chapter on Afghanistan is particularly enlightening in this regard.

Findings of the Main Study

Although the problems that exist in fragile states at first appear utterly daunting, a great deal can in fact be achieved there. Development programs need to be based not just on established principles but also on an assessment at the outset of distinctive conditions at and just above the local level within fragile states. Among these conditions, power dynamics are especially important because they are bound up with governance issues—which, as expected, we found to be immensely important.

This assessment must be conducted in consultation with citizens. Once it has been completed, the resulting programs should be implemented with a willingness both to learn from periodic consultations and to adjust approaches accordingly. In most cases, an incremental approach that incorporates lessons from trials will be beneficial.

Such an approach lends itself to the difficult transition from initial, quick-impact, top-down programs to address dire emergencies to longer-term, bottom-up efforts to promote development and institutional reform. That transition requires changes in the ways in which both officials and citizens think about governance, state-society relations, and development. Emphasis should be placed on initiatives that governments fearful of change are at least somewhat inclined to undertake, because officials are likely to gain a sense of ownership of these programs.

We were surprised to discover that the potential for constructive action at and just above the local level was greater than at higher levels in these political systems. When institutions become seriously incapacitated, human and interpersonal resources and bonds more often survive at the local level than do the looser, more impersonal relationships that exist at higher levels. These resources and bonds have considerable potential for establishment of trust, accommodation, and a sense of mutuality, and they provide a platform on which to mount grassroots efforts at reconstruction.

Almost all of the successful programs that we studied entailed consultative mechanisms to draw local preferences, knowledge, and energies into the policy process and to provide external resources to local communities. These mechanisms worked especially well when they were coupled with efforts at democratic decentralization, which linked changes to formal institutions that can help to structure and sustain them.

Governments everywhere are reluctant to devolve powers and resources onto elected bodies at lower levels, but when they do so, they usually make major compensatory gains in popularity and legitimacy. Such generosity turns out to be nonthreatening and in their interests. The resulting changes in the thinking and behavior of government actors can promote the transition from coercive regimes to developmental states.

Encouraging governments' inclination and capacity to pursue development in an open, consultative manner is essential. This task is often best pursued through pilot projects within a few small arenas that can demonstrate to insecure governments the benefits to themselves and citizens of open, consultative governance.

The positive results of these projects often inspire adoption of similar approaches in other government agencies, regions, and development sectors. Publicizing the successes of pilot experiments can encourage such spillover. More systematic efforts to scale up such successes may also bear fruit, but this process is often slow and difficult in fragile states.

This discussion has focused on achieving changes within governments. The utility of civil society organizations should not be dismissed, but governments nearly always reach far more localities than these organizations. And even where regimes are fragile, they command far more resources. It therefore makes sense for donors to concentrate mainly on influencing governments.

To influence governments and make development sustainable, donors should integrate development programs with mainstream government institutions—at both local and higher levels—as soon as possible. This task often entails a difficult move away from initial efforts to tackle emergencies through special parallel agencies that bypass mainstream institutions. But if development programs are kept separate from mainstream bureaucratic agencies and elected bodies at the local level, the programs can prevent those groups from evolving into elements of a new, constructive order that can make improvements possible and sustainable. Integration of programs with mainstream government structures has the added benefits of empowering governments and making them amenable to open, consultative, and participatory approaches.

Finally, difficulties will beset the processes described above. But evidence from our studies of very different, but consistently difficult, cases indicates that fortitude is justified: much can be achieved.

Notes

1. In undertaking a preliminary analysis, donors may consider using or adapting an approach developed at the Harvard School of Public Health (Bossert 2005) for rapidly appraising conditions in developing countries.
2. See Manor (1999, chapter 6).
3. Sarah Cliffe, World Bank, stressed this point to us in Washington, DC, on April 28, 2005.
4. See also Romeo (2002).
5. See in this connection, Katorobo (2003).
6. On the key issue of strengthening human resources, see Harbison (1973) and Schultz (1961).
7. This definition is adapted from one of the earliest—and still one of the best—analyses of this issue (in the context of nongovernmental organizations): Edwards and Hulme (1992).
8. See Malhotra (2004).
9. This paragraph draws heavily on comments by David Warren, Senior Social Privatization Specialist, World Bank.
10. See World Bank (2002).
11. This point emerged at a World Bank workshop on social funds in Washington, DC, in June 2000.
12. David Warren made this point in informal comments on papers from this project in November 2005.
13. This point is discussed in much greater detail in Manor (2004a).
14. See Crook and Manor (1998, chapter 5). The Rawlings regime failed to provide minimal powers and resources to the elected assemblies, so they eventually inspired disillusionment. But that does not occur where governments behave less cynically.
15. The four are Bangladesh, Brazil, India, and the Philippines. See Manor (2004b).

Bibliography

Bossert, T. 2005. "Reaching the Health MDGs with Human Resource Reforms: Financial, Educational and Management Capacities." *IDS Bulletin*, September, 74–82.

Crook, R. C., and James Manor. 1998. *Democracy and Decentralisation in South Asia and West Africa: Participation, Accountability and Performance.* Cambridge, UK: Cambridge University Press.

Edwards, M., and D. Hulme. 1992. "Scaling Up NGO Impacts on Development: Learning from Experience." *Development in Practice*, May, 77–91.

Grindle, M. 2004. "Good Enough Governance: Poverty Reduction and Reform in Developing Countries." *Governance: An International Journal of Policy, Administration and Institutions* 17 (4): 525–48.

Harbison, F. H. 1973. *Human Resources as the Wealth of Nations.* New York: Oxford University Press.

Katorobo, J. 2003. "Democratic Institution Building in Post-Conflict Societies." UNDESA paper for the Fifth International Conference on New or Restored Democracies, Ulaanbaatar, Mongolia, June 18–20.

Malhotra, M. 2004. "Lessons: Scaling Up Successful Efforts to Reduce Poverty." http://www.worldbank.org/reducingpoverty/docs/conceptual.pdf.

Manor, James. 1999. *The Political Economy of Democratic Decentralization.* Washington, DC: World Bank.

———. 2004a. 2004. *Civil Society and Poverty Reduction in Less-Developed Countries: A Practitioner's Guide.* Stockholm: Sida.

———. 2004b. "'User Committees': A Potentially Damaging New Wave of Decentralization." *European Journal of Development Research*, (Spring): 192–213.

Quinn, M. 2002. "More Than Implementers: Civil Societies in Complex Emergencies." International Alert, London.

Ottaway, M. 2001. "Strengthening Civil Society in Other Countries: Policy Goal or Wishful Thinking?" *The Chronicle Review*, June 29 (Carnegie Endowment for International Peace, Washington, DC).

Romeo, L. 2002. "Local Governance Approach to Social Reintegration and Economic Recovery in Post-Conflict Countries: Towards a Definition and a Rationale." Paper prepared for the UNDP/UNCDF workshop titled A Local Governance Approach to Post-Conflict Recovery, New York, October 8.

Schultz, T. W. 1961. "Investing in Human Capital." *The American Economic Review*, LI, March 1961, 1–17. American Economic Association Presidential Address.

World Bank. 2002. *Social Funds: Assessing Effectiveness.* Washington, DC: World Bank.

CHAPTER 2

A Framework for Assessing Program and Project Aid in Low-Income Countries under Stress

> The international aid system faces real dilemmas and remains ill equipped
> to respond to the peculiar challenges of quasi-statehood that characterize
> chronic political emergencies and their aftermath.
>
> —Macrae (2001, Foreword)

The inability of international organizations to respond effectively to
"quasi-states" prompted a World Bank initiative to develop more systematic knowledge of how development agencies might most effectively
engage with low-income countries under stress (LICUS).[1] The World
Bank's Task Force Report on LICUS reviews at length the issues involved
in helping poor countries "whose policies and institutions offer limited
scope for poverty reduction through donor-supported programs and
projects" (World Bank 2002a).

A World Bank research initiative is studying how LICUS achieve
turnaround, defined as a durable cessation of violent conflict, sustained
economic growth, and sustained improvement in the level of human

---

This chapter was written by Martin Greeley.

development. Phase one of that effort created a detailed mapping of the choice, content, and sequencing of reforms in seven turnaround countries (Institute of Development Studies 2006). The framework and case studies presented in this volume represent phase two, which seeks to provide clear policy and operational implications for future aid.

The chapter has two main sections. The first section reviews the literature on aid and assesses conventional approaches to aid effectiveness in LICUS. This literature argues that achieving development results from aid, in the form of growth, depends on good policies. As LICUS are characterized by poor policy environments, by definition they will not use aid effectively. But growth is not the arbiter of aid effectiveness in LICUS contexts; measures of progress are different, as the framework outlined in this chapter makes clear. Moreover, this literature does not always distinguish among aid modalities. In contrast, the case study approach adopted here is designed to examine whether specific aid modalities can offset the special difficulties of operating in LICUS.

The second section presents a LICUS program/project assessment framework. This framework is designed to assess "successful" initiatives in LICUS and to enhance understanding of key issues. "Success" is defined as reducing poverty, improving service delivery, or both; achieving sustainable change in governance; achieving positive spillover by catalyzing change outside the area, sector, or theme of the original intervention; or stemming the negative spillover effects from one country to a neighboring country or the wider region.

World Bank country offices assisted in identifying programs and projects believed to have been successful in at least one of these respects. The assessment framework for these interventions includes three elements: **Results**—what was delivered, or attempted, and possibly led to positive spillover; **Design Considerations**—why this approach was adopted; and **Implementation**—how it facilitated achievement of development results (table 2.1).

The framework first identifies the types of success or results achieved, provides the evidence for it, and assesses its development significance. Identifying development results is the first element, because programs and projects were selected on the basis of development results and the main analytic focus is to derive lessons for the future by understanding how success came about. The first two domains for results are delivered outcomes and governance outcomes, although the case study treatment of governance outcomes varies, since not all interventions had explicit governance objectives.

Table 2.1 Framework for Assessing Program and Project Aid in LICUS

Development results	Non-governance outcomes	Governance outcomes
	What was delivered? Did it benefit the poor? What are the growth implications?	For all interventions, were there effects on governance or the wider political economy? For interventions targeting specific governance outcomes, what was achieved? How might these achievements contribute to poverty reduction and growth?
	Engendering positive spillover Within the local, domestic, or regional economy, were there positive social, political, or economic benefits beyond the direct development results?	
Design considerations	Elements of political economy and governance: What was planned and why? Was it coordinated? Was the intervention attuned to the LICUS context, and did the design recognize the opportunities for and threats to effectiveness posed by the domestic political economy?	
Implementation processes	Program management How did quality of implementation improve achievement of development results?	

Source: Author.

A third results domain is spillover—whether the intervention generated benefits (or costs) beyond its immediate objectives. One hypothesis is that in LICUS, well-designed and implemented interventions can generate significant spillover within a country that is an important component of the total benefits from the intervention. Spillover can take several forms. Economic externalities, in the form of backward and forward links and consumption multipliers, are one type of positive externality.

In the case studies in this volume, spillover includes social and political as well as economic dimensions. Political spillover may occur within a country, or it may contribute to regional stability where cross-border problems (migration, informal trade, and smuggling, for example) are significant and politically sensitive. Economic reforms promoting growth and livelihoods may mitigate these problems. Alternatively, an intervention may generate direct positive spillover. Women's groups formed in a microfinance program, for example, may become active in supporting better health-seeking behavior within their community. Positive spillover can also occur through the replication of "model" interventions by the government or by other donors.

The second element of the framework seeks to provide insights into how design considerations contributed to the achievement of development results. The design element centers on a review of the design process and a set of political economy considerations that should inform the development of aid activities for LICUS. Evidence on and reviews of these considerations are critical in assessing LICUS aid interventions. The third element, on implementation, focuses on process issues involved in the specific interventions. It uses eight criteria to assess the quality of implementation processes and their contribution to development results.

The underlying contextual distinction of LICUS status is best captured by the notion of quasi-statehood. This refers to the combined conditions of recent recovery, at least partially, from a complex emergency, often war, and newly recreated and poorly developed state sovereignty. It is associated with continuing political complexities, often with the risk of fresh conflict. It is characterized by widespread and severe poverty and limited or no provision of basic social services. The organs of the state are weak, because they have poor and limited human resources. They typically operate with a damaged infrastructure and very few material resources.

Insecurity and poor governance are two of the special difficulties of LICUS, especially following conflicts. Specific aid interventions can help reduce insecurity directly, through policing and judicial services, or through aid interventions, such as those that increase economic growth or that may reduce insecurity indirectly.[2] But the main focus of aid interventions, beyond their direct outcomes, is on improving governance. In LICUS this means strengthening the willingness and capacity of elected officials, state institutions, and government workers to improve social welfare though public actions. An extensive body of literature has examined improved governance in post-conflict and other LICUS contexts (for a good review, see Katorobo 2003).

The conditions associated with quasi-statehood vary. In some cases, these conditions affect a specific region, such as northern Uganda. In other cases, these conditions may not be directly related to conflict but to extreme poverty, political complexity, weak services, limited human resources, and a poor policy environment, as measured, for example, by the condition's score on the Country Policy and Institutional Assessment (CPIA).[3] In different contexts, the relative importance of the different conditions for aid effectiveness will therefore vary, but there is a common need for external support because of extreme and widespread poverty and limited domestic resources and capacity.

Quasi-states also suffer from weak modalities for effective intervention because of the fragility of the political process, weak policy-making capacity, and very limited financial and organizational resources to operationalize development programs. Donor resources can be especially influential in such contexts, and their disbursement can affect domestic politics. Interventions that can contribute to fledgling opportunities to strengthen governance are of special importance. The potential of external assistance to be a positive catalyst is clear, and the need to provide such a catalyst is urgent, but the design- and implementation-related conditions outlined above make it difficult for donors to be effective.

Overarching Issues Affecting Aid Modalities

Three aid modality issues affect the effectiveness of intervention in LICUS contexts: constrained state capacity, lack of aid coordination by multiple donors, and scarce local public expenditure resources. There appears to be consensus that working through the state is desirable; coordinating with other donors, particularly like-minded donors, is important; and resource transfers should support a fiscal policy and budget reflecting sustainable public resource management. These three issues are of special significance in LICUS contexts, in which the current orthodoxy may not be applicable. The success of an external intervention is unlikely unless design and implementation take account of these issues. The issues reinforce the need to pay attention to lessons from "successful" interventions in settings with LICUS-like conditions, conditions that require a fresh approach to assessing development interventions. Such an approach must focus on the political economy of aid, specifically on the role of development resources in the domestic political economy.

Replacing Relief with Development
In many fragile states the focus of external assistance changes as establishment of sovereignty triggers replacement of relief by development assistance. Although funding of relief may continue, donor engagement shifts to the longer-term prospects for growth and poverty reduction. In the context of quasi-statehood, however, equating establishment of sovereignty with commitment to a reform agenda is often incorrect. Moreover, commitment to state-based resource flows poses risks when the policy framework and capacity are weak. Proposed interventions must be assessed in the context

of the stage reached in the shift from relief to development, and specifically in reference to the state's capacity to deliver services effectively.

Coordinating Donors

The central tenet of aid-effectiveness literature is that the coherence of support will be undermined if donors do not exercise some degree of coordination. Coordination begins with shared understanding of initial conditions and causes, which leads to identification of sequencing priorities, design of activities, and implementation. Some LICUS (such as Mozambique) have suffered from donors' failure to avoid burdening domestic government with multiple donor demands and conditions in return for resources. The OECD-DAC (2001, 4) underlines the importance of donor coordination in difficult partnerships and emphasizes the need to share analysis, establish one set of criteria for assessment, agree on the most appropriate conditions for engagement, task lead agencies, and build on the comparative advantages of both bilateral and multilateral agencies. It also underlines the importance of maintaining dialogue with the government and flexibility while remaining focused on poverty reduction. The issue of coordination is linked to the possible positive spillover from "model" interventions.

Dealing with Resource Constraints

Resource constraints are a common problem in LICUS. Assessment of design must involve reviews of how this constraint has been addressed in projects and focus on recurrent costs. Government revenues may not be available on any relevant scale in the short term; project design may have to include an analysis of required resource commitments over time and options for relaxing resource constraints.

This analysis may not support the normative donor approach, which emphasizes sustainability. Sustainability may not be an appropriate goal, because mechanisms of revenue generation are inadequate or because sustainability is temporarily subordinated to poverty reduction or improved governance. In these cases, it will be necessary to determine what approach to sustainability was adopted and why donors did not insist on sustainability. Severe and immediate poverty is likely to be one reason; limited revenue collection capacity and corruption could be others.

Reviewing LICUS Contexts and the Aid Effectiveness Literature

In the wake of assesments by Burnside and Dollar (1997) and World Bank (1998), the World Bank identified recipient countries' policy environment as a catalyst for improving aid effectiveness, as measured by growth and poverty reduction. On the basis of this finding, Collier and Dollar (1999) used CPIA data to measure policy quality and evaluate how improved aid allocations across countries could improve poverty reduction. Other donors have been influenced by this work, and commitment to policy-based support, selectivity, and results- or performance-based allocations is growing globally. The key message—that trying to buy good policies is inefficient and that from the standpoint of allocative efficiency too much aid is currently allocated to countries with poor policy environments—does not bode well for LICUS.

Lensink and White (1999) have critiqued this message because it ignores the degree of country variability in the relationships being modeled. Neither cross-country regressions nor raw CPIA scores[4] help agencies identify specific opportunities for providing effective aid in particular countries. However, recent evidence supports the policy-based approach to aid effectiveness and underscores the challenges in making aid effective in poor policy environments (World Bank 2003b).

Very poor LICUS merit aid because of the direct relationship between aid and poverty reduction, but this aid will be less effective than in countries that score well on the CPIA. Devarajan, Dollar, and Holmgren (2001) show that policy formation is driven primarily by the domestic political economy and that there is no association between aid and improved policy in poor policy environments. These are cross-country comparative results. It seems plausible that in LICUS, opportunities to influence policy development will be important. The research is a warning, however; although aid has sometimes improved policy, success is particularly elusive in LICUS.

World Bank (2002b) find that aid to LICUS is more effective in promoting growth than the global cross-country regressions indicate but only for a limited period, roughly from the fourth to the seventh year after peace has been achieved. The authors of this chapter recognize that the result is tentative and that country-specific analysis may produce different findings.[5] Collier and Dollar (1999) note that aid is allocated for reasons other than direct growth and poverty reduction. In LICUS contexts, aid may reduce the risk of conflict or its re-emergence (Collier 1998) and induce private sector investment.

Clemens, Radelet, and Bhavnani (2004) establish that the type of aid matters. Using three categories (relief; contribution to long-term growth, such as investment in education; and aid for immediate growth, such as infrastructure and productive sector aid), they show that aid for short-term impacts is highly effective, regardless of the policy environment.

These findings underscore the importance of assessing the relative merits of different aid modalities and recognizing the contribution of aid to objectives other than immediate growth.

The key explanatory variable in this aid effectiveness framework—the strength of policies and institutions—is of little value in explaining variation in donor effectiveness in LICUS, because all of these countries have poor policies and institutions. Therefore, the overall conclusion from the literature is that for humanitarian, security, and economic reasons, aid should be allocated to LICUS, but the current policy quality framework for examining aid effectiveness offers little insight into the assessment of effectiveness in LICUS contexts.

In an approach to aid effectiveness that is more relevant to LICUS, four drivers of change have been proposed. The framework, presented at a World Bank–supported conference on poverty in Shanghai in May 2004, identifies a conceptual framework for scaling up poverty reduction (World Bank 2004b). Based mainly on experience in Asia, it builds on success stories there to identify the factors that help reduce poverty. The framework employs two strategic pillars—the investment climate and social inclusion—and specifies four drivers of change or success factors: learning, experimenting, and communication; institutional innovation and implementation; the political economy of change; and external catalysts. All of these success criteria are relevant in LICUS. But it is important to recognize that this agenda was developed in fully functioning states.

The notion of scaling up implies that some success has been achieved. It is by no means clear that specific projects or programs, such as the cases examined in this volume, can demonstrate the type of results that would lend themselves to scaling up. Initial activities to get a sector moving again may not be grounded in longer-term institutional development options; transition plans may be necessary. These activities may be "zero-generation" reforms that are designed to make some progress quickly and to achieve a degree of political buy-in. In many LICUS, social inclusion is a more central strategic pillar than the investment climate, which may be more broadly interpreted as growth-promoting outcomes. The LICUS context and the condition of quasi-statehood require a strategic emphasis on political economy.

Reviewing Poverty Reduction Strategy Papers and the New Aid Architecture

Since 1999, the Poverty Reduction Strategy Paper (PRSP) process has been used to guide Poverty Reduction and Growth Fund (PRGF) and

IDA Poverty Reduction Support Credit (PRSC) allocations and enhanced entitlement by highly indebted poor countries (HIPC). Core concepts driving the new architecture are country ownership and civil society engagement in the provision of policy-based aid. PRSPs have been prepared in some LICUS, including three of the case studies included in this volume (Cambodia, Mozambique, and Uganda). The International Monetary Fund (IMF) and the World Bank have special arrangements for LICUS in early recovery (World Bank 2001). These arrangements involve some relaxation of the production and content rules for the interim PRSP, but countries still have to follow this route to acquire entitlement to debt relief and PRGF and PRSC resources.[6]

These new aid instruments are likely to be of limited application in LICUS in the early stages of recovery. But under current aid policies, PRSPs are inevitably going to be attempted in most LICUS, as partnership arrangements deepen and "normal" aid conditions begin to emerge. It is not always clear whether adoption of these new instruments is really driven by local assessment of the most appropriate aid modalities or by international aid rules regulating resource transfers and instruments for debt reduction. Nevertheless, promotion of PRSPs may still be strategically important in LICUS, for both political and resource reasons.[7] PRSPs may also improve donor coordination, a central concern for aid effectiveness in LICUS.

The PRSP approach is inherently challenging where governance is poor, budget management is weak, human resources are limited, and civil society is fractured and institutionally bereft. Nevertheless, the substantial learning associated with global review of PRSP experience on participatory approaches to poverty analysis, direct budgetary support, sector aid, and monitoring and evaluation may inform aid activities in LICUS. The PRSP approach also suggests that participation by the poor in policy making and implementation is crucial to achieving positive policy outcomes. Such participation may be especially difficult in LICUS, where the institutions of civil society are inherently weak and rights of representation are contested. To some degree, therefore, the opportunities for learning from research on and experience with PRSP processes and the new aid instruments will depend on the precise conditions of quasi-statehood and on the length of time that has passed since sovereignty was restored.

The conventional wisdom on assessing aid effectiveness is not readily applicable or indeed relevant to LICUS, where the underlying PRSP presumptions about revenue management, participation, and a poverty reduction focus may not hold. The conditions of quasi-statehood mean that the basis for assessment and the options for aid modalities are systemically different. These conditions proscribe straightforward application of the scaling-up framework, although there is some degree of overlap in success factors in the framework developed below.

Framework for Program and Project Assessment in LICUS

Which aid interventions can best contribute to development in LICUS contexts? To answer that question we need to know the ways in which a given intervention was informed by analysis of the local political economy and the extent to which it improved, by example or more directly, the political and economic context for development. To address these information needs, our framework for assessing interventions considers design considerations and implementation processes, as well as development results,[8] which are the justification for selection of the case studies in this volume. The bases for assessing these results are shown in table 2.2.

The table lists six non-governance outcomes and five governance outcomes that might result from interventions. In LICUS contexts, assessment of poverty reduction and growth outcomes is most critical. Rigorous assessment of these outcomes may not be feasible in the earliest years of support to LICUS governments. But where the productive sectors have been part of the focus of the intervention, some poverty reduction and growth conclusions may be feasible and should be attempted.

The framework seeks to be comprehensive but is not intended to be restrictive. The relative importance of specific design considerations and process issues varies, and judgment is required to provide an assessment that plausibly explains "success."

The framework is applied to a variety of LICUS, some of which have recently emerged as sovereign states or have established sovereignty unevenly and others of which have a longer history of sovereignty. The programs and projects represent a range of interventions; some are regional, some are more localized, and some are quite narrow in scope and focused on service delivery. The framework is therefore neither a template nor a checklist but instead a guide to improving the comprehensiveness of individual assessments, the basis for comparative analysis, and the identification of lessons for future interventions.

The framework entails no specific research methods. When there is no opportunity for survey work or detailed qualitative assessments using focus

Table 2.2   Framework for Evidence on Development Results of Aid Interventions in LICUS

	Description, including scale and scope	Quantitative and qualitative results	Means of assessment	Poverty sensitivity and growth implications	Means of assessment
Non-governance outcomes					
Service provision					
Capacity building					
Natural resource management					
Infrastructure development					
Policy reform and economic management					
Private sector development					
Governance outcomes					
Political stability strengthened					
Domestic leadership strengthened, nationally or regionally					
Ethnic tensions reduced					
Security enhanced					
Human rights strengthened					

Source: Author.
Notes: Scale refers to the significance of a given outcome in relation to other project/program outcomes; scope refers to the significance of the outcome in national or regional contexts. Means of assessment refers to the evidence informing the analysis of outcomes and draws in part on monitoring and evaluation reports and other documentation of project achievements.

groups, effective use of secondary data must be made. Researchers should collect information from a cross-section of stakeholders and attempt to corroborate it whenever possible. To establish the credibility of their results, researchers should report on their research methods and design considerations, which may reflect a high degree of individual discretion.

Assessing Development Results

The first hypothesis to be tested with the case studies presented in this volume is that well-designed aid can be effective where governance is poor, as in LICUS. To assess an intervention's effectiveness, the case study authors ask the following questions:

- How well did actual results match outcomes specified at the outset of the project or program? Did poor people benefit from the intervention?
- Was beneficiary satisfaction assessed?
- Did the results reflect poverty reduction priorities, and did they have any implications for growth processes?

The second hypothesis to be tested is that analysis of political dynamics in the design of interventions will strengthen an intervention's capacity to reduce poverty and spark growth in LICUS. Some of the interventions analyzed here had specified governance outcomes. Other interventions addressed governance constraints indirectly. Because any sustained improvement in governance is unlikely to be wholly attributable to specific interventions, the authors of the case studies presented here made judgments about the significance of the intervention's contribution by asking the following questions:

- Did the intervention strengthen political stability? That is, did it address the interests of disaffected groups in ways that promoted their participation in domestic political processes and enhanced the legitimacy of the political system?
- Did the intervention strengthen domestic leadership? That is, did it deliver results that strengthened the populace's confidence that leaders were pursuing effective policies?
- Did the intervention reduce ethnic tensions? Such tensions are often associated with quasi-statehood. Interventions can reduce them through careful attention to cultural differences, to the spatial distribution of ethnic groups, and to the economic basis of each group's livelihoods.
- Did the intervention enhance security? LICUS conditions are often associated with ready access to arms, even in post-conflict situations. Interventions can reduce the resulting insecurity by providing economic opportunities and new aspirations to past combatants and other marginalized groups that are a threat to security.
- Did the intervention strengthen human rights? To lessen rights violations, interventions can make reduction of the violations a basis for inclusion of groups responsible for the violations in the development agenda.

The third hypothesis to be tested is that interventions may have spillover effects, such as reducing displacement and cross-border migration, limiting cross-border insurgency and its political costs, or decreasing the incidence of disease or environmental degradation (for example, logging). Spillovers may come about through an intervention's specified outcomes, such as new economic opportunities that reduce crime. They may be the result of individual beneficiaries' strengthened capacities in areas unconnected to the intervention. Crucially, they may arise from use of a well-designed and -executed intervention as a model for governance arrangements, participatory processes, or other elements of other interventions.

Positive spillovers are of special importance in LICUS because of the fragility of the state and the need for broad-based social, political, and economic progress. In most cases such spillovers will be difficult to establish. Nevertheless, the authors of the case studies presented here explicitly address the spillover issue by asking the following questions:

- Is there any evidence of positive spillover?
- What form does it take?
- How strong is the evidence in support of it?
- What development lessons can be drawn?

Assessing Design Considerations' Contribution to Development Results

LICUS are characterized by extreme shortages of domestic resources for public expenditure. Therefore, any moderately large intervention will likely have some measurable impacts. The issue is how impacts can be strengthened through circumvention or removal of weaknesses in governance and state capacity. Such strengthening depends crucially on the extent to which a political economy and social analysis informed the design of a given intervention.

Diagnosis of Political Economy and Social Conditions
LICUS are commonly characterized by severe poverty in income terms, in access to food, and in provision of health and education services. These conditions will determine poverty reduction priorities, but more pressing needs are likely to exist on a wider set of fronts. Addressing these needs is especially difficult in LICUS, because weakness in both the state and civil society, together with conditions of insecurity, creates problems of capacity with respect to policy development, design of activities, and implementation.

The authors of the case studies in this volume attempted to identify the political and governance obstacles to effective development that a given intervention had to address. They began by asking a set of questions about the specifics of the intervention's design:

- What were the main design considerations, what were the program/ project objectives, and what was the scale and geographical coverage?[9]
- Which issues were analyzed as the program was being developed?
- What flexibility was built in, how was risk anticipated, and how did the design plan to or actually enable the intervention to deal with deterioration in the implementation environment?

Attention to Domestic Ownership

Aid interventions will suffer without meaningful domestic "ownership." Although such ownership is needed to maximize aid effectiveness, it is not easy to achieve in LICUS, where institutions are so weak. Given the absence of effective institutions, design of aid interventions should reflect the input of local partners in civil society that espouse inclusivity (Quinn 2002).

In the case studies, the researchers had to assess the extent to which design was sensitive to the aspirations of reformers and to opportunities for strengthening progressive domestic ownership. To do this they asked two questions:

- Into which elements of the design process was domestic ownership incorporated?
- In areas in which reliance on international expertise was great, did the design anticipate movement toward greater local ownership during implementation?

Attention to Horizontal Inequality

Stewart (2000) develops the concept of horizontal inequality to refer to different culturally formed groups that are often party to earlier conflict. The concept relates closely to consideration of domestic ownership. Stewart's analysis of nine case studies examines how states supported by donors have promoted divisive policies that have undermined development progress and threatened conflict or renewal of conflict. She shows that "current political conditionality is concerned with establishing democracy, not inclusive government, while current economic and social conditionality is directed towards promoting growth and efficiency and poverty reduction but not reducing horizontal inequality."

The case study authors attempted to identify the significance of horizontal inequality and the steps taken to ameliorate it. This inequality is not restricted to an understanding of "culturally formed groups" as merely ethnically based groups. It also includes gender inequality and sometimes specific occupational groups. For the case studies, two questions are, therefore, important:

- How did knowledge of ethnic or other group differences inform design?
- Were interventions chosen and designed to promote inclusiveness and reduce group tensions?

Choice of Implementing Agency

Successful design depends on identification of an appropriate organization to spearhead the intervention. In many countries, line ministries might shoulder this task. In LICUS, project implementation units, special state bodies, and NGOs may be more appropriate choices. In other circumstances, local governments may be the most sensible option, especially when community-based organizations are the endpoint for aid delivery (Romeo 2002).

As development activities gather momentum in LICUS, the role of NGOs is commonly reassessed. That role is often diminished as international donors seek to partner with sovereign states and influence and support the states' development strategies. The capacity to maintain a strong and immediate focus on alleviating poverty and human suffering through external intervention, and the use of directive strategies such as ring-fencing of aid-supported expenditure, can easily be undermined by optimistic assessments of state institutions to manage resources and implement policies effectively. Zero-generation reforms, in particular, have to be based on a nuanced analysis of longer-term development options and current needs. Therefore, case studies authors asked two questions:

- What factors influenced the choice of implementing agency, and what alternatives were considered?
- What capacity constraints were identified, and what measures were taken to address them in the intervention's design?

Public Support for the Intervention

Interventions may reflect priorities of past regimes (priorities that are no longer relevant), or they may benefit specific elements of the new leadership. A significant portion of LICUS aid supports reconstruction, but reconstruction of institutions and infrastructure that have been lost or damaged may not be appropriate priorities (Le Billion 2000). Maintaining a heritage of large city hospitals may be less urgent for welfare than starting afresh with community-based clinics. Moreover, the public may not support interventions that have unwelcome associations with unpopular regimes or policies. Therefore, the case study authors attempted to determine whether interventions, especially any reconstruction priorities, were informed by knowledge of such associations.

Inclusion of Civil Society and Local Institutions

Increasing the participation of civil society in decisions about the use and control of public resources is accepted as a development norm but is difficult to achieve in LICUS.[10] Because local civil society institutions there are often weak, strengthening of these institutions is often an indispensable part of post-conflict interventions.

Civil society research identifies a need for diversification among partners and responsiveness to local processes and contexts in allocating aid for strengthening civil society. In the projects examined here in which civil society plays a central role, researchers sought to establish the extent to which engagement with civil society was based on external analyses and agendas or was informed by domestic assessment of opportunities to rebuild inclusive civil society institutions. In all the case studies, the researchers asked two questions:

- Was civil society involved in the design of the intervention?
- Did it have a role in implementation (monitoring service delivery or ensuring accountability of resources, for example) and, if so, how did that role contribute to achievement of development results?

Attention to Aid Modalities

As noted above, the choice of aid modality is particularly important in LICUS contexts. Constrained domestic capacity, multiple donors, and scarce local public expenditure resources were identified as sensitive and important issues. To assess whether the appropriate aid modality was chosen, case study authors asked three questions:

- To what extent was state absorptive capacity assessed and what sorts of attempts were made to address weaknesses?

- What specific donor coordination activities were part of the design process?
- What attention was given to the sustainability of the intervention, and how feasible was the resource plan?

Assessing Implementation Management's Contribution to Development Results

In LICUS contexts, progressive management of aid interventions, including capacity for flexibility in operationalizing interventions, is crucial. Those responsible for this management may have little knowledge of how external actors and their resources interact with local institutions and communities. Their actions may meet with skepticism or mistrust. The framework below identifies four key aspects of program or project management that will influence the quality of implementation.

Resource Mix and Adequacy

Externally provided resources are an important part of the whole resource envelope in most LICUS contexts and their effective management is challenged by competing demands and multiple priorities. The mix of resources—funding, policy advice, and technical assistance—plus the interaction among them and the sequencing of their use will influence achievement of desired outcomes. The quality of technical assistance is likely to be of importance in establishing implementation priorities and managing monetary resources.

Coordination

Aid in the form of monetary resources, but also technical assistance and policy advice, is usually the core resource in the revitalization of a development agenda in LICUS cases and will typically involve multiple donors. If this collective effort is to be efficient, implementation should be based on agreed division of labor, partnership arrangements, and consistency in policy advice.

Revenue and Budget Management

An appropriate approach to financial sustainability, as emphasized in the introductory discussion on aid modalities, is a key concern in LICUS contexts, particularly for service delivery. The ring-fencing of resources may offer a short-term strategy to ensure service delivery, but program or project management has also to provide guidance on the longer-term options for sustainable service provision.

Implementation Process and Activities

With respect to implementation, case study authors attempted to describe what was done, what was achieved, what difficulties were faced, and what lessons can be learned with respect to the following implementation activities:

Policy dialogue. LICUS are defined by weak policy environments, and donors have a role as catalysts to promote policy reform—that requires dialogue.

Stakeholder participation. Stakeholder analysis identifies those who influence decisions. This analysis must be performed with sensitivity in LICUS contexts and must be ongoing. Assessment of implementation management should include how any opposition to proposed implementation was addressed.

Inclusivity, including gender sensitivity. Related closely to stakeholder participation, inclusivity is of special importance in most LICUS because of the risks to effective implementation that may result from excluding groups that are disaffected from the political leadership, or that are politically weak but of importance for welfare improvement. Often special initiatives will be required to ensure the inclusion of women in implementation; absence of such inclusion may reduce aid effectiveness.

Learning and sharing. One of the most important ways that aid interventions can promote development gains is through acquisition and dissemination of knowledge about effective and ineffective implementation processes and activities. Donor resources are crucial in promoting learning from implementation experience and in promoting a shared agenda of learning. Assessment of implementation management should include assessment of the extent to which development effectiveness was monitored and communicated for learning purposes.

Public relations. Public relations is an especially important element of aid to LICUS, where donors seek to effect positive change both directly through program activities and indirectly as catalysts for improving the environment for development effectiveness. Strategic management of partnership relations, both of willing partners and of those potentially or actually in opposition to interventions, is likely to be crucial.

Summarizing Case Study Contents

Each case study includes a description of country and development context, country statistics, study design, the aid program or project, and fieldwork methods and sources.

In accordance with the framework presented in table 2.2, each case study includes an assessment of development results—actual outcomes as compared with desired outcomes; the intervention's political impact and contribution to improved governance; and the intervention's implications for poverty reduction, such as an assessment of inclusiveness and a growth assessment, including any likely outcomes for natural resource sustainability. Development results include spillover effects.

Each case study includes an assessment of design considerations—political, economic, social, cultural, security, and strategic context and broad options. This assessment includes an analysis of political economy—domestic ownership, horizontal inequality, choice of implementing agency, public support for the intervention, and civil society and local institutions—and of aid modalities.

Each case study includes an assessment of implementation management and concludes with a summary of findings discussed in relation to the three hypotheses noted above and to issues on attribution (see note 8).

Notes

1. "'Quasi-states' are those states where capacity to govern their territory is compromised . . . by a lack of resources and institutional failure" (Macrae 2001, p. 4). This definition applies equally to most of the countries classified as LICUS. The World Bank classifies 26 countries as LICUS and another 8 as close to that status. Half of the 26 countries are post-conflict countries. In the other half, chronic poor governance impedes human development and growth. Only a few of these 34 countries are "policy poor but resource rich" and do not need finance (World Bank 2002a).

2. A World Bank note (2003a) identifies three routes—higher incomes, faster growth and low dependence on primary commodities—through which economic performance may reduce conflict but states that there is no a priori link.

3. CPIA (Country Policy and Institutional Assessment) is carried out annually by the World Bank and is used to guide IDA allocations between countries.

4. This is confirmed by a review of performance measurement as summarized in World Bank (2003b).

5. The authors of the World Bank note (2002b) do suggest that their result has implications for the timing and longevity of International Development Agency (IDA) special conditions in post-conflict countries. IDA conditions include special procedures on governance, human security, and the use of post-conflict progress indicators but only for three to five years.

6. See also World Bank (2004a). Early experience with this instrument, the Transitional Results Matrix, is being evaluated.

7. In Sierra Leone, for example, the Interim PRSP was used as a domestic political instrument to strengthen sovereignty and mobilize resources to promote political inclusion and reduce insecurity.

8. In assessing interventions, researchers have to address two underlying problems of attribution. The first is the counterfactual, or what would have happened in the absence of the intervention. Program/project outcomes could have resulted from reforms elsewhere; for example, lower neonatal mortality may not be due to improved health service delivery but to security improvements that allow expectant mothers access to services. The second problem is the extent to which the intervention was really additional or would have been implemented anyway, for example, by an international NGO.

One approach to these problems is theory-based impact assessment in which hypotheses link the intervention to the outcome through a set of causal links; for example, microfinance service provision, to loans taken, to increased use of agricultural inputs, to higher output, to more income and less hunger. Evidence of each link would constitute a credible case for attributing impact to intervention. Another approach is to focus on the outputs most clearly linked to the intervention and to seek hard evidence in support of causality in these cases. The credibility of the intervention-based explanation will be strengthened if the evidence base for alternative explanations is weaker or nonexistent.

9. In a service delivery program this would include anticipated numbers of beneficiaries and so forth. For a governance related program, it would be which institutions are being strengthened and so forth.

10. A Carnegie Endowment for International Peace study of post-conflict conditions (Ottaway 2001, 2) suggests that "in disbursing civil society assistance, donors often exclude important, vibrant players. . . . (U)ntil recently, (they) have paid little attention to social movements, professional and religious groups, and other organizations that may lie closer to the grassroots in many countries."

References

Burnside, Craig, and David Dollar. 1997. "Aid, Policies, and Growth." Policy Research Working Paper 1777, World Bank, Washington, DC.

Clemens, Michael A., Steven Radelet, and Rikhil Bhavnani. 2004. "Counting Chickens When They Hatch: The Short-Term Effect of Aid on Growth." Working Paper 44, Center for Global Development, Washington, DC.

Collier, Paul. 1998. "The Economics of Civil War." World Bank, Washington, DC.

Collier, Paul, and David Dollar. 1999. "Aid Allocation and Poverty Reduction." Policy Research Working Paper 2041, World Bank, Washington, DC.

Devarajan, Shantayanan, David Dollar, and Torgny Holmgren, eds. 2001. "Aid and Reform in Africa: Lessons from Ten Case Studies." World Bank, Washington, DC.

Katorobo, James. 2003. "Democratic Institution Building in Post-Conflict Societies." UNDESA commissioned paper for the Fifth International Conference on New or Restored Democracies, Ulaanbaatar, Mongolia, June 18–20.

Le Billion, Philippe. 2000. "The Political Economy of War: What Relief Agencies Need to Know." Humanitarian Practice Network Paper 33, Overseas Development Institute, London.

Lensink, Robert, and Howard White. 1999. "Assessing Aid: A Manifesto for the 21st Century?" Evaluation Report, Sida, Stockholm.

Macrae, Joanna. 2001. "Aiding Recovery? The Crisis of Aid in Chronic Political Emergencies." London: Zed Books Ltd.

OECD-DAC (Organisation for Economic Co-operation and Development, Development Assistance Committee). 2001. "Poor Performers: Basic Approaches for Supporting Development in Difficult Partnerships." OECD-DAC, Paris, November.

Ottaway, Marina. 2001. "Strengthening Civil Society in Other Countries: Policy Goal or Wishful Thinking?" Carnegie Endowment for International Peace, Washington DC, reprinted with permission from *The Chronicle Review*, Weekly Special Section of *The Chronicle for Higher Education*, Washington, DC, June 29.

Quinn, M. 2002. "More Than Implementers: Civil Societies in Complex Emergencies." A discussion paper. International Alert, London, U.K., August.

Romeo, Leonardo. 2002. "Local Governance Approach to Social Reintegration and Economic Recovery in Post-Conflict Countries: Towards a Definition and a Rationale." Discussion Paper for the UNDP/UNCDF Workshop "A Local Governance Approach to Post-Conflict Recovery," October 8, New York.

Stewart, F. 2000. "Crisis Prevention: Tackling Horizontal Inequalities." Queen Elizabeth House, University of Oxford.

World Bank. 1998. *Assessing Aid: What Works, What Doesn't, and Why*. Washington, DC: World Bank.

———. 2001. "Assistance to Post-Conflict Countries and the HIPC Framework." World Bank, Resource Mobilization Department, Washington, DC, jointly produced with the IMF, Policy Development and Review and Treasurer's Departments, April.

———. 2002a. "World Bank Group Work in Low Income Countries Under Stress: A Task Force Report." World Bank, Washington, DC, September.

———. 2002b. "Aid, Policy, and Growth in Post-Conflict Countries." Dissemination Note 2, World Bank, Social Development Department, Conflict Prevention and Reconstruction Unit, Washington, DC.

————. 2003a. "Aid, Policy, and Peace." Dissemination Note 9, World Bank, Social Development Department, Conflict Prevention and Reconstruction Unit. Washington, DC, February.

————. 2003b. "Annual Review of Development Effectiveness." World Bank, Operations Evaluation Department, Washington, DC.

————. 2004a. "Guidance Note on Transitional Results Matrices: A Pre-PRSP Tool for Guidance in LICUS." World Bank, Washington, DC, August.

————. 2004b. "Scaling Up Poverty Reduction: Case Studies and Global Learning Process." World Bank, Washington, DC. http://www.worldbank.org/wbi/reducingpoverty/docs/conceptual.pdf.

CHAPTER 3

The Transition Support Program in Timor-Leste

When the first government of the Democratic Republic of Timor-Leste was established, on May 20, 2002, the development challenges before it were enormous. Four centuries of Portuguese colonial rule, two and a half decades of Indonesian occupation, and a violent transition from Indonesian rule in September 1999 had left the country devastated and its people living in extreme poverty (World Bank 2002a).

To help the new government address these challenges, the World Bank and several other donors initiated the Transition Support Program (TSP) in mid-2002. The program has two main purposes. The first is to provide bridging finance to the government to allow it to fund its expenditures until substantial oil and gas revenues from the Timor Sea come on stream (World Bank 2002b). The second is to provide a forum for donors and the government to negotiate an annual program of policy measures and activities reflecting the country's policy and operational priorities, as outlined in the National Development Plan and other government plans (World Bank 2003a). The content of this program has varied from year to year.

The purpose of this chapter is twofold. First, it assesses the extent to which the TSP has contributed to positive development results in

This chapter was written by Andrew Rosser.

the areas identified in the methodological framework for this book—governance, delivery of basic services to the poor, negative spillover effects from violent conflict and disease, and economic growth and poverty reduction. Second, it explains how, insofar as the TSP has contributed to positive results in these areas, it has done so.

Some argue that the TSP's main contribution has been to improve the quality of governance in Timor-Leste. The program has facilitated positive outcomes in all of the areas mentioned above by providing a key source of finance for government activities in these areas and by according high priority to activities that reflect the country's development needs. But its principal contribution has been to ensure the continued viability of the state and to establish a mechanism for development planning. The TSP's positive contribution to the country's development is explained by a variety of factors related to the design and implementation of the program as well as contextual political factors.

The first section of the chapter describes development in Timor-Leste before the TSP. The following sections outline the TSP, assess its positive contribution to the country's development, and examine the factors that enabled the TSP to contribute to development. The last section summarizes the chapter's main findings and discusses the TSP's replicability in other contexts.

Development in Timor-Leste before the Transition Support Program

The territory now known as Timor-Leste has long been one of the most underdeveloped, conflict-ridden, and poorest parts of Southeast Asia.[1] For much of the Portuguese colonial period, the territory was a neglected trading post. The Portuguese invested little in infrastructure, education, or health facilities and ruled harshly. In the late nineteenth century, the Portuguese tried to increase economic exploitation in their colonies, including Portuguese Timor, to assist the economic development of the homeland. Greater effort was put into extracting raw materials, cultivating cash crops for export, and developing an internal market for home-produced and imported goods. To facilitate this exploitation, the Portuguese moved to establish greater political control over their territories. This policy encountered significant opposition from the Timorese, culminating in a major rebellion between 1910 and 1912 that led to the deaths of about 3,000 local inhabitants. During World War II, the island of Timor became the site of a guerrilla war between invading

Japanese forces and a few hundred Australian and Dutch troops who had been trapped on the island. As soon as the war was over, the Portuguese reclaimed their former territory and returned to practices of forced labor and economic exploitation (Schwarz 1994; Taylor 1999).

Under Indonesian rule, "East Timor," as the territory was known during this time, fared even worse. Indonesia's invasion of the territory in 1975 and the subsequent warfare between the Indonesian military and Timorese independence fighters led to the deaths of 120,000–200,000 people out of a pre-1975 population of 650,000 (Sebastian and Smith 2000). Reflecting the broader economic success of the Indonesian economy, the territory experienced strong economic growth during the Indonesian occupation—indeed, between 1983 and 1997 its economy grew at a rate faster than the Indonesian national average. At the same time, its economy experienced marked structural change, in particular a dramatic shift out of agriculture into other economic activities. But both of these changes were due mainly to an expansion of the public sector, including the military presence in the territory, rather than investment in manufacturing, mining, and other industries. At the same time, although the Indonesian government funded the development of a health and education system and introduced measures to promote agricultural production in the territory, East Timor's social indicators remained weak compared with the rest of Indonesia. By the mid-1990s, East Timor still had the highest incidence of poverty in Indonesia, the highest rate of illiteracy, and health indicators that were below national averages (Hill 2001). For these reasons, some observers have dismissed official Indonesian claims to have promoted development in the territory as a myth (see, for instance, Gunn 1997).

In early January 1999, the Indonesian cabinet decided to initiate a process that might lead to a referendum on East Timor's future. The decision followed receipt of a letter from Australian Prime Minister John Howard to Indonesia's President B. J. Habibie, suggesting that the East Timorese should be given a greater say in their own affairs. This decision probably reflected a calculation on the cabinet's part that the outcome of the referendum would favor Indonesia rather than a desire for separation (Sebastian and Smith 2000). On May 5, 1999, Indonesia, Portugal, and the United Nations agreed that a referendum should be held under UN auspices to determine whether the East Timorese accepted a proposal for greater autonomy within Indonesia. If the vote went against the autonomy proposal, it was agreed that steps would be taken to initiate East Timor's transition to independence. In the end, the result of the referendum was an overwhelming rejection of the autonomy proposal, with more than 78 percent of voters favoring independence.

Supporters of independence for East Timor were given little time to celebrate the result. Operating under the protective wing of local military commanders, pro-Indonesia militias unleashed a massive campaign of violence and destruction immediately after the referendum. This included widespread killing, sexual assaults, the destruction of up to 80 percent of public and private infrastructure, disruption to health and education services, and the displacement of many thousands of people from their homes. Of those displaced, a large number were forcibly relocated to West Timor, the neighboring Indonesian province, where they were kept in camps controlled by militia (Sebastian and Smith 2000). The scale of the violence and destruction forced the United Nations to act. On September 15, 1999, through Security Council Resolution 1264, the UN authorized the establishment of a multinational force "to restore peace and security in East Timor, to protect and support [the UN Mission in East Timor] in carrying out its tasks and . . . to facilitate humanitarian assistance operations"(Burchill 2000, 180).

When troops from the International Force for East Timor (INTER-FET), as this multilateral force was known, arrived in East Timor in late September 1999, they found a devastated country. As one sign of this, East Timor's economy may have contracted by as much as one-third during 1999 (World Bank 2002a).

With the establishment of the United Nations Transitional Administration for East Timor (UNTAET) in October 1999 and its assumption of authority over the territory in February 2000, things began to turn around. Most people who were displaced during September 1999 returned home, including many of the people who had been relocated to West Timor. An influx of UN workers, the initiation of various donor-financed reconstruction efforts, and a recovery in agricultural production led to a marked increase in economic activity. In 2000 the economy grew by an estimated 15 percent; in 2001 it grew another 18 percent (World Bank 2002a, 2003d). By April 2001 almost all children between the ages of 6 and 10 had returned to school, and more than 200 functioning health facilities had been established. The security situation remained stable as well. Having fled with the arrival of the INTERFET forces, many members of pro-integration militia groups began to use West Timor as a base from which to make periodic incursions into East Timorese territory and commit acts of violence. The stationing of substantial UN peacekeeping forces in border areas served to keep this problem under control, even if it did not bring it to a halt (Australian Strategic Policy Institute 2002).

Significant progress was also made in promoting self-government. Under UNTAET, bodies such as the National Consultative Council and its successor, the National Council, provided a mechanism for input by East Timorese into the policy-making process. But their role was relatively limited. Dissatisfaction with the extent of East Timorese involvement in the policy-making process combined with a belief that East Timor would remain politically stable for the foreseeable future persuaded the UN administration to move ahead with the transition to independence. In March 2001 the head of UN administration, Sergio Vieria de Mello, announced that elections for the country's first parliament would be held later that year, on August 30. The elections proved largely problem free and delivered a decisive victory to the Fretilin Party. In April of the following year, the country's first presidential elections were held, also proving to be virtually free of trouble. These were won by Xanana Gusmao, the former head of the East Timorese resistance. Between the two elections, the Constituent Assembly enacted a constitution for the new republic and work began on a national development plan. The plan, prepared following a large-scale consultation process, was approved by the parliament just after independence (World Bank 2002a; ETAN 2001).

Reflecting the economic and political progress that had been made since late 1999, the Timorese Living Standards Measurement Survey, conducted in December 2001 as part of a broader poverty assessment, found that an overwhelming majority of East Timorese felt that they had more power over their lives than before 1999. Improvements in people's economic circumstances were less positive, with the bulk of respondents reporting that their economic circumstances had changed little since 1999. However, more people reported that their economic circumstances had improved since 1999 than deteriorated (35 percent against 23 percent) (World Bank 2002a).

By the time of independence and the start of the TSP in May 2002, then, Timor-Leste appeared to have begun a process of recovery. The country still faced a number of serious development challenges, however. Although the economy grew strongly during 2000 and 2001, many children had returned to school, and a series of health centers had been established, the country's development indicators remained poor (table 3.1), and 40 percent of the population continued to live below the poverty line (World Bank 2002a). Although some rehabilitation of buildings occurred between 1999 and 2002, the country's infrastructure remained

Table 3.1 Development Indicators in Timor-Leste before and after 1999
(percent unless otherwise indicated)

Indicator	Pre-1999	Late 2001
GDP per capita (current dollars)	390	389
Rural household with animal holdings	90	80
Average animal holding per household (number)	2.1	2.2
Net primary enrollment	65	75
Net secondary enrollment	27	30
Net female primary enrollment	68	76
DPT immunization	13	9
Access to piped water or pumps	30	42
Access to potable water	66	50
Electrification	35	26

Source: Rohland and Cliffe 2002.

in desperate need of further rehabilitation and development. Although the country now had an elected government with a high degree of legitimacy, it lacked a judicial system, oversight mechanisms, and various other key political and bureaucratic institutions. It also lacked a strong human resources base and policy frameworks in areas such as education, health, agriculture, and private sector development. The human resources situation was particularly serious. During the Indonesian occupation, non-Timorese held almost all positions of administrative responsibility and economic opportunity. Most of these people fled East Timor in 1999, leaving the country with a severe shortage of skills (World Bank 2002a). Finally, although the country had avoided serious political instability and had managed to contain former militia elements, the security situation remained fragile. The country faced a security threat stemming from disaffection among former members of Falintil, the guerrilla force that had fought the Indonesians during the occupation. While many former Falintil fighters were recruited into the new defense force after 1999, some were excluded. Facing bleak job prospects, some of these fighters became involved in robbery, extortion, and other illegal activities (Australian Strategic Policy Institute 2002). Others became politically active, at times using violent methods to express their opposition to the new government and its policies (Smith 2004).

Overview of the Transition Support Program

The bridging finance provided by the TSP has been channeled to Timor-Leste through the Consolidated Fund for East Timor (CFET), essentially an account that the government uses to fund budget expenditures.[2] The CFET was initially established under UNTAET as one of several modalities through which aid was delivered to East Timor. The other modalities included bilateral agencies and NGOs operating under the humanitarian consolidated appeal; the Trust Fund for East Timor (TFET), which mobilized resources for reconstruction and development activities in health, education, agriculture, transport, power, and other key sectors; nonhumanitarian projects implemented by UN agencies; and bilateral projects implemented through contractors and NGOs (Rohland and Cliffe 2002).[3] Like most of these modalities, it was retained after independence. In contrast to these other modalities, however, the CFET came to constitute an increasing proportion of expenditures after independence, mainly because of reductions in other forms of assistance. Whereas the CFET accounted for only 18 percent of these expenditures in 2001, by 2004 it accounted for 39 percent (World Bank 2004a).

Government expenditures supported by the TSP have focused largely on recurrent expenditure items, such as salaries, wages, goods, and services. Recurrent expenditures accounted for 79 percent of CFET expenditure in 2003 and an estimated 90 percent of CFET expenditure in 2004 (table 3.2). In sectoral terms, the expenditure program has focused on education, health, economic affairs, public order and safety, and general public services (table 3.3). The funds provided to the government through the TSP have not been designated for specific purposes. Hence one can assume that they have been spent according to the overall pattern of government expenditure.

Table 3.2 Consolidated Fund Expenditure in Timor-Leste, Fiscal Year (FY) 2003–05
(millions of dollars)

Component	FY2003 (Actual)		FY2004 (Mid-year budget update)		FY2005 MTFF	
	Millions of dollars	Percent	Millions of dollars	Percent	Millions of dollars	Percent
Recurrent expenditures	56.1	79.3	67.1	90.6	66.7	88.9
Salaries and wages	21.9	30.9	25.8	34.9	28.2	37.5
Goods and services	34.2	48.4	38.0	51.3	36.8	49.0
Minor capital	0	0	3.2	4.4	1.7	2.3
Capital expenditures	14.6	20.7	7.0	9.4	8.4	11.1
Total expenditures	70.8	100.0	74.1	100.0	75.1	100.0

Source: World Bank 2004a.
Note: Figures may not sum because of rounding.

Table 3.3 Consolidated Fund Expenditure in Timor-Leste, by Function, FY 2003–05
(percent of total budget)

Function	FY 2003 (Actual)	FY 2004 (Estimated)	FY 2005 (Budget)
General public services	16	16	17
Defense	7	8	8
Public order and safety	15	14	13
Police services	12	12	11
Judicial services	2	1	1
Economic affairs	22	22	21
Agriculture, forestry, fisheries	2	2	2
Fuel and energy	12	9	8
Transport	5	8	9
Environmental protection	—	—	—
Housing and community development	3	3	3
Health	11	11	13
Recreation, culture, religion	1	1	1
Education	23	21	22
Social protection	—	—	0
Unclassified	2	2	1
Total	100	98	100

Source: World Bank 2004a.
— = not applicable.

Although the World Bank has had primary responsibility for managing the TSP, its funds have come from a range of sources, including Australia, Canada, Ireland, Norway, Portugal, Sweden, the United Kingdom, the United States, and the World Bank. This funding has been crucial to plugging the financing gap in CFET since 2002 (table 3.4). External grants provided through the TSP covered 47 percent of CFET expenditure in FY2003 and an estimated 47 percent of CFET expenditure in FY2004. They are budgeted to cover 41 percent of CFET expenditure in FY2005. This financing gap has emerged because government revenues from domestic sources and Timor Sea oil and gas have been insufficient to cover the government's expenditures. Initially, it was envisaged that this financing gap would exist for three years (FY2003–05) and that the program would, therefore, have to run for the same length of time. By 2004, however, it appeared that it would take more than three years for substantial oil and gas revenues to come on stream. Donors and the government therefore agreed to extend the program until 2007 (World Bank 2004b). As it turned out, dramatic increases in international oil prices during 2004–05 have obviated the government's need for external

Table 3.4 Consolidation Fund Financing, FY 2003–05

Component	FY 2003 (Actual)	FY 2004 (Estimated)	FY 2005 (Budget)
Revenues	48.8	57.4	67.1
Domestic revenues	19.3	26.1	23.0
Timor Sea revenues	29.5	31.3	44.1
Consolidated fund expenditures	70.8	74.6	75.1
Overall balance	−22.0	−17.2	−8.0
Net financing	22.0	17.2	8.0
External financing (grants)	33.8	35.7	30.8
Consolidated fund reserves	−8.7	−13.9	2.9
Timor Sea account	−3.1	−4.6	−25.7
Financing gap	0	0	0
Memorandum: Balance at end of period			
Timor Sea account	10.5	15.1	40.8

Source: World Bank 2004a.
Note: Figures are based on FY2004 mid-year budget update.

assistance to fund its budget in the immediate future by dramatically increasing its revenues from the Timor Sea.

In addition to plugging the financing gap, the TSP has provided a forum for donors and the government to negotiate a set of policy measures and activities based on the National Development Plan and other government plans. During the UNTAET period, donors held six monthly meetings to establish benchmarks for the political transition, the administrative handover, economic and social reconstruction, and public finances and to monitor progress against these benchmarks (Rohland and Cliffe 2002). Building on this model, the TSP has entailed the construction of a program of policy measures and activities, including target completion dates. Incorporated into an action matrix, the program has essentially been a subset of the policy measures and activities proposed by individual government departments and agencies in the annual action plans that they have prepared as part of annual planning and budget processes. This program of policy measures and activities has not necessarily been funded through the TSP: the government has been able to draw on resources provided through bilateral mechanisms, TFET, and other multilateral mechanisms to fund the technical assistance and other inputs required to complete the program. The main contribution of the TSP has been in identifying a set of core measures and activities that donors and the government agree reflect the country's main development priorities, as articulated in the National Development Plan and other government plans (World Bank 2003a).

The 2003 Transition Support Program (TSP I)

During FY2003 the TSP focused on "the creation of the institutions, leg-islative framework, and management systems needed for core government functions—planning and policy development, financial management, oversight, and the judiciary—and establishment of a regulatory framework for private sector investment" (World Bank 2003c). The program was quickly put together and consisted largely of measures that the govern-ment felt it was able to tackle immediately. It consisted of four compo-nents, each of which was linked in one way or another to activities and objectives outlined in the National Development Plan.[4]

Continued Poverty Reduction Planning and Quick Wins. This component included measures such as (1) establishment of an institutional framework for updating and operationalizing the government's development strategy, which consisted of planning focal points in each line agency, action plans for FY2003 in key sectors (education, health, and justice), and a high-level coordination structure for participatory implementation and monitoring of the National Development Plan and subsequent planning exercises; (2) preparation of a road map for operationalizing the National Development Plan beyond FY2003, a map that identified gaps in the current policy, strategic framework, and consultation strategy; and (3) development of a policy framework for the education, health, and social protection sectors (especially veterans affairs) and implementation of priority activities that are expected to bring immediate benefits.

Governance and Private Sector Development. This component included measures such as (1) preparation of various pieces of legislation to form part of a private sector regulatory framework, including commercial and notary codes and an investment law; (2) establishment of a basic legal framework for the judiciary, including a magistrate's code and legislation on public prosecutors and public defenders; (3) approval of a legal frame-work for public sector personnel management and conduct, through an interim ministerial decree on civil service discipline and the submission of a civil service statute to Parliament; (4) establishment of an institutional framework for an ombudsman's office; and (5) a preliminary study on administrative decentralization.

Public Expenditure Policy and Management. This component consis-ted of measures such as (1) preparation of a medium-term capacity build-ing plan for financial management functions and contracting of a staff;

(2) a medium-term program for developing statistical reporting systems; (3) a review of sector pay; (4) execution of the FY2003 budget, in line with initial allocations and various restrictions, including a cap on the total payroll of 16,400 public sector employees, maintenance of the current pay policy, and allocations of less than 20 percent of core CFET funds to police and defense spending and at least 35 percent to education and health; (5) revision of the budget framework law and introduction of procedures for management of the capital program; (6) presentation of framework legislation for the oil and gas fund; (7) strengthened expenditure controls and information systems for asset management, procurement, and personnel management; and (8) submission of independent audit reports.

The Power Sector. This component included (1) approval of management arrangements for the power authority, on the basis of options that included management contracts; (2) improvements in cost recovery by increasing the installation of meters, approving an amended tariff directive, and presenting monthly performance reports; and (3) preparation of draft framework legislation for an autonomous power authority.

The 2004 Transition Support Program (TSP II)
For FY2004, the action matrix for the TSP was rather different, which reflected, in part, the introduction of the government's stability program following the outbreak of rioting in Dili in December 2002 that left two people dead, a number of others injured, and several buildings damaged, including Prime Minister Alkatiri's residence (Smith 2004). The stability program called for greater attention to security and job creation. The program also reflected greater attention on the part of government and donors to the medium- to long-term development priorities of the country. Whereas the first TSP focused on measures and activities that the government could implement immediately, the second TSP focused more on measures and activities that the government needed—in the eyes of the government and donors—to implement over time.[5]

Good Governance. Oversight institutions. This subcomponent focused on planning and following up on internal investigations, establishing the Office of the Ombudsman, and developing formal legislative procedures. Specific measures included preparation of a strategy for investigating complaints regarding the civil service by the Inspector General; a review of the status of previous investigations; establishment of the

Office of the Ombudsman (Provedor de Direitos Humanos e da Justica); implementation of a campaign by the ombudsman on payments of fees and fines for basic public services; and development of guidelines on the policy and legislative process, with formal procedures for policy review, consultation, and legislative drafting within the executive.

Local government. This subcomponent focused on operationalizing the recommendations of a study on the options for local government. Specific measures included a presentation to the Council of Ministers of legislation on state local administration and local authority, together with an implementation strategy for establishing local government structures; presentation of a draft proposal on funding mechanisms for local authorities and a framework for capacity building and financing by development partners; and presentation of a strategy on community authorities in *sucos* (clusters of villages) and villages, intended to legitimize community authorities.

Public sector management. This subcomponent focused on establishing the management and information systems needed to operationalize the civil service statute. Specific measures included finalization of the civil service statute and disciplinary regulation, dissemination of the statute, training of senior management in the application of disciplinary procedures, presentation and review of a draft human resources policy, design of supporting information systems, establishment and training of human resource units in priority line agencies, and implementation of personnel registries in priority institutions to ensure that basic personnel records are maintained for permanent staff.

Poverty reduction planning. This subcomponent focused on consolidating the annual planning process and establishing the civil society monitoring mechanism. It included the following specific measures: an informal workshop to review the experience of the prioritizing and sequencing exercise, the preparation of annual action plans and quarterly reporting matrixes, an update of the prioritizing and sequencing exercise, the preparation of annual action plans for FY2005, and the promotion of a high-level consultative mechanism as a fully independent body.

Public expenditure management. This subcomponent focused on updating the legal framework for the financial management system, building capacity, and improving expenditure performance. It included the following specific measures: formulation of a government budget for FY2005 in line with national priorities, monitoring the implementation of the power sector management contract to assess progress in cost recovery, development of a human resource development strategy for financial management functions, submission of a revised budget and financial management law to Parliament, revision of Treasury manuals in line with the law, improvements in the timeliness of procurement in line with targets, development of a procurement strategy, training of procurement staff, submission of a revised procurement law, preparation of trade statistics using the Automated System for Customs Data (ASYCUDA) system, and preparation of updated national accounts for 2002.

Police forces. This subcomponent focused on strengthening the capacities of the institutions responsible for internal and external security. Specifically, it sought to develop a strategy for transitioning from United Nations Mission of Support in East Timor (UNMISET) control of the police force to government control and for the long-term institutional development of the police force; to prepare a Police Act; and to establish effective support functions for the police in human resources management, finance, logistics, and other areas.

Justice sector. This subcomponent focused on finalizing the legal framework for the judiciary, improving system performance, and establishing basic systems for registration. Specfically, it sought to finalize legislation on public prosecutors and public defenders, hold sessions in the Judicial Superior Council, improve the ratio of cases taken to court to cases brought to trial, and establish systems for registration and the delivery of registration services.

Improved Service Delivery. *Education*. This subcomponent focused on developing an education policy framework and improving the quality of education through curriculum development, strengthening of financial management functions, and piloting of mechanisms to transfer resources directly to schools (for a similar transfer scheme in Mozambique, see chapter 6 of this volume). It involved preparing and approving an education sector policy framework and draft education law, developing a primary education curriculum and distributing supporting teaching guides to all primary schools, developing and implementing a three-year training program for presecondary education teachers, training senior management and district personnel in financial management procedures, and developing and piloting a mechanism for channeling funds through school councils.

Health. This subcomponent focused on further expanding services, strengthening service management at the field level, and defining policies to operationalize core services. It involved improvements in service delivery, as measured by performance against targets for delivery of DPT3 and measles vaccination, attended deliveries, and outpatient visits; formulation of district health plans to provide a framework for performance monitoring and management of services; and formulation of micro-policies operationalizing the following sector programs: expanded programs for immunization, mother and child health and nutrition, health promotion, maternal health, malaria, tuberculosis, other communicable diseases, non-communicable diseases, and human resources.

Vulnerable groups. This subcomponent focused on issues related to veterans and ex-combatants. It sought to define criteria for recognizing veterans and ex-combatants, identify and register veterans, and define a sustainable policy for veterans and ex-combatants.

Job Creation. *Private sector development.* This subcomponent focused on finalizing key private sector regulatory instruments and implementing land registration systems and short-term job creation initiatives. Specifically, it sought to finalize company and investment laws, develop land administration and cadastre systems aimed primarily at urban properties, implement a community-based road maintenance program, promote backward linkages to onshore investment from the Timor Sea, and launch a "Sending Labor Abroad" program.

Agriculture. This subcomponent focused on developing a policy framework for the agricultural sector, regulating the fisheries sector, and implementing a number of quick-win projects to support rural employment and improvements in farm income. It involved developing a draft policy framework for the agricultural sector; developing a regulatory framework and strategy for community-based management of fisheries; and implementing pilot initiatives for commercial crops, farm-level processing of agricultural products, and community watershed management.

Not all of these measures and activities were completed by the end of the relevant program year. But many were completed, and many others were in the process of being completed. In FY2003, 31 out of 47 actions listed in the action matrix for that year were either fully or partly completed or in implementation by the end of the year. For FY2004, the figure was 35 out of 50 activities. A relatively small proportion of activities in each year was partly or fully rescheduled or otherwise incomplete— 16 out of 47 activities in FY2003 and 15 out of 50 activities in FY2004 (table 3.5).

Table 3.5 Status of Actions under TSP I and TSP II

Component	Actions fully or partly completed	Actions being implemented	Actions partly or completely rescheduled	No substantive work undertaken, work suspended or cancelled	Total
TSP I: FY2003					
Continued poverty reduction	7	2	4		13
Governance and private sector development	5	2	5	1	13
Public expenditure policy and management	2	7	3	3	15
Power sector	1	5	0		6
Total	15	16	12	4	47
TSP II: FY2004					
Governance	6	13	7	2	28
Service delivery	8	1	3		12
Job creation	4	3	3		10
Total	18	17	13	2	50

Sources: World Bank 2003d, 2004c.

Development Results

The TSP has made a positive contribution to development outcomes in all of the areas identified in the methodological framework for this book—improving governance and the delivery of basic services to the poor, addressing the negative spillover effects from violent conflict and disease, and increasing economic growth and reduced poverty—by providing a key source of finance for government activities in these areas. The TSP has not been the only source of finance on which the government has drawn. It has also drawn on the TFET and on funding from bilateral and multilateral donors. The TSP has been the main source of funding, however, particularly with regard to recurrent items, such as salaries and wages and the purchase of goods and services.

The TSP's contribution has been positive because its activities have genuinely reflected the country's development needs. As a result, they have stood a greater chance of being successfully implemented. Donors and the government have defended the content of the TSP by stressing that it draws on the National Development Plan, which was formulated through a broadly consultative process involving tens of thousands of people from all parts of the country. They argue that because the National Development Plan reflects the aspirations of the people of Timor-Leste, the TSP does as well.

The program has received some criticism, however. Some commentators argue that it has placed too much emphasis on education and health (which are required to receive at least 35 percent of CFET expenditure) and insufficient emphasis on agriculture and infrastructure (interview with Joao Saldhana, head of Timor Institute of Development Studies [formerly East Timor Study Group] Dili, September 2004). Others, particularly within the NGO community, have criticized the TSP for promoting "a model of development that promotes dependency on exports and foreign investment" (La'o Hamutuk 2003; see also Anderson 2003).[6] It is likely that future versions of the TSP will try to accommodate the first of these criticisms, given that there is support within the government and among some donors for greater emphasis on agriculture and infrastructure. Given donors' broad commitment to market-oriented economic policies, their power over Timor-Leste's government, and deep suspicion within certain sections of the government toward the NGO community, it is unlikely that future versions of the TSP will accommodate the second criticism.

Whatever view one takes of these issues, the main contribution of the TSP to Timor-Leste's development has arguably been in the area of governance. First, and most fundamentally, it has facilitated the transition to self-government. It is difficult to see how self-government would have been possible had it not been for the financial support provided through the TSP. Without the TSP, Timor-Leste would have had to remain a UN protectorate or face collapse. Of course, the provision of finance through the TSP was not sufficient in itself to prevent state collapse—the country has faced a variety of threats that could, under certain conditions, have led to disaster. But the TSP reduced the likelihood of this occurring, at least in the short term, by providing the government with the resources it needed to provide basic services, maintain security, manage the economy, and perform the other basic functions of a state.

The TSP has also provided a mechanism for development planning. The two-week joint donor missions for the TSP that have been held every six months since it began have been crucial in this respect. These missions have involved a series of meetings and discussions among government officials (initially senior bureaucrats, later cabinet members); representatives from bilateral and multilateral donors; and the members of the TSP Mission Team (usually donor-financed consultants and a few key donor officials). These missions have provided a forum in which the government and donors have been able to discuss policy issues, resolve donor coordination problems, review the government's progress in implementing an array of measures and activities agreed on with donors during earlier TSP missions, and formulate a new set of measures and activities for the coming year. All of the people interviewed for this study, in both the government and the donor community, who were familiar with the TSP indicate that the missions had been effective in these respects.

Explaining the TSP's Contribution to Timor-Leste's Development

Much commentary on general budgetary support has suggested that this form of aid is most likely to be effective where governments have a high degree of institutional capacity, particularly with respect to the management of public finances. Where governments lack this, it is argued, they may not be "ready for the responsibilities that general budgetary support imposes" (Overseas Development Institute n.d.). This idea is not very helpful in terms of explaining the TSP's contribution to Timor-Leste's development, because the capacity of the government there has been extremely low (World Bank 2002a). Non-Timorese held almost all positions of administrative responsibility during the Indonesian occupation; their departure from East Timor in 1999 left the bureaucracy with a severe shortage of people with senior management experience and technical skills. As one indicator of the magnitude of the skills deficit at this time, only 30 qualified doctors remained in the country after the Indonesian exodus (Joint Assessment Mission 1999, 1). Since independence, capacity problems in the government have been exacerbated by the fact that positions in the bureaucracy have generally gone to people with strong connections to the major political party, Fretilin, rather than to those with previous administrative experience. By one estimate, only 5–10 percent of officials in the current government held positions in the bureaucracy under the Indonesians (interview with Joao Saldhana, Dili, September 2004).

How, then, can the TSP's contribution to Timor-Leste's development be understood? Eight main factors explain the program's success.

Design and Implementation Factors. Five of the eight factors are related to the way in which the program was designed and implemented. First, the TSP was based on a careful diagnosis of the development problems facing the country at independence and a detailed understanding of the development priorities of the people of Timor-Leste. By the time the

TSP was designed, the World Bank had completed two major studies on the country's development since 1999—a country economic memorandum (World Bank 2002a), which examined the broad economic challenges facing the country, and a Financial Management Accountability Note, which examined challenges related to public finance.[7] The government had produced a National Development Plan that outlined a development strategy based on preferences expressed by citizens during a large-scale public consultation exercise in 2001. Taken together, these documents gave donors and the government a clear idea of the challenges ahead and people's priorities concerning which of these should be given the most and earliest attention. Incorporating this information into the TSP meant not only that the program was soundly based in a technical sense but also that it probably had a degree of legitimacy in the eyes of the Timorese.

Second, the design of the TSP took into account some key constraints imposed by the political and social context, particularly the government's lack of institutional capacity and the fragility of the security situation. The first of these constraints was addressed by measures aimed at strengthening the government's capacity to engage in development planning and to manage public expenditures. These measures were incorporated into the TSP from the outset. The second of these constraints was addressed by incorporating activities related to the re-integration of veterans and ex-combatants, although it probably did not give sufficient attention to this issue initially. Measures related to security became a central part of the TSP only after the government's introduction of the stability plan following the December 2002 riots. By including these measures, the government and donors minimized the extent to which institutional capacity–related and security-related problems could hinder the country's development and the contribution of the TSP to it.

Third, the program was implemented in a flexible manner. The action matrix was not fixed but was subject to continuing negotiation and revised on numerous occasions. When government priorities changed following the 2002 riots, for instance, the government, with the support of a number of bilateral donors, was able to increase the range of security-related measures in the program. This flexibility also made possible the transition from a short-term focus in the TSP for FY2003 to a longer-term focus in FY2004.

Fourth, the TSP was designed and implemented in way that achieved a certain degree of local ownership. The activities incorporated into the TFET were designed largely under UNTAET and embodied relatively little input from the Timorese. By contrast, the government has had a considerable say in how the TSP has operated, by virtue of its involvement in the preparation of departmental annual action plans and its role in negotiating the content of the action matrix during TSP missions. At the same time, the TSP grant agreements between the government and the World Bank have not imposed any formal conditions on the government's use of these funds beyond requiring that it implement an array of reforms and activities; produce certain reports; and refrain from using the funds to purchase arms, uranium, and various other items on a "negative list." According to one source, the World Bank initially tried to persuade the government to sign a three-year TSP grant agreement that would have required it to maintain a stable macroeconomic environment. But the government rejected this proposal, opting instead for annual TSP agreements that did not include this conditionality. Because the World Bank has disbursed funds for the TSP in a single tranche at the beginning of each financial year, it has been unable to exercise leverage over the government by threatening to withhold funds. This has further enhanced the government's role in deciding how funds are used and increased feelings of local ownership over the program. It seems reasonable to conclude that this has translated into a greater willingness on the government's part to implement the activities agreed to in the action matrix.

Of course, one cannot say that there have been no conditionalities in the TSP. There clearly have been, insofar as future donor funding has not been guaranteed. In this context, the government has been forced to pursue a development strategy that is broadly consistent with donor interests in order to keep them on their side in case it needs their help in the future. There has always been some possibility that the government would require TSP funding beyond FY2005, the initially envisaged end point for the program. Although the government has expected to be able to fund its expenditure program from sizable oil and gas revenues in the future, the precise timing of these revenues is uncertain. To be sure, donors are unlikely to walk away from Timor-Leste. But aid flows to Timor-Leste are already declining (World Bank 2004a). And in a world in which aid is being diverted to countries associated with the "war on terror," it is possible to imagine donors reducing their aid to Timor-Leste in the future if they no longer have confidence that the government is committed to economic development and democratic reform.

To the extent that there has been conditionality, it has clearly been a constraint on the degree of local ownership. In September 2004, the government proposed that donor-government development cooperation move away from general budgetary support toward "enhanced co-financing" of projects, whereby the government plays a central role in the management of projects and there is greater on-shore procurement (Government of Timor-Leste 2004). According to one observer, the government's motivation for proposing this change was to increase the degree to which donor-funded activities increase capacity within the government. Another observer suggested that it had more to do with government concerns about conditionality in the TSP. If this is true, it suggests that while the TSP may have gone some way toward building local ownership, it has not been entirely successful in this respect. At the same time, the government has clearly not wanted to abandon the TSP—indeed, it has asked donors to continue the program despite the government's new financial autonomy as a result of oil price increases. This suggests that any concern the government has about conditionality is outweighed by a desire to maintain the benefits of the program: assistance with prioritizing policy measures and development activities, greater coordination of donor interventions, and so forth.

Fifth, the program has facilitated donor coordination by bringing together a wide range of donors to discuss Timor-Leste's development and negotiate the country's priorities with respect to development, including several donors that do not contribute financially to the TSP. By bringing donors together over a jointly determined set of priorities, the program has influenced the allocation of aid funds provided not just through the TSP but also through other mechanisms. All donor representatives interviewed during fieldwork commented positively on the spin-offs from the TSP with respect to donor coordination.

The design and implementation of the TSP also had some serious weaknesses. Two in particular are worth noting. First, while the National Development Plan may have been prepared through participatory and inclusive mechanisms, the TSP was not. Civil society involvement in the initial design was minimal, and in subsequent TSP missions it has been very low, in part because of government unwillingness to consult civil society organizations and in part because of the disorganization and lack of capacity of those groups. This has resulted in some criticism of the TSP from local civil society organizations, which undermines the degree of public support for the program. According to one World Bank official, the Bank has consistently sought to increase consultation with civil society actors during the TSP process, but it has been hampered by the government's unwillingness to allow these actors much of a role. Civil society organizations are invited to participate in the TSP missions only during the second week of the missions. Their representatives have complained that this is too late, because many important decisions have already been made by this point, leaving little prospect of influencing the outcome of negotiations.

Second, donors and the government seriously overestimated the amount of funding that the government could absorb through the TSP. The government has found it difficult to spend money, in part because of dysfunctional procurement processes, resulting in low levels of budget execution. This has reduced the effectiveness of the TSP.

Contextual Political Economy Factors. The other three of the eight factors contributing to the success of the TSP relate to the nature of Timor-Leste's political economy since independence. First, the government has had strong incentives to cooperate closely with donors, especially in relation to the TSP. It has lacked access to alternative sources of government finance or investment capital, at least during the period in which the TSP has been operating. Highly dependent on aid, the government has been unable to ignore donors as, for instance, a number of oil-exporting countries did during the oil boom years (Winters 1996).

This dynamic has been reinforced by another aspect of the country's political economy, the fact that the country is vulnerable in security terms. The government has needed donors to help maintain political and social stability. Donors have helped in this respect by funding security-related activities in the TSP and by funding troops on the ground. Indeed, the presence of international peacekeeping forces was crucial to restoring political and social stability after the violence of September 1999.

While the country has remained broadly stable since that time, it faces a range of potential security threats. On the external side, there is the possibility that former militia elements, probably in conjunction with elements in the Indonesian military, may try to destabilize Timor-Leste. Indonesia is highly unlikely to re-invade—it could not afford the international condemnation that would surely follow such a step. But elements within the military could try to destabilize Timor-Leste through covert means, to show the people of Aceh and Papua—the other areas in the Indonesian archipelago in which separatist movements have been active—the possible consequences of seeking independence.

On the internal side, unemployed youth and the growing popularity of martial arts groups constitute a potential, albeit at this point minor, threat. Recognizing its vulnerability in these respects, the government successfully negotiated an extension of the Peacekeeping Force's presence in Timor-Leste until May 2005. It has also secured greater support for the development of its security forces from Australia, including a new A\$32 million package of assistance focused on the police and a A\$37 million program focused "on capacity building through in-country training and professional advice, as well as assistance to the Office of Defense Force Development" (Department of Foreign Affairs and Trade 2004). All of this implies that it has been in the government's interests to cooperate broadly with donors, including in relation to development policies.

Second, authority has been concentrated in the hands of the Council of Ministers, a body equivalent to a cabinet. Fretilin, the party that won the 2001 parliamentary elections, has a large majority in Parliament, having won 55 out of the 88 seats in the 2001 election. The party has remained fairly unified, rarely challenging decisions made by the Council of Ministers. There are signs that Fretilin Members of Parliament are becoming increasingly assertive with respect to the Council of Ministers. The most notable example in this respect is their recent rejection of the government candidate for ombudsman, a position that constitutes one of the main accountability mechanisms in the government (Suara Timor Lorosae 2004). Despite these signs, however, the general pattern has been for Fretilin Members of Parliament to fall in behind the Council of Ministers (Holloway 2004).

At the same time, civil society organizations have generally been ineffective in carrying out advocacy work, partly because of their own weaknesses and partly because of a lack of channels through which they can access the policy-making process (Holloway 2004). In this context, the only real veto point in the whole process has been the presidency. Under the Constitution, the president has the authority to veto any statute within 90 days of its passage by Parliament (Shoesmith 2003). Because the president could exercise this veto power over legislation included in the action matrix, he could interfere with the TSP. To date, this interference has not occurred, which has meant that the government has been able to make decisions relatively quickly and with considerable credibility. If it has agreed to do something during the TSP missions, there has been relatively little prospect of a policy reversal at some latter date.

Third, although Timor-Leste has continued to face potential security threats, it has remained stable. Indeed, as the Joint Assessment Mission in 1999 notes:

> East Timor is different from other postconflict situations in one very important aspect. There is no apparent need for pacification between different

ethnic, cultural, or religious segments of the population. . . . In a way it would be most useful to treat the problem as a post-natural disaster situation, where a vicious hurricane destroyed all buildings and most crops and removed all records and institutional memory (World Bank 2002a, 5).

Since Timorese society has remained relatively cohesive in the post-occupation period and the country's political leaders have not been distracted by ethnic, cultural, or religious fighting, they have been able to focus on development. This has doubtless facilitated the process of development policy making, not just surrounding the TSP but in other areas as well.

Conclusion

The TSP has made positive contributions to Timor-Leste's development on several fronts. It has provided a key source of finance for government activities aimed at improving governance, improving service delivery to the poor, reducing negative spillover effects from violent conflict and disease, and promoting economic growth and poverty reduction. It has increased the priority given to activities that reflect the country's development. It has ensured the continued viability of the state and established a mechanism for development planning.

This positive contribution can be explained by certain features of the program's design and implementation and by aspects of Timor-Leste's political economy. Design and implementation features include the flexible implementation of the program, the way in which these features facilitated local ownership and donor coordination, and the fact that its design reflected a good understanding of the country's development problems and of the people's development priorities. It addressed key constraints stemming from the political context. These constraints include the government's strong incentives to cooperate closely with donors, the concentration of decision-making authority within the government, and the relative stability of the country since independence.

Could the TSP be successfully replicated in other countries, particularly other low-income countries under stress (LICUS)? To what extent was the program's success contingent on the political and social conditions that existed in Timor-Leste? This case suggests that general budgetary support can work in LICUS where governments do not have high levels of institutional capacity. But could it work in a country where the political elite is fractured, where there is a strong threat of continued violent conflict, or where the government has little incentive to cooperate with donors, perhaps because it has access to revenues from natural resources? The answer is not clear, although the answer is probably no. If this is the case, it implies that the TSP is more an exceptional case than a model that could be adopted more generally.

Notes

1. Because Timor-Leste has been officially known as Timor-Leste only since independence, in May 2002, this name is used to refer to the territory only since that time. "East Timor" is used to refer to the territory under the UN administration and Indonesian rule, because that it is what they called it. The UN referred to it using the English "East Timor," while the Indonesians called it "Timor Timur," which translates as "East Timor."

2. The author wishes to thank Adrian Fozzard, Senior Public Sector Specialist, World Bank, for his advice on this point.

3. Rohland and Cliffe (2002) add a fifth modality to this list, the United Nations' assessed contribution budget. Funds provided through this mechanism covered costs associated with the presence of UN peacekeeping troops and civilian staff. Because this funding was channeled through CFET to fund UNTAET's budget, it is not listed here as a separate modality.

4. The description of the components draws heavily on World Bank (2003b).

5. The description of the components also draws heavily on World Bank (2003c, 2004c).

6. According to one World Bank official, the NGO La'o Hamutuk has changed its position with respect to the TSP since making this comment and now broadly supports the program, because "they can see that the agenda is pushing the key governance issues, such as transparency and accountability" (personal communication with Adrian Fozzard, Senior Public Sector Specialist, Poverty Reduction and Economic Management Sector Unit, World Bank, November 2004).

7. Interview with Adrian Fozzard by phone, September 2004.

Bibliography

Anderson, T. 2003. "Aid, Trade and Oil: Australia's Second Betrayal of East Timor." *Journal of Australian Political Economy* 52 (December): 113–27.

Australian Strategic Policy Institute. 2002. "New Neighbour, New Challenge: Australia and the Security of East Timor." Australian Strategic Policy Institute, Canberra.

Burchill, S. 2000. "East Timor, Australia, and Indonesia." In *Guns and Ballot Boxes: East Timor's Vote for Independence*, ed. D. Kingsbury, 169–84. Clayton: Monash Asia Institute.

Department of Foreign Affairs and Trade. 2004. "East Timor: Country Brief." http://www.dfat.gov.au/geo/east_timor/east_timor_brief.html.

East Timor and Indonesia Action Network (ETAN). 2001. "Official, East Timor Elections on 30 August." http://www.etan.org/et2001a/march/18-24/19 enews.htm.

Government of Timor-Leste. 2004. "Overview of the Sectoral Investment Program." Internal document, Dili.

Gunn, G. 1997. *East Timor and the United Nations: The Case for Intervention.* Lawrenceville, NJ: Red Sea Press.

Hill, H. 2001. "Tiny, Poor, and War-Torn: Development Policy Challenges for East Timor." *World Development* 29 (7): 1137–56.

Holloway, R. 2004. "NGO Advocacy in Timor-Leste: What Is Possible?" *In Aspects of Democracy in Timor-Leste*: NGOs Advocating for Social Change, ed. R. Holloway, 7–15. Dili: Catholic Relief Services.

Joint Assessment Mission. 1999. "Health and Education Background Paper." November.

La'o Hamutuk. 2003. "A Review of the First Year of the Transition Support Program." *La'o Hamutuk Bulletin* 4 (2): 10–11.

Overseas Development Institute. n.d. "Choice of Aid Modalities Keysheet." London: Overseas Development Institute.

Rohland, K., and S. Cliffe. 2002. "East Timor Reconstruction Program: Successes, Problems, Tradeoffs." World Bank, Conflict Prevention and Reconstruction Unit Working Paper 2, Washington, DC.

Schwarz, A. 1994. *A Nation in Waiting: Indonesia in the 1990s.* Sydney: Allen and Unwin.

Sebastian, L., and Smith A. 2000. "East Timor Crisis: A Test Case for Humanitarian Intervention." *Southeast Asian Affairs* (2000), 64–83.

Shoesmith, D. 2003. "Timor-Leste: Divided Leadership in a Semi-Presidential System." *Asian Survey* 43 (2): 231–52.

Smith, A. 2004. "Timor-Leste: Strong Government, Weak State." *Southeast Asian Affairs* (2004): 279–94.

Suara Timor Lorosae. 2004. "Fretilin Tak Pecah." August 20, 1.

Taylor, J. 1999. *East Timor: The Price of Freedom.* London: Zed Books.

Winters, J. 1996. *Power in Motion: Capital Mobility and the Indonesian State.* Ithaca, NY: Cornell University Press.

World Bank. 2002a. *East Timor: Policy Challenges for a New Nation.* Washington, DC: World Bank.

———. 2002b. "Program Appraisal Document for a Proposed Post-Conflict Grant in the Amount of $5 Million to the Democratic Republic of East Timor for a Transition Support Program." World Bank, Washington, DC.

———. 2003a. "Draft Initial Project Information Document." April 7, World Bank, Washington, DC.

———. 2003b. "Project Information Document." Working paper, May 21, World Bank, Washington, DC.

———. 2003c. "Revised Project Information Document." Working paper, June 19, World Bank, Washington, DC.

———. 2003d. *Timor-Leste: Poverty in a New Nation: Analysis for Action.* Washington, DC: World Bank.

———. 2003e. "Second Transition Support Program Appraisal Mission: Draft Aide Memoire." Working paper, World Bank, Washington, DC.

———. 2004a. "The Democratic Republic of Timor-Leste: Public Expenditure Review." Working paper, World Bank, Washington, DC.

———. 2004b. "Draft Initial Project Information Document." April 20. Working paper, World Bank, Washington, DC.

———. 2004c. "Third Transition Support Program Appraisal Mission: Draft Aide Memoire." Working paper, World Bank, Washington, DC.

CHAPTER 4

The Seila Program in Cambodia

Cambodia's Seila program emerged in a context in which conflict was ongoing and political and economic reforms were at an early stage. At the national level, political conflict remained intense, while on the ground, almost 90 percent of the population engaged in subsistence agriculture amid physical, political, and economic insecurity. The rural economy was characterized by shattered infrastructure that inhibited access to markets and services, unclear land rights and widespread land-grabbing, and a largely nonexistent private sector offering little off-farm employment. Throughout the 1990s, natural resources, particularly forests and fishing lots, were rapidly privatized through nontransparent means, with disastrous implications for the incomes of the landless and the poor.

In terms of governance, the picture was murky. In the 1980s, Cambodia's provinces were governed by provincial administrations, with a great deal of de facto autonomy from the center. This autonomy was not a product of a federal regime but rather of the lack of infrastructure, poor telecommunications, and difficulty of travel. With the overhaul of the state apparatus after 1993, following the promulgation of a new Constitution, rapid centralization of powers occurred. Subsequently, the government announced a

---

This chapter was written by Caroline Hughes.

desire to decentralize power once again, although no organic law yet exists identifying the structure, functions, or revenue-raising powers of different layers.

In the provinces, government is organized through a number of vertical structures. The central administrative structure is the provincial administration, under an appointed governor, who oversees the offices of the various district chiefs. District chiefs oversee a system of communes, the lowest layer of government. Before 2002 appointed chiefs headed communes. In 2002 the first commune elections took place to choose multimember commune councils from party lists in a proportional representation system. Cambodia's ruling party, the Cambodian People's Party, won a landslide victory in these elections, although almost all commune councils have representatives from more than one party.

Below the commune is the village, headed by a village chief who receives a stipend from the commune, although his role is not recognized in the Constitution as that of a government official. Research has shown that for most rural Cambodians, the village is the only sphere of society, the economy, or politics in which villagers take much interest or about which they have much knowledge (Biddulph 2001,14). Commune government is frequently referred to as a monolithic *tnak loeu* (higher level), although attitudes toward the commune level may be changing as a result of the recent commune elections.

The functions of these layers of government are complicated by the existence alongside them of provincial and district departments of various line ministries, such as rural development, planning, agriculture, forestry and fisheries, education, and health. The horizontal coordination between these line ministries is highly variable and generally poor. Complicating matters further, the Ministry of Health administers health districts that are not coextensive with administrative districts, while ministries such as the Ministry of Agriculture, Forestry, and Fisheries and the Ministry of Rural Development, which engage in natural resource management, frequently deal with resources, such as forests and fisheries that are common to a number of villages or communes.

In the northwest of the country, where the programs that culminated in Seila originated, are a number of so-called "reconciliation zones"— zones previously administered by insurgents of the National Army of Democratic Kampuchea (NADK) that have been reintegrated. In these zones, commune and district officials are often former NADK cadres, retained in their administrative roles. In the early 1990s, these provinces accepted large numbers of refugees returning from border refugee camps, where many had lived since the late 1970s or early 1980s. Warfare continued until 1999, leaving landmines and a devastated economy. This setting provided the context for the Seila program.

This chapter is based on three sources of information. The main source is documentary evidence, gained from the comprehensive literature of research studies, evaluation reports, and project documents collected by Seila over the years (these sources are available online at http://www.seila. gov.kh). A second source is a series of interviews with representatives of donor organizations, NGOs, ministries, and Seila officials that was conducted in Phnom Penh in September and October 2004. A third source is discussions with representatives of the provincial government and commune councils, which were conducted during two brief field trips to Kompong Cham and Pursat Provinces in October 2004.

The Seila Program's Evolving Goals and Objectives

The Seila program was established in 1996, initially as a framework for matching the delivery of capital for infrastructural projects from a variety of donors and the national government with local, participatory needs assessments in five provinces in Cambodia. Since 2001 the program's goal has been redefined in order to integrate it with the government's decentralization and deconcentration reforms, under which a three-tiered system of planning and budgeting—focusing on the commune/*sangkat*, province/municipality, and national levels— was created.[1]

Resources mobilized or programmed under the Seila framework are channeled through annual planning processes and horizontal and vertical consultations at the commune, district, province, and national levels. The resources are then systematically transferred to national ministries and institutions, provinces, and commune/*sangkat* councils, which are responsible for implementing a wide range of services and investments in accordance with their respective mandates.

The Cambodian government's Seila program document of December 2000 defines it as "a national effort to achieve poverty reduction through improved local governance." As such, it incorporates three goals:

- alleviating poverty, by delivering discretionary budgetary support for provincial and commune authorities to provide basic infrastructure and services at the village level, which are in compliance with participatory systems of planning and prioritization, and are implemented locally

- strengthening institutions at the provincial and commune levels, by providing technical assistance in managing the administration and financing participatory development schemes
- piloting and experimenting with models of decentralization and deconcentration in support of government policy for wider initiatives in this area

The program's outputs are as follows:

- provision of efficient and effective public goods and services for local development
- effective implementation of strengthened local institutions and of decentralized and deconcentrated systems
- improvement of national policy and regulations for decentralization and deconcentration (UNDP 2001a)

A central concept behind Seila's strategy is the notion of good governance, which is regarded as a prerequisite for poverty reduction and sustainable development. Good governance encompasses these:

- local democratic institutions (both representative and participatory) that provide opportunities for citizens (including the poor and marginalized) to be actively involved in local decision making and in the monitoring and auditing of local public expenditures
- local administrations with greater development and services responsibilities and with correspondingly greater autonomy, resources, and capacities to adopt their own poverty alleviation policies and to deliver their benefits
- effective and efficient partnership arrangements for development management and service delivery between central and local authorities, civil society organizations, and the private sector (UNDP 2001b)

Strengthening governance has involved developing procedures for procurement, participatory planning, financing, and public–private partnerships in local development projects; training staff at the provincial and commune levels in implementing these procedures; and establishing teams of facilitators to monitor their implementation on an ongoing basis. More broadly, it has involved establishing a framework for disbursing donor funds through subnational state agencies, giving these agencies the resources, discretion, and capacity to take a leading role in promoting participatory development practices. An important indicator of the success of the program is the fact that this funding framework has attracted significant interest from donors, who have increasingly channeled their contributions through the Seila framework.

If one is to appreciate the significance of the program's achievements, it is important to note that these objectives were not explicit in the program's initial design. Rather, they developed along the way, in the light of experience and necessity. Several aspects of the Seila program emerged almost by chance, which is significant in terms of the implications for the design of similar programs. In characterizing the Seila program, then, one must take account of the development in the program's scope and objectives, as well as its changing institutional structure.

Seila emerged from an initial effort, by the United Nations Development Programme (UNDP), to channel funds for repairing infrastructure and improving services to areas in Northwest Cambodia where former refugees were being repatriated under the Cambodian peace process of 1991–93. UNDP had accumulated 16 years of funding for Cambodia, funds that needed to be spent. In a project titled the Cambodia Area Rehabilitation and Regeneration Project (CARERE 1), it focused on providing quick-impact projects to benefit communities to which refugees were returning. Many aspects of these projects were unsuccessful, particularly in promoting the local ownership necessary to render the infrastructure projects delivered sustainable. However, this program laid the groundwork for Seila by getting development workers on the ground in five provinces; giving them experience in working with the state apparatus in these areas; and, in one province, permitting experimentation in participatory planning by creating elected village development committees, a concept that was taken up in the next phase of the project.

CARERE 2, which ran from 1996 to 2000, built on CARERE 1, with some key differences. It set out to provide long-term frameworks for planning and development rather than short-term emergency response and humanitarian relief. CARERE 1 was a traditional project, in which local structures were largely bypassed to deliver goods to the local population. This approach was altered in 1996, when CARERE 2 was established, as a support project to a set of government development activities, themselves organized through the Seila program. CARERE 2 replaced emergency relief and infrastructure delivery for resettled people with experimentation in decentralized local development and reconciliation. The Seila half of the program entailed the establishment of planning and development mechanisms within government for the spending of funds allocated by donors. The CARERE 2 half of the program lent support that emphasized capacity building for the government officials involved with Seila.

Initially, the objectives of CARERE 2 were framed as follows:

- build capacity in the five provinces for integrated area development planning
- build capacity for Seila to mobilize and manage financial resources
- build capacity for Seila to perform activities related to the whole project cycle
- improve the socioeconomic well-being of the population in target zones
- establish a comprehensive documentary resource base on the Seila experience

After a mid-term evaluation in July 1998, these objectives were rearticulated as follows:

- establish decentralized government systems that plan, finance, and manage development
- create a secure environment conducive to reconciliation between government and communities
- assist government and nongovernment entities in providing essential basic services
- inform national policy on decentralized development with lessons from the CARERE/Seila experience

The changing focus suggested by these alterations in objectives reflected growing awareness that the strength of the program lay in its relationship with government and its ability to promote changing governmental attitudes, increase government effectiveness, and provide the means for experimenting with new forms of local governance. Thus, the goals of the program changed: in 1996 CARERE 2 was envisaged as a program to alleviate poverty and to contribute to the building of peace through capacity building in the state apparatus. By 1998, the goal had become broader and the vision of reformed governance more ambitious. The notion that CARERE itself should deliver improved standards of living had fallen away entirely. Instead, it was seen as supporting government in raising living standards. In addition, issues of participation and state-society relations had entered the program's central rationale, giving the program more of a specifically political agenda. Seila now aimed—through support for decentralized governance—to contribute to poverty alleviation and spread of peace in Cambodia, by strengthening the bonds linking civil society to the structures of the state and by empowering the Cambodian rural population to become fully participating members in the development process (Rudengren and Ojendal 2002, 6).

CARERE ended in 2001. The Seila program continued, supported by a new multidonor support program called the Partnership for Local Governance (PLG), established in 2001. Seila's new objectives focused primarily on instituting decentralized systems and strategies for poverty alleviation through good governance.

The PLG project document emphasizes that the significance of Seila, from a donor perspective, is that it focuses on the policy and institutional environment of poverty reduction, which is neglected by many stand-alone projects. The central concern of Seila is to support provincial and commune planning and coordination mechanisms. This support is achieved through provision of budgets and support for experimentation in developing new procedures. It describes Seila as a program to

> provide subnational (provincial and commune) authorities with some regular general purpose financial transfers (the Local Development Fund and Provincial Investment Fund) that would support . . . the practical experimentation and adoption, by the same local authorities, of technically sound and participatory planning, programming and budgeting practices. Such practices are meant to be institutionally sustainable, which is potentially statutory (nationally/locally regulated) and independent from specific/sectoral, domestic or external funding sources. They are in turn expected to provide the supporting framework for . . . subnational decision making and accountability on the allocation of resources and actual implementation, of multiple, centrally funded and monitored, sectoral or purpose-specific development programs (PLG 2001,11–12).

By this time, Seila was viewed primarily as a program aimed at reforming local governance. It was also being increasingly used as a mechanism for channeling and coordinating broader, sector-specific donor assistance, although this was seen as supplementary to the core function. To a great extent, Seila was being promoted as the future of Cambodian local government and as the testing ground for the policies of decentralization and deconcentration of government function that by 2001—with the first local elections looming—were very much on the political agenda.[2]

Structures of the Seila Program

The decentralized governance system that was put in place created government structures at the national, provincial, district, commune, and village levels. Initially, this was done in the four provinces in the northwest where the concentration of refugees was greatest. Subsequently, as the passage of time reduced the saliency of the issue of refugee reintegration and as enthusiasm for Seila grew among donors and within powerful sections of government, Seila was expanded. It now covers all provinces of Cambodia.

Seila consists of a structure of institutions and a set of processes (figure 4.1). The structure focuses on the provincial and commune levels, although it operates under a national task force and reaches through the district level down to the village level. The Seila Task Force, comprising delegates from seven ministries—Economics and Finance, Agriculture, Planning, Rural Development, Water Resources, Women's Affairs, and Veteran's Affairs—is responsible for overall policy making with regard to Seila. It is supported by a national secretariat and is responsible for mobilizing and coordinating aid, allocating funds, and conducting the overall monitoring and evaluation of the program. The secretariat executes the Seila program through contracts with provincial governments and relevant line ministries. It has 20 professional staff members.

The provincial level is the highest level at which planning of projects occurs. A provincial rural development committee is established, chaired by the governor of the province, and including the directors of key line departments within the Ministries of Rural Development, Planning, Finance, Agriculture, Women's Affairs, and Veteran's Affairs and the representatives from districts in the province. The Provincial Rural Development Committee makes overall plans for development at the provincial level, through the Provincial Development Plan, and establishes budgets for the plan with the assistance of a Provincial Investment Fund. Implementation of the plans is the responsibility of the Executive Committee (ExCom), which is chaired by the governor. This committee is made up of the directors of the line departments. It is supported by a secretariat with four units: a contract administration unit, a technical support unit, a finance unit, and a local administration unit, which fields provincial and district facilitation teams to assist in the overall process. The units report to ExCom and deliver services to the commune development committees. Advisors from the PLG support project assist these provincial structures.

The next key level of management of development is the commune level. A commune development committee uses participatory processes

Figure 4.1 Institutional Structure of the Seila Program

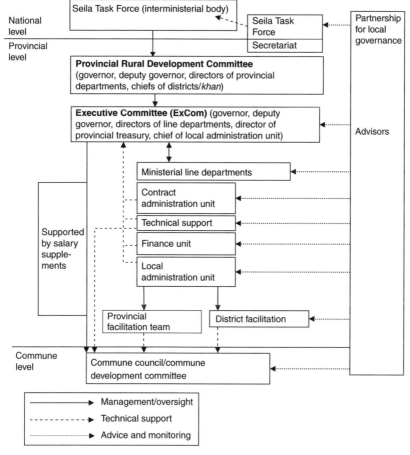

Source: Adapted from Rudengren and Ojendal (2002), appendix 2.

to develop a commune needs assessment and a commune development plan. This plan is then taken to the district level for an "integration workshop," during which the various commune plans are coordinated and prioritized and funding is sought, either from the provincial level or from NGOs, donors, or line departments. A small amount of funds is also available directly to communes through the Commune/*Sangkat* Fund. In 2002, when local elections were held in Cambodia, the commune development committee was replaced by the commune council's Planning and Budgeting Subcommittee, a committee working in conjunction with elected commune councils. In the original Seila provinces, the community development committees worked with village development committees to establish needs and action plans. However, the election of commune councils and the understanding that the commune level will be the lowest level of government to which decentralization will extend has meant that village development committees must remain informal and be program creations rather than elements of government.

Alongside these governmental structures exists a support structure of advisors and facilitators, originally established as CARERE 2 in 1996. They include a provincial office with its own staff, many of them expatriates. Gradually, expatriates were replaced by national staff, so that by the end of CARERE 2, in 2000, all support staff were nationals. After 2001, the CARERE offices were integrated into the provincial administration. Support to Seila is now delivered through the four secretariat units and through PLG advisors, who support the provincial administration in management, finance, planning, monitoring, local capacity building, and infrastructure as well as in specific sectors, such as agriculture. PLG staff work with the Seila units in the provincial administration to provide support to commune councils and to offer capacity building to provincial staff. There are currently 176 PLG staff working at the provincial level, ranging from 2 in the municipality of Kep to 25 in Ratanakiri Province. The mid-term review of Seila/PLG describes the PLG support staff as "the keystone for the whole support structure." The staff are described as not merely providing technical advice but also "ensuring sound management, transparency and accountability—in short, good governance" (UNDP/DFID/SIDA 2004, 13–14).

The Seila Process

The Seila program entails processes at a number of levels. It has developed specific procedures for participatory planning and for management of provincial and commune development. These procedures are codified in manuals for use by local authorities and facilitated by the provincial and district facilitation teams attached to the Seila secretariat in each province. The procedures include both participatory needs assessments and planning processes, which are designed to bring ordinary villagers into the process of development, and transparent mechanisms for the disbursement of funds provided by donors.

The key funds provided at the provincial level are the Provincial Investment Fund and provincial operational budgets, composed entirely of donor funding and consequently "off budget" as far as the national treasury is concerned. Since 2002, a proportion of funds has also been channeled to the Commune/*Sangkat* Fund, which is financed by external grants and loans and by annual national budget appropriations.

The process of bringing villagers' ideas into contact with donors' money requires an intermediate coordination mechanism, which will allow the provincial level of government to retain oversight over the various projects, funds, and activities pursued at the commune level and to prioritize projects across communes and districts. In an 11–step process, commune councils develop their own three-year investment plans and five-year development plans. They then draw annual priorities from plans, which are submitted to district planning units. At the same time, line ministries at the provincial level prepare their own work plans. All of these plans are brought together at the annual district integration workshop, in which commune, district, and provincial representatives meet, along with nongovernmental and international organizations planning to work in the province. Priorities and distributions of resources are determined, as communes present their needs, line ministries and other organizations select activities to support, and temporary contracts between the two sides are signed. These agreements then feed into provincial and district planning for the year.

Seila has also developed processes for building capacity in order to enable local government institutions to become adept at using the planning and management procedures. An important element of this approach has been the notion of learning-by-doing. The process has involved what one evaluation team described as a leap of faith—the willingness to commit funds to government structures that had not yet proved their capacity to use them in a manner that accorded with donor conceptions of good practice. In the context of early postwar Cambodia, where the state was widely and to a great extent accurately regarded as abusive, corrupt, and politically biased, this leap of faith was unusual among donors. The Seila program gave these state structures the opportunities to reform and, in particular, to become more responsive to their constituents precisely because it gave them funds with which to deliver government services.

The procedures used by advisors under CARERE and subsequently the PLG staff for planning and managing development and for capacity building within government have also been subject to a learning-by-doing creed. Seila has been notable for its flexibility and for its willingness to adapt, experiment, and reform. This flexibility has been built into the program through continuous monitoring and evaluation, both internal and external, and through operational feedback.

Development Results

The Seila program evolved away from the original CARERE 1 orientation of delivering quick-impact infrastructure and services toward support of poverty alleviation by reforming the institutions and procedures of local government. Analyzing the program's delivered outcomes, then, requires attention to both its impact on poverty alleviation and its impact on local governance. Addressing the question of spillover in this context is problematic, because an early spillover—the changing of attitudes locally and centrally toward appropriate methods of government and the nature of state-society relations—was swiftly adopted as a goal of the program. Furthermore, the program has increasingly been pitched as a framework for experimentation and data collection, which can support wider government policy making. By this means, further spillovers are co-opted as delivered outcomes, making spillovers and intended results difficult to distinguish. Consequently, this section addresses the results of the Seila program in terms of the nature of successes claimed, the impact on poverty and the poor, the impact on local government, and the impact on central government, attempting in each case to illuminate the relationship between intended and unintended outcomes.

Several far-reaching evaluations of Seila have declared the program an unusual success in the Cambodian context. One study concluded that Seila "has succeeded in being a development program . . . while at the same time having a progressive and profound long-term policy impact for the future of public administration and development in Cambodia . . . . Here is an example of how aid always was supposed to work, but in reality rarely did" (Rudengren and Ojendal 2002, 1).

A 2002 evaluation of CARERE 2/Seila (Evans and others 2000) listed a wide-ranging set of positive outcomes, which included these:

- developing and making operational a concept for regional and local planning and development
- making substantial progress toward building sustainable capacity at the province, district, and community levels in five provinces
- visibly changing attitudes toward democratic values and good governance, including increasing the activism, self-reliance, and self-esteem of communities that were formerly passive recipients of assistance
- increasing the responsiveness and self-reliance of provincial and district government staff and strongly influencing central government policy on deconcentration and particularly decentralization

- providing an effective mechanism for approaching former Khmer Rouge communities and dealing with ethnic diversity in pursuit of the government's reconciliation efforts
- delivering essential basic services to needy communities in more than 2,000 villages
- attracting funding from a range of donors

Some of these outcomes are incontrovertible. Seila processes for planning and managing development are being implemented in a number of Cambodian provinces. Seila has attracted funding and passionate commitment from a range of donors, including various UN agencies, the World Bank, the Swedish International Development Agency (SIDA), the United Kingdom's Department for International Development (DFID), Australian Agency for International Development (AusAID), the Danish International Development Agency (DANIDA), and others. Funding channeled through Seila has increased from $12 million in 1996 to $23 million in 2003; funding from various donors from CARERE 1 to the end of CARERE 2 also rose (tables 4.1 and 4.2). Some of Cambodia's largest bilateral donors—notably the Japanese and French governments and the European Union—have chosen not to direct funding primarily through Seila.

Other claims of success require closer analysis. Chief among them is the extent of the contribution Seila has made to its overall goals of reducing poverty and improving governance.

Impact on Poverty Reduction and Aid to the Poor

Seila delivered essential basic service to poor communities in more than 200 villages, an achievement that Evans and others (2000) consider a major success. Between 1996 and 2000, more than $75 million worth of technical and program support and investments in local services and infrastructure was channeled through the program, by 11 multilateral and bilateral donors, the central government, and NGOs. Since 2000, the scope of Seila has widened to cover the entire country, and more money has been plowed into the system.

Other evaluators have been more circumspect in attributing success in this respect. Rudengren and Ojendal, for example, note that although Seila has provided tangible goods, such as bridges, roads, and wells, to the population, there is little quantifiable evidence to suggest that it has had a quantifiable impact on poverty. Rudengren and Ojendal (2002, 34) conclude the following:

> For a major development program on poverty alleviation to not be able to account for quantifiable advances in poverty reduction, after five years of

Table 4.1 Financial Support to CARERE and Seila, 1992–2001

Donor	1992–93	1994–95	1996–98	1999–2001	Total	Percent
UN System						
UNDP	4,744,000	7,085,000	17,810,000	4,862,000	34,501,000	33.3
UNCDF	0	0	1,988,000	2,042,000	4,030,000	3.9
UNWFP	0	0	0	2,860,000	2,860,000	2.8
UNHCR	2,627,000	0	0	340,000	2,988,000	2.9
Subtotal	7,392,000	7,085,000	19,797,000	10,105,000	44,379,000	42.8
Bilateral donors						
Australia	0	476,000	0	820,000	1,296,000	1.2
Canada/IDRC	0	0	226,000	100,000	326,000	0.3
Caisse Française	0	791,000	0	0	791,000	0.8
EU	0	0	2,893,000	0	2,893,000	2.8
Finland	449,000	0	0	0	449,000	0.4
Netherlands	1,768,000	3,421,000	6,050,000	4,463,000	15,702,000	15.1
Norway	0	915,000	0	00	0	0.9
Sweden	0	1,459,000	13,436,000	5,653,000	20,548,000	19.8
United Kingdom/ DFID	125,000	0	236,000	950,000	1,311,000	1.3
United States	1,780,000	0	0	0	1,780,000	1.7
Subtotal	4,121,000	7,062,000	22,840,000	11,986,000	46,010,000	44.4
International financial institutions						
IFAD	0	0	0	5,700,000	5,700,000	5.5
World Bank	0	0	0	4,099,000	4,099,000	4.0
Subtotal	0	0	0	9,799,000	9,799,000	9.4
Domestic resources						
Local contributions	0	0	400,000	920,000	1,320,000	1.3
National budget	0	0	0	2,191,000	2,191,000	2.1
Subtotal	0	0	400,000	3,111,000	3,511,000	3.4
Total	11,513,000	14,147,000	43,038,000	35,001,000	103,699,000	100

Source: UNDP 2001.
Note: EU = European Union, IDRC = International Development Research Centre, IFAD = International Fund for Agricultural Development, UNWFP = United Nations World Food Programme.

operation, may seem devastating. This certainly has been controversial, endlessly noted in monitoring reports, and a constant concern of donors. Some more targeted attempts at poverty alleviation for particularly disadvantaged groups have been attempted, but with limited success. The explanation for the relative indifference for more tangible poverty alleviation is, firstly, that the program works on a structural level with state–civil society relations and through addressing issues pertaining to social fragmentation, and is thus only indirectly addressing poverty. Second, small-scale infrastructure investments have received the bulk of the investment budget. Thus poverty is targeted. Third, poverty is an elusive concept—although income level may not have risen across the board in the concerned areas, life has probably become easier (through feeder roads), health is likely to have increased (through better access to water and clinics), or basic education been raised (through more schools being built), and so forth.

Seila was reoriented at an early stage toward governance rather than direct poverty alleviation. The presupposition of the Seila philosophy is the claim that poverty alleviation is best approached by promoting participation, transparency, and accountability in government. Evaluating Seila on its own terms suggests that the best indication of its utility to the poor is the extent to which the poor are empowered by Seila processes and the extent to which the needs they express are met through the Seila system. More broadly, the question is whether the governance approach is an appropriate means of tackling poverty in early postconflict situations.

Qualitative assessments of Seila's impact on village politics and on the extent to which the process offers opportunities for the poor to participate have been undertaken. The findings offer only equivocal evidence of a positive impact. One study, conducted in 1999/2000, concluded that "Seila's impact on local governance is largely determined by local power relations," that where Seila had an effect, it was due to the fact that the program exposed villagers to actors from outside and prompted the emergence of new leaders. The study argued that "Seila can contribute to active citizenship if people are aware of their rights and responsibilities, that Seila can contribute to establishing accountable village representatives with a limited mandate, and that Seila can strengthen commune governance if other actors do not counteract that objective" (Hasselskog, Krong, and Chim 2000, 11). These results suggest that Seila has an effect on state–society relations but that it is highly qualified by incidental factors.

A 2001 study on the impact of Seila on the involvement of civil society in local governance found that villagers were aware of Seila activities in their own village but were less well aware of activities taking place at the commune level, thus limiting their ability to demand accountability from commune-level officials (Biddulph 2001). A 2003 study on the implications of Seila for empowerment of villagers suggested that awareness of the importance of the commune level of government had grown in Cambodian villages (Biddulph 2003, 10). The study also reported widespread participation in planning, along with satisfaction with project choice and anticipation of benefiting from projects implemented. These findings suggest that elites have not captured the Seila process, a finding backed up by other research. However, the empowerment study also found generally low awareness of the nuts and bolts of the planning process, poor availability of detailed information, dissatisfaction among officials with training processes, and some concerns over technical standards that may result from "collaboration between contractors and provincial technical officers" (Biddulph 2003, 7). In other words, Seila has delivered tangible, popular, and useful benefits to villagers, including the very poor, in response to articulated needs, but it has been less successful in delivering transparency, accountability, and, consequently, empowerment with respect to commune, district, and provincial government. This has significant repercussions with regard to local ownership.

A significant finding of these studies is that villagers were much more likely to take ownership of local projects if they had made a financial contribution. The Seila process allows for mobilization of local contributions toward development projects. This finding raises the question of whether the Seila framework's overall orientation toward the disbursement of donor funds could not have been better linked to the gathering of local contributions and whether a spillover effect of having done so might have raised more urgent attention on the part of central government to issues of revenue raising by local governments.

Another issue is the emergence of a village-based civil society. Arguably, the input of villagers into state planning processes might be more effective if it were channeled through community-based organizations. The participatory planning processes of the Seila program offer opportunities for community-based organizations to come to the table. They also offer opportunities for NGOs to engage in commune-level affairs (through the district integration workshops) and for links to be formed between grassroots organizations and national and international NGOs. Attention has been paid, at least in the original provinces supported by Seila, to forming and strengthening elected village development committees to represent grassroots community interests. It is unclear, however, whether members of these committees represent a range of village interests and concerns; their relationship with the village and commune authorities is highly variable (Hasselskog, Krong, and Chim 2000). The Seila program did not allocate resources directly to strengthening community-based organizations representing sectional interests. Fostering local interest groups—by offering arenas within which the needs, concerns, and preferences of different villagers can be defined and developed—could improve the quality of planning outcomes.

The relationship between Seila structures and longstanding civil (rather than governmental) authority structures within villages is also unclear. The lack of community-based organizations may have contributed to difficulties in disseminating information about Seila activities and procedures at the village level. Efforts have been made to involve local pagodas—a focus of civil society in rural Cambodia villages—in Seila activities. A 2001 study reported that there had been some success in eliciting the assistance of monks in mobilizing contributions for Seila projects but less success in using monks as advisors or facilitators (Biddulph 2001).

The 2004 Mid-Term Review of the Seila/PLG project partly frees Seila from the need to show evidence of an impact on poverty reduction. The review notes that Seila aims to reduce poverty by improving governance and that the government and PLG donors had agreed that "the Seila program would not produce its own poverty strategy, but instead would define an approach for how to contribute to and strengthen the implementation of the National Poverty Reduction Strategy 2003–05." (SPM Consultants and Oxford Policy Management 2004, 15). The reviewers note that Seila processes have the potential to be pro-poor. "The modest financial resources that have been provided through the Commune/*Sangkat* Fund, promoted and supported by the Seila program, may be allocated in a way that ensures that at least some of the benefits reach the very poor, though this is far from automatic" (SPM Consultants and Oxford Policy Management 2004, 15).

The report also notes that guidelines for the district integration workshops reflect the strategic objectives of the government's National Poverty Reduction Strategy, as do guidelines for allocation of Provincial Investment Funds.[3] However, the report notes, decentralization policies are not likely to reduce poverty significantly, because the funds transferred to commune councils are meager and there is little downward accountability.

No quantifiable evidence is available on Seila's overall contribution to economic growth. However, it is clear that Seila has channeled money into useful projects. Cambodia emerged from the civil war with a shattered infrastructure. The provision of basic infrastructure—bridges, wells, schools—is likely to have provided significant benefit to the communities. Qualitative studies suggest that these benefits extended to the very poor (Biddulph 2003).

Impact on Governance

In line with the reorientation of Seila's approach away from poverty reduction toward improved governance, the conclusions of the Mid-Term Review of February 2004 focus on governance outcomes. The review suggests that successes have been achieved in several areas such as these:

- "relevance . . . [in] contributing to improved governance, service delivery and poverty reduction"
- "effectiveness" in providing technical assistance at the provincial level, although this aid was constrained by a lack of a clear government policy framework determining the powers and functions of provincial governments
- timeliness in implementing program activities
- an "impression" of "significant positive impact on the government's decentralization program . . . less so with respect to promoting deconcentration"
- significant strengthening of capacities and improvement of systems for accountability and transparency

The review also notes a high level of dependence on donor financial and technical assistance support, which is expected to continue for a number of years.

With regard to attitudes and governance, it is difficult to separate the particular contribution of Seila from other motors driving political and administrative change. The Cambodian government has officially stated that it regards Seila as supportive of deconcentration and decentralization. It considers Seila a laboratory in which policies can be experimented with, one that provides a database and a body of experience.

However, there are wider political issues within which any contribution from Seila must be framed. Although already enacted decentralization policies for introducing elected local bodies at the commune level bear Seila's imprint, policies for devolving central government powers to the provincial and district level are still in the earliest stages of development.

Seila's role in this process is unclear. Important actors in the policy-making process are not convinced that Seila should be viewed as the template for wider deconcentration reform.

More problematic is establishing evidence for less-tangible outcomes, such as the sustainability of capacity built at the provincial, district, and commune levels; the democratic attitudes promoted among the population and local government; and the significance of Seila in driving government policy making. Providing evidence for these outcomes—particularly evidence for changing attitudes on the part of government and the population—is difficult, not only because of the intangible nature of these outcomes but also because Seila was implemented in the context of wider political, social, and economic changes over the course of the 1990s.

Analyzing the success of Seila in these cases requires examining the political economy of the situation within which Seila has been implemented, the incentive structures of key actors, and the ways in which Seila has fitted into or transformed them. Such an approach offers insight into the extent to which Seila has had an impact that is likely to be valued highly enough to promote changed behavior and far-reaching enough to prove sustainable over the long run.

Reform of Provincial Government
The initial impetus for CARERE 2/Seila emerged in response to experimentation under CARERE 1 in the northwestern provinces, which were heavily hit by fighting during the civil war and remained divided into government and insurgent zones until the end of the war. The earliest village development councils and provincial rural development committees were piloted there, under the auspices of CARERE and the Ministry of Rural Development. CARERE 1 developed a close relationship with five provincial administrations, in an environment where provincial governors had recently lost considerable power because of rapid centralization under the terms of the 1993 Constitution. To promote macroeconomic stability, the government has pursued fiscal centralization since 1993, thus depriving provincial governments of revenue. In the northwestern provinces in particular, institutions for managing rural development in the context of ongoing war, the regular displacement of population, and the return of thousands of refugees were not merely lacking but absent.

Seila's success in reforming provincial government emerged to a great extent from this context. Seila was successful because it provided funding and functions to a level of government that had lost its purpose. Provincial governors in the northwest faced a difficult political and economic situation.

They were under pressure from two directions. National reform toward elections and subsequent political instability meant that their positions—and those of their parties—were highly uncertain. Within their provinces, they were under pressure to maintain control of government zones in the face of continued armed insurgency, inflowing refugees and ongoing displacement, and minimal financial flows. Rapid economic reform away from the command economy toward a free market and the centralization of revenue raising had altered the policy context for development beyond recognition. At the same time, inflows of aid were almost uniformly bypassing the state. In the early 1990s, the majority of rural development work in the northwestern provinces was being delivered by NGOs that dealt with local associations as partners. The current governor of Pursat and former governor of Battambang was interviewed for this study and commented, "NGOs used to come here to do projects and we didn't know about it." Some reports suggest that a similar situation existed between the provincial governor's office and the provincial offices of line ministries. The relations between these agencies varied considerably from province to province.

In this context, provincial governors needed to find a way to reassert their authority with respect to other political and economic actors, to legitimize their position with respect to a more politically diverse population through the provision of tangible benefits, to stave off economic disaster and popular disaffection, and to give them some flexibility to react to the unfolding situation. The Seila program—which offered discretionary local development funds, mechanisms for managing them, a role in coordinating nongovernmental development initiatives, and new participatory institutions that could bind villagers to the state—fitted well with the needs of provincial governments. In the CARERE 2/Seila phase, in particular, Seila mechanisms also offered some of the only neutral ground for engagement between provincial administrations and the newly integrated zones that had been administered by insurgents during the civil war. In the two provinces visited for this study, Kompong Cham and Pursat, senior staff members emphasized the importance of Seila in giving the provincial government a role, allocating resources to them, and restoring their authority over other development actors.

This situation was conducive to success from the perspective of both provincial governors and donors. A lack of pre-existing rural development practices, the extreme dearth of local finance, and the strong incentives for cooperation on the part of provincial government gave maximum leverage to donors. As a result, they were able to engage state actors in intensive training and to insist that detailed mechanisms for planning, procurement, management, and financing be followed. Given the widespread mistrust among donors of the Cambodian state apparatus and its rapidly growing reputation for corruption and politicization, this was an important element in attracting donors to both offer funds to the core of the Seila program and, increasingly, to channel supplementary funding through the Seila framework.

With regard to the possibility of political hijacking or elite capture, Seila benefited from the fact that it began life as a program operating primarily at the provincial level, with small-scale funding. During the early to mid-1990s, the provincial level was much less politicized than the national level of government. During CARERE 1 and the early years of CARERE 2 until the national elections of 1998, the national level of politics was driven by internal tension between the partners in the coalition government, the National Front for an Independent, Peaceful, and Cooperative Cambodia (FUNCINPEC) and the Cambodian People's Party (CPP). The Seila Task Force—the national body managing policy making for Seila—was convened in December 1997, after the July battle in which the CPP defeated FUNCINPEC armed forces and before the return of many of the FUNCINPEC and opposition politicians who fled Cambodia in the aftermath of that battle. Furthermore, even once established, the Seila Task Force lagged behind provincial and local actors who were already driving the program. An evaluation of Seila conducted in 2000 found that the national-level Seila Task Force was the least effective of the various levels of government with regard to their Seila roles (Evans et al. 2000, 2).

Part of the reason for Seila's success has been the fact that it began life below the political radar, at a level of government that was removed somewhat from the heat of political wrangling. Seila's initial disbursements of funds were too small to be the target of attempts at elite capture on a large scale. As one interviewee put it, "By the time the funding had reached a significant level, the accountability mechanisms were in place." Accountability mechanisms are a major issue, given the high level of corruption within the Cambodian state apparatus and the disastrous effect that corruption has had on a large number of donor-sponsored development and resource management projects.[4]

The nature of these successes, however, provokes another question. Given that Seila fitted neatly with the needs of provincial governors, to what extent did Seila actually foster change within provincial governments? A number of evaluations have concluded that Seila has fostered change, a conclusion enthusiastically endorsed by the governor of Pursat, who asserted, "The Seila program has changed my life." Proponents of Seila argue that the learning-by-doing approach offered an expression of trust in the state, to which a state hungry for increased legitimacy and the capacity to be more effective eagerly responded (Rudengren and Ojendal 2002). Some people interviewed for this study also suggested that the discretion awarded to state actors over Seila funds increased the sense of ownership. According to one of them, there is a crucial difference in the way that local level officials talk about projects produced with Seila funds and projects delivered by external agencies. "They say, this road is the ADB road, but that road is our road."

Provincial governments across Cambodia have been implicated in a range of corrupt and abusive activities. One person interviewed for this study quoted a provincial governor as saying, "Provincial governors have two hats, a black one and a white one. When we work with Seila we wear our white hats." This quote raises the question of how far the response to Seila has prompted spillover into wider governmental attitudes and how far it is simply a response prompted by the particular conditions of Seila funding. This question is difficult to answer. Several evaluations have noted that the attitudes of provincial officials have been transformed by Seila, with provincial government becoming more responsive and self-reliant (Evans et al. 2000, 16; see also Rudengren and Ojendal 2002, 16). But a survey conducted in 2001 among government officials in Seila and non-Seila provinces suggested that there was little difference between them in terms of government officials' understanding of international definitions of good governance (Holloway and others 2001).

The survey found that Cambodian government officials generally fall short of international standards. It noted, however, that "there are some systems, for example, the Seila program, which have demonstrated that transparency in governance and development is possible at a cost. Officials who work in Seila systems meet this standard" (Holloway and others 2001, 46). This survey suggests that while attitudes toward good governance across Seila and non-Seila provinces might be monolithic, practices are not. The maintenance of such practices is vitally dependent on their continued support and monitoring through the system. Salary supplements and ongoing supervision by PLG advisors represent two examples of support that keep Seila officials on the straight and narrow. But has there has been any spillover? Have attitudes changed fundamentally—or just in line with current Seila incentives? Are the capacities and structures built through Seila sustainable in the absence of this kind of ongoing support?

The business of working through the annual round of Seila planning and management mechanisms has undoubtedly changed the framework within which provincial government operates, making the "white hat" approach to government possible. New institutions have been created, notably the village, commune, and provincial rural development committees, that permit the circulation of information upward from the grassroots and horizontally between provincial government and line departments. Coordination has been facilitated by an increase in mutual understanding of concerns and interests and by the establishment of personal relationships between different actors in the system. Seila funds give the provincial governments the ability to formulate plans and, to a limited extent, a vision of the future development trajectory of the province. As provincial staff in the two provinces visited (Kompong Cham and Pursat) made clear, this formulation expands the independence, authority, and effectiveness of provincial government, and it permits governors to enjoy a sense of job satisfaction and popularity with the people.

Since 1993 the electoral strategy of the current ruling party has been heavily dependent on the ability of the ruling party to raise large sums of money to sponsor politicized, party-owned rural development projects, which are used to garner votes at election times. Provincial governors are required to contribute both to raising the necessary funds, through a range of practices associated with corruption and natural resource exploitation, and to promoting the politicization of much government-sponsored rural development. There is little sign that the ruling party is rethinking this electoral strategy. The continuation of this side of provincial governance casts some doubt over whether the relative transparency and accountability with which Seila operates remains a function of close scrutiny by PLG advisors rather than changed attitudes within provincial government. This question will become acute in the future as Seila processes become further mainstreamed and as the proportion of provincial funding channeled through the processes increases.

Associated with this debate is another over whether Seila has set up parallel structures. Proponents of Seila point to the fact that it is almost unprecedented in Cambodian rural development to work through the state and, in particular, to trust the state with funds. The program's learning-by-doing approach, which held that state actors had to be given budgets in order to learn how to use them, has been hailed as both revolutionary and progressive. Seila's advocates also point out that the so-called

Table 4.2 Financial Support to Seila, 2001–05

Donor	Seila Program 2001–2005: Donor Financing					Total	Percent
	2001	2002	2003	2004	2005		
National Budget – Royal Government of Cambodia	1,447,368	6,017,248	11,312,282	13,041,814	14,959,567	46,778,279	27.5
Multilateral Grants	10,095,820	11,658,737	14,364,690	15,413,768	14,696,596	666,229,611	39.0
UN-Donor Partnership for Local Governance	5,695,820	6,569,647	11,113,516	11,649,684	12,240,223	47,268,890	27.8
UN World Food Program	4,400,000	4,706,090	2,307,210	2,546,845		13,960,145	8.2
UNICEF/Seth Koma		340,000	918,964	1,217,239	2,206,373	4,682,576	2.8
UNDP/DSP					250,000	250,000	0.1
UNV/Community Development in Angkor Park		43,000	25,000			68,000	0.0
Bilateral Grants	1,263,400	2,004,187	3,320,979	4,928,617	3,578,681	115,095,864	8.9
Germany/GTZ	1,113,400	1,700,000	1,905,126	2,056,153	1,110,102	7,884,781	4.6
Australia/AusAID	150,000	150,000	1,022,858	766,634	436,135	2,525,627	1.5
Denmark/DANIDA			392,995	2,105,830	1,232,444	3,731,269	2.2
Japan/Small Grants Facility		154,187				154,187	0.1
Canada/CIDA					800,000	800,000	0.5
Loan Programs	4,964,488	5,033,449	7,769,436	12,004,944	11,296,724	441,069,041	24.2
IFAD/ADESS	1,735,081	2,261,508	1,780,843	1,172,966	756,799	7,707,197	4.5
IFAD/CBRD	2,131,330	2,771,941	2,988,593	4,068,622	2,360,465	14,320,951	8.4
IFAD/RPRP				1,515,156	2,866,860	4,382,016	2.6

						Total	%
International Fund for Agricultural Development Total	3,866,411	5,033,449	4,769,436	6,756,744	5,984,124	426,410,164	15.5
World Bank/RILG[a]			3,000,000	5,248,200	5,312,600	13,560,800	8.0
World Bank/NVDP	500,000					500,000	0.3
World Bank/Social Fund of the Kingdom of Cambodia	598,077					598,077	0.4
World Bank Total	1,098,077		3,000,000	5,248,200	5,312,600	14,658,877	8.6
NGO and Private Sector Grants		292,583	160,000		343,000	795,583	0.5
AustCARE		143,000				143,000	0.1
GRET			85,000		20,000	105,000	0.1
Concern					323,000	323,000	0.2
Private Donation	149,583		75,000			224,583	0.1

Source: Table provided by Partnership for Local Governance (2005).

Note: ADESS = Agriculture Development Support to Seila; CBRD = Community Based Rural Development; RPRP = Rural Poverty Reduction Project; GTZ = German Agency for Technical Cooperation; CIDA = Canadian International Development Agency; DANIDA = Danish International Development Agency; UNDP = UN Development Programme; RILG = Rural Investment and Local Governance; NVDP = Northeast Village Development Project; blank cells = zero.

a. World Bank reimbursements to CS Fund included under both RGC and WB/RILG but subtracted from total to avoid double counting.

Seila institutions, such as the provincial rural development committee and the commune development committee, are staffed by members of the respective levels of government. The 2004 Mid-Term Review suggested that the question of parallel structures could be resolved simply by "debranding": Seila structures are called Seila because they were originally associated with the Seila project. Now that mainstreaming has proceeded sufficiently, this notion of separation should be abandoned. Critics have argued that Seila impinges on the mandate of the Ministry for Rural Development and captures rural development funds for capital projects that could be better spent raising salaries and promoting capacity within ministry line departments (Batkin 2001). They argue that Seila is ringfenced, to an extent, from the broader business of provincial government, because many Seila funds are off budget.

With the exception of contributions to the Commune/*Sangkat* Fund's treasury account, the bulk of Seila funds are off-budget transfers, which are maintained and handled separately from other financial flows, and accountable to donors. However, the deconcentration of functions is likely to bring Seila mechanisms into the heart of subnational financing. Given the notorious politicization of the Cambodian state and the tendency to skim budgets to pay for items such as election campaigning, the delivery of mainstream government budgets through the Seila-type mechanisms will constitute a significant test of the integrity of these mechanisms. Corruption in Cambodia is systemic and institutionalized. The pressure on provincial governments to deliver political support at crucial times runs counter to the Seila ethos and makes it difficult for provincial governors to "switch hats" easily. Seila offers an opportunity for donors to increase their monitoring of government practices and to reorient them toward a more transparent and accountable system. However, given that to a great extent corruption in the Cambodian government forms the basis of the current social and political order, resistance to such monitoring and reorientation can reasonably be expected once Seila is mainstreamed.

Seila staff are currently motivated by the payment of salary supplements. This is regarded as indispensable to ensure "efficient and honest performance" (SPM Consultants and Oxford Policy Management, 2004, 3). A key issue affecting all donor programs in Cambodia is the fact that since 1993, civil service salaries have been so derisory that civil servants frequently spend most, if not all, of their time away from their posts doing other jobs. Salary supplements ensure regular attendance, the essential prerequisite for any kind of institutional functioning. Combined with ongoing supervision by PLG, they represent the "carrot and stick" used to limit attempts at siphoning off Seila funds. Reliance on salary supplements, however, raises the question of how Seila mechanisms can be mainstreamed. Unless there is a significant increase in civil service salaries generally—something that donors are currently promoting but that the government has resisted—it is unclear how the level of efficiency and integrity currently attained by Seila processes can be continued.

Donors are active participants in and proponents of Seila, particularly through the PLG, although functions initially performed by expatriates have by and large been taken over by national staff members who are paid by donors. Were donor input to decline, it is unclear whether the staff administering Seila processes would continue to retain authority over them or whether the staff or the processes they administer would be sidelined.

In brief, Seila's successes in terms of governance outcomes are to a great extent the result of the way the program was slotted into the political and economic context of northwest Cambodia in the early to mid-1990s. The program responded to the incentive structures of provincial governments and was able to entrench its own working practices in newly forming institutions within the state. However, close scrutiny by PLG advisors has created a firewall between Seila institutions and funds and other institutions and funds within provincial governments. If this firewall were removed, by either the mainstreaming of Seila processes or a decline in donor interest, it is unclear whether the habits, training, and advantages offered by Seila would trump the systemic and institutional dynamics of corruption that are pervasive in the Cambodian state apparatus. The assertions in the 2004 Mid-Term Review that continued donor support will be required for many years and that PLG monitoring of transparency and accountability are key to Seila's success suggest that the program's spillover effects remain uncertain.

Impact on Commune Government

Seila has played a significant role at the commune level, a level of government that was in significant ways reinvented in the 1990s. The precise role of commune government was unclear in the 1990s and varied from commune to commune. The 1993 Constitution specified the commune level as the lowest level of government, thus removing the village as a legal or administrative entity. In 2002 commune elections were held, replacing the old appointed commune chiefs with new (or in many cases the same) elected commune chiefs and commune councils.

Under CARERE 1 and 2, participatory planning processes were conducted with village-based, elected village development committees. With the election of commune councils, the village development committees have become the central actors in participatory planning. This process makes sense in the context of democratization, because it aligns representation, participation, and accountability within Seila mechanisms with the broader electoral regime. It contrasts, however, with survey findings on the perceptions of voters. Seila's own evaluations have regularly shown that villagers tend to have a strongly village-focused perspective. One study of these attitudes, conducted after the commune elections in 2003, found that villagers were more likely now than previously to suggest that the commune level of government might be responsible for various development activities, representing a heightened profile for commune government. The same study, however, found that most villagers were unaware that there was a commune council or what it did (Biddulph 2003).

Commune government, to a great extent, must be invented. Seila may have allowed commune councilors and chiefs to build on their higher profile following the elections by providing a set of processes to access a Commune/Sangkat Fund for local development. Through participatory planning, commune councils have an opportunity to interact with their electorates and to build accountable relationships with them.

There have been certain difficulties, however, with this approach. A frequent criticism of the Seila program has been that its procedures are time-consuming and cumbersome and tax the capacities of both commune officials and villagers.[5] This is particularly the case when the possibility for funding all aspects of the commune's plans is uncertain. Field visits to Kompong Cham and Pursat Provinces revealed anecdotal evidence of ennui in Pursat but not in Kompong Cham. Both the marginal utility of going through the process of participatory planning (in terms of gaining information about villages and their needs and gaining status and legitimacy in the eyes of constituents) and the marginal utility of the projects delivered in response are likely to decline over time. Set against this, however, is the claim that villagers get into the habit of being consulted on development projects and that this habit is difficult to break once established. Evidence backing up this claim is sparse.

Promotion of Decentralization and Deconcentration
An evaluation by SIDA noted that "the CARERE 2/Seila program has itself been the catalyst spurring public interest and the government's current policy thrust toward deconcentration and decentralization. It has

done this by creating a model for coordinated planning and development of communes and provinces and demonstrating that it works" (Evans and others 2000, 4). While a clear incentive structure may be prompting the enthusiasm of provincial governors for Seila, the political driving force behind the Cambodian government's wider decentralization and deconcentration policies is less evident.

Decentralization and deconcentration have been on Cambodia's political reform agenda since the mid-1990s. Overall, progress in fulfilling this agenda has been slow. Decentralization took a leap forward with the holding of commune elections in 2002. But subsequent action in devolving significant powers to the commune level and establishing a sound basis for local revenue raising by commune councils has been limited. One person interviewed for this study, a member of the Decentralization and Deconcentration Working Group, described the current mood in government as one of consolidation with respect to decentralization.

Given the landslide victory of the CPP in the 2002 commune elections, it is tempting to regard this effort at decentralization as political opportunism. The replacement of appointed commune chiefs with elected councils was tentatively slated for 1996 but repeatedly postponed. When elections finally occurred, most observers regarded them as a credible step forward in democratization, but it was clear that significant benefits accrued to the CPP by virtue of its increasingly firm grip on power.[6] The elections were well timed and delivered political benefits to the ruling party, and they went some way toward meeting the expectations of democracy promoters at home and abroad. However, studies since 2002 have suggested that the quality of the relationship between villagers and commune authorities has changed since the elections. Studies have noted increased awareness of commune government on the part of villagers, increased accountability of commune authorities to villagers, and cross-party solidarity within commune councils with respect to higher levels of government (Biddulph 2003; Rusten and others 2004; Hughes and Sedara 2004).

Seila's stated role is to provide experience and expertise in support of decentralization and deconcentration policy making. A subdecree issued in June 2001, laying out the role of the Seila Task Force, defines this role as supporting the "design of decentralized and deconcentrated mechanisms and systems to manage sustainable local development" and the undertaking of "human resource development for decentralized and deconcentrated mechanisms and systems implementation within the Seila framework." One key achievement of the Seila program, according to one person interviewed for this study, is the fact that it offered a safe environment for experimentation and risk taking. In highly politicized postconflict situations, the tolerance for government officials who champion policies that later turn out to have been misguided is very limited. This tolerence militates against innovative and experimental attitudes within government. Seila was useful in advancing the agenda for decentralization and deconcentration because it illustrated that participatory planning and decentralized management of development projects could work without being politically threatening.

Seila undertook a number of activities with respect to decentralization. It funded technical assistance to the National Council for the Support of Communes to develop regulations and guidelines for their use. Donor-financed support through Seila continues to test and evaluate these systems. Seila implemented training courses for commune councils and clerks. It revised the design of Seila structures at the provincial level to transfer responsibilities for commune capacity building to the provincial offices of local administration, established under the Ministry of Interior, taking them away from the Ministry of Rural Development. The Commune/*Sangkat* Fund, which was disbursed to commune councils from the central government as their primary source of funding, evolved from the local development funds piloted by Seila, initially with grants from the UN Capital Development Fund. In these respects, Seila operates as a source of capacity building, piloting, and design innovation, upon which government has drawn in framing decentralization processes.

Deconcentration has been slower to unfold. Some ministries, notably the Ministry of Health and the Ministry of Education, have already deconcentrated their functions to a significant degree. But the overall framework for deconcentrating power and distributing power between agencies at the provincial and district levels has not been established. Several people interviewed for this study put forward sound pragmatic reasons for advancing with caution. One is concern over the viability of communes at their current size, particularly if communes are given revenue collection duties. Another is concern over the capacity of local government and the fear of overstretching Seila/PLG, which has just expanded to cover all 24 provinces and municipalities, without a concomitant increase in the administrative staff.

Substantial disagreements have arisen between national ministries regarding the appropriate nature of future arrangements; some observers have suggested that Seila itself is a bone of contention. At the national level, the Seila Task Force, with its mandate for generating policy for decentralized government in pursuit of poverty alleviation, overlaps with other agencies established to oversee local government, namely, the Council for Administrative Reform, the National Council for the Support of Communes, and the Department of Local Administration within the Ministry of Interior. This overlap is said to make it difficult to determine who has responsibility for taking the lead in promoting deconcentration policies and formulating organic law. While there may be some overlap at the national level, this overlap is far less the case at the provincial level, where, for example, the Provincial Office of Local Administration—reporting to the Department of Local Administration—is likely to be staffed by the same people as the local administration unit that supports Seila's ExCom.

It is too early to say whether Seila will have a significant effect on the form of the government's deconcentration strategy or what that effect will be, although plans are already being drawn up to determine what kind of role Seila could play. It is clear, however, that Seila is well positioned to play a key role in deconcentration, and it is likely that many of Seila's working practices will find their way into the eventual deconcentration schema.

Overall Assessment

Measuring Seila's success in terms of delivered outcomes and spillovers is problematic in that the program has tended to reinvent itself in accordance with spillovers as they arise and, in doing so, has moved away from tangible development goals toward intangible ones. While a number of evaluators have been highly impressed by the extent to which the program has promoted changed attitudes on the part of provincial officials, it is difficult to pin this contribution down. Qualitative studies aiming to establish the extent to which Seila has provided intangible goods, such as empowerment and good governance, have tended to find only sketchy evidence. Where attitudes seem to have changed, it has frequently been because a supportive incentive structure has been created (for example, by paying salary supplements to government officials). It is difficult to find hard evidence of sustainable change.

In the short term, Seila has clearly contributed to improved provincial and commune governance. It has created structures for rural infrastructure delivery where they did not exist. Through these structures, Seila has delivered rural infrastructure that benefits the very poor. It has trained thousands of civil servants and elected people's representatives in mechanisms for implementing development projects in a manner that is acceptable to donors and is likely to elicit further funds from them. It has offered opportunities for provincial governments to regain authority over development processes, following the free-for-all of the early 1990s. Finally, it has created opportunities for donors to coordinate with one another and for all development actors to coordinate with village-produced development plans and to align them with the National Poverty Reduction Strategy. It has achieved all of these things in a manner that is viewed by donors as transparent and noncorrupt. There is some doubt, however, as to the extent to which villagers have been empowered by these systems. The test for Seila will be whether it can maintain its integrity once funding moves on budget, evaluation and monitoring regimes weaken, and support for incentives such as salary supplements tails off.

Implications for Design and Implementation

Seila has succeeded to a great extent by virtue of its flexibility and its ability to mainstream areas in which it has had the most impact, to make incremental shifts over time into new areas, and, in so doing, to continue to provide incentives for government to remain engaged. This success suggests that initial questions of design were less important than the willingness and ability to redesign opportunistically in the light of the changing context.

This conclusion is important in a postconflict society for two major reasons. First, the nature of politics in postconflict societies is such that prominent programs channeling donor funds are likely to be the target of a great deal of local attention, of attempts at co-optation or elite capture of resources, and of contestation for control. Seila avoided these pitfalls by growing incrementally from a modest program in terms of scope and resources into a national program with major implications for the future direction of government policy.

Second, by virtue of a number of fortunate factors—the accumulation of 16 years' worth of UNDP funding for Cambodia and the willingness of particular donors to experiment—the program avoided overmanagement and was able to evolve through experimentation and feedback rather than through the application of a tested methodology for delivering agreed-upon outputs from the beginning. While accountability demands that delivered outcomes be measured, truly experimental programs are constrained only by the need to stick rigidly to initial project documents. The Seila program's willingness to shed goals and adopt new ones makes its success difficult to quantify, but it allowed the program to experiment.

At the same time, the basic themes of the Seila program—learning-by-doing, using intensive efforts at capacity building, are placing high value on engagement with the state apparatus—have been apparent from the start. These aspects of the program appeared risky initially, given the deep distrust of state structures on the part of donors in the early 1990s. With hindsight, however, an appreciation of the dire situation facing provincial governments in Cambodia in the early to mid-1990s suggests that Seila was, in part, successful because it intervened at a level of government where donor-state relations were most inclined toward donors. Strong incentives to cooperate in order to obtain money, training, and authority permitted Seila to establish and enforce exemplary mechanisms for ensuring that provincial governors' experiments with donor funding were kept broadly within the parameters of donors' perceptions of legitimate expenditure. The theme of state engagement subsequently emerged as highly significant to the program's success, especially once political tensions at the national level were reduced. Donors, meanwhile, gained a channel through which both funds and ideas could be coordinated and disseminated to a level that was far more receptive to donor exhortations than the national level, particularly in the mid-1990s.

To a great extent, then, design and implementation were not discrete phases of the program but rather intertwined. The overall project design and the design of individual elements, such as the detailed procedures for planning and project management, changed in response to implementation difficulties and successes as well as to the changing context. Modifications to the initial program included changes in response to donor priorities, as exemplified by the shift from CARERE 1's emphasis on the rehabilitation of vulnerable refugees to CARERE 2's capacity-building focus to the PLG's focus on feeding into decentralization policies for the future. The incorporation of National Poverty Reduction Strategy priorities into Seila guidelines is another example of flexible adaptation. By offering a channel through which donors could convey their concerns to government and responding to changing donor concerns, Seila has maintained its relevance and has come to occupy a central place among donor initiatives in Cambodia.

Conclusion

Seila is a flourishing program, in terms of its political influence, geographical scope, popularity with donors, and ability to disburse money effectively to small-scale infrastructure projects that have been designed with input from local people. It has transformed provincial government from complete disarray to a functioning layer of administration, with a vision for development and a certain degree of funding, capacity, and institutional structures to implement that vision. Its success is reflected in the fact that it is increasingly favored by donors as a mechanism for channeling funds to rural Cambodia and that it is increasingly favored by government as an arena within which decentralization and deconcentration policies can be piloted. Whether or not Seila has transformed attitudes among officials and villagers remains unclear, given that the program includes strong incentives for compliance.

Much of the program's success has been the result of its flexibility, its emphasis on learning-by-doing, and its incremental development. These features have allowed Seila both to carve out a niche in Cambodia and to adapt to the context in which it operates. To an extent, Seila's initial success was fortuitous. Its learning-by-doing approach and its focus on process have allowed the program to capitalize on that success by focusing on areas of greatest strength and adapting to the changing focuses of donor and government concern.

Several lessons can be drawn for postconflict contexts from Seila's experience:

- Flexibility and adaptation are as important as initial design.
- Experimentation and the ability to recognize, promote, and capitalize on successful experiments are important.
- Identifying and responding to the needs and concerns of stakeholders are critical to keeping them engaged.
- It is advisable to start with a low level of resources until systems are firmly in place and then to increase them incrementally.
- It is useful to develop close relationships with key political players at all levels.
- Intensive and proactive donor input is needed to keep all actors engaged.

Notes

1. A *sangkat* is an urban commune, rather like a London borough.
2. In the Cambodian context, the term *decentralization* is used to refer to the creation, regulation, and support of elected commune governments; the term *deconcentration* is used to refer to the codification of an expanded role for

provincial and district levels of government. It involves delegating activities from the central level and establishing funding mechanisms to support such delegation.

3. The report also notes, however, that the strategies in the National Poverty Reduction Strategy are very broad.

4. Prominent examples include the Forest Monitoring Project, the Demobilization Project, and the current scandal over the World Food Program's Food for Work Project.

5. Since 2002, these procedures have been adopted by the National Council for Support to Communes as the mainstream procedures for commune/*sangkat*-level financing and have ceased to be specifically Seila processes.

6. For example, the role of the national media in the commune elections was a significant bone of contention, as less than 3 percent of news coverage of the elections was devoted to non-CPP parties' activities, compared with 12 percent devoted to the CPP and 75 percent to the CPP-led government (National Democratic Institute 2002).

Bibliography

Batkin, Andy. 2001. "Support to Decentralization: Assisting NCSC to Implement its Action Plan." October. Royal Government of Cambodia Ministry of Interior Department Of Local Administration/Asian Development Bank/GTZ (Deutsche Gesellschaft fur Technische Zusammenarbeit), Phnom Penh.

Biddulph, Robin. 2001. "Civil Society and Local Governance: Learning from Seila Experience." July. United Nations Office for Project Services, Kuala Lumpur.

———. 2003. "PAT Empowerment Study: Final Report." Phnom Penh.

Evans, Hugh. 2003. "Seila Support to Deconcentration Framework: An Update and Agenda." Revised Draft. United Nations Development Programme Phnom Penh.

Evans, Hugh, Lars Birgegaard, Peter Cox, Lim Siv Hong, and Cambodia Area Rehabilitation and Regeneration Project. 2000. "SIDA Evaluation 00/8." SIDA (Swedish International Development Cooperation Agency), Stockholm.

Government-Donor Partnership Working Group. 2004. "Practices and Lessons Learned in the Management of Development Cooperation: Cases from Cambodia." Sub-Working Group 3, Phnom Penh.

Hasselskog, Malin, Chanthou Krong, and Charya Chim. 2000. "Local Governance in Transition: Villagers' Perceptions and Seila's Impact." UNDP (United Nations Development Programme)/Cambodia Rehabilitation and Regeneration Project, Phnom Penh.

Holloway, John, James D'Ercole, Chom Sok, and the Researchers from Crossroads Consultancies. 2001. "Survey on Governance: Survey of Knowledge, Attitudes, Practices and Beliefs on Standards in Good Governance in Seila." United Nations Office for Project Services, Kuala Lumpur.

Hughes, Caroline, and Kim Sedara. 2004. "The Evolution of Democratic Process and Conflict Management in Cambodia, A Comparative Study of Three Cambodian Elections, Working Paper 30." Cambodia Development Resource Institute, Phnom Penh.

National Democratic Institute. 2002. "The 2002 Cambodian Commune Elections." National Democratic Institute, Phnom Penh.

PLG (Partnership for Local Governance) 2001. "Project of the Royal Government of Cambodia, Partnership for Local Governance." UNDP (United Nations Development Programme), Phnom Penh.

———. 2005. Data on financial support to Seila. UNDP, Phnom Penh.

Royal Government of Cambodia Seila Task Force. 2000. "Seila Program Document, 2001–05." Seila Task Force, Phnom Penh.

Rudengren, Jan, and Joakim Ojendal. 2002. "Learning by Doing: An Analysis of the Seila Experiences in Cambodia." SPM Consultants, Stockholm.

Rusten, Caroline, Kim Sedara, Eng Netra, and Pak Kimchoeun. 2004. "The Challenges of Decentralization Design in Cambodia." Cambodia Development Resource Institute, Phnom Penh.

SPM Consultants and Oxford Policy Management. 2004. "Seila Program and Partnership for Local Governance, Mid-Term Review." February. UNDP (United Nations Development Programme), DFID (Department for International Development), SIDA (Swedish International Development Cooperation Agency), Phnom Penh.

UNDP (United Nations Development Programme). 1995. "CARERE Prospective Evaluation Report." UNDP, Phnom Penh.

———. 1998. "Final Report: Mid-Term Review of CARERE 2." UNDP, Phnom Penh.

———. 2001a. "CARERE 2 Terminal Report." UNDP, Phnom Penh.

———. 2001b. "Partnership for Local Governance, Project Document." UNDP, Phnom Penh.

———. 2001c. "Peace-Building from the Ground Up: A Case Study of UNDP's CARERE Programme in Cambodia 1991–2000." UNDP, Phnom Penh.

———. 2004. "Report on the Elections of the Commune Councils." UNDP, Phnom Penh.

UNDP, DFID (Department for International Development), SIDA (Swedish International Development Cooperation Agency). 2004. "Seila Program and

Partnership for Local Governance Mid-Term Review." UNDP, DFID, SIDA, Phnom Penh.

UNDP/United Nations Office for Project Services/Cambodia Area Rehabilitation and Regeneration Project. 1996. "Building the Foundation of the Seila Program: The 1996 Work Plan of the Cambodia Rehabilitation and Regeneration Project (CARERE)." UNDP, Phnom Penh.

World Bank. 2004. "The Bank's Approach to Supporting 'Local Governance and Accountability' in Cambodia: Some Thoughts and Proposals." World Bank, Poverty Reduction and Economic Management Unit, Phnom Penh.

CHAPTER 5

The First and Second Health Sector Rehabilitation and Development Projects in Timor-Leste

When troops from the International Force for East Timor (INTERFET) arrived in 1999 to restore peace and security and to facilitate the establishment of a transitional UN administration, the health situation in the territory was precarious.[1] Although the Indonesian government had funded the development of a health system during its occupation between 1975 and 1999, the system did not perform well. When the Indonesians left East Timor, the territory's health indicators were among the poorest within the archipelago. The violent withdrawal of the Indonesian military in 1999 resulted in the destruction of most of the country's health infrastructure and supplies and the departure of most of the country's senior health managers and doctors (Hill 2001; World Bank 2002; Joint Assessment Mission 1999; Morris 2001). When the Joint Assessment Mission—a team of specialists representing the bilateral donor countries, the Asian Development Bank, the World Bank, and the UN agencies—visited East Timor shortly after the 1999 violence, it concluded that the territory faced a serious risk of communicable disease outbreaks and thus a considerable increase in "excess mortality" (Joint Assessment Mission 1999).

This chapter was written by Andrew Rosser.

To address these problems, the donors and the Interim Health Authority—the initial name given to the UN transitional administration authority responsible for health matters—agreed that two health projects should be included among the range of aid projects funded by the Trust Fund for East Timor (TFET), which is a multidonor fund established to mobilize resources for reconstruction and development activities in health, education, agriculture, transport, power, and other key sectors. The first of these, the Health Sector Rehabilitation and Development Project (HSRDP I), began in mid-2000; the second, the Second Health Sector Rehabilitation and Development Project (HSRDP II), began in mid-2001. HSRDP II was supported by a separate grant from the European Union. The World Bank administered both projects (Tulloch and others 2003; World Bank 2000a, 2001a).

This chapter assesses the extent to which the HSRDPs contributed to positive development outcomes on improving governance, improving delivery of basic services to the poor, addressing negative spillover effects from violent conflict and disease, and improving economic growth and poverty reduction. It then tries to explain why contributions to positive outcomes occurred. It begins by discussing the development of East Timor's health sector before the introduction of the HSRDPs. It then describes the HSRDPs. The next two sections assess the projects' contribution to the development of the territory's health sector and examine the factors that enabled them to contribute to development. The last section presents conclusions, examining the extent to which the HSRDPs might be replicable in other contexts.

The Health Sector in East Timor before 2000

East Timor faced a grim situation in the health sector before the end of the Indonesian occupation in 1999. The Indonesians constructed an extensive system of government hospitals, clinics, and health posts, staffed by about 160 doctors and 2,000 nurses and midwives (World Bank 2002). The focal point of this system was the community health center (*puskesmas*). Located in all subdistricts, these centers provided a variety of primary health services and coordinated outreach care activities by health subcenters, mobile clinics, and village midwives. These activities included national programs in maternal and child health, family planning activities, and campaigns against malaria and tuberculosis. Tertiary care was provided through eight small district hospitals; a central referral hospital in the capital, Dili; and the Central Health Laboratory. Overseeing the system was the provincial health department, although most key policy and programmatic decisions were made in Jakarta (Joint Assessment Mission 1999; Morris 2001).

Although this system provided a mechanism for delivering health services, it did not perform well. It suffered from a number of serious problems: it was chronically underfunded; public subsidies were not allocated in a pro-poor way, despite the fact that one of the stated objectives of the system was to deliver health services to the poor; it provided, in many cases, poor-quality health services; it was unresponsive to the needs and demands of beneficiaries; its quality assurance systems and regulatory framework were inadequate; and it did not produce adequate information for planning and evaluation purposes (World Bank 2000a). Perhaps its most serious problem, however, was that it was underutilized: the number of outpatient visits per capita per year was just over one, and the number of outpatient visits per staff member per day employed in the health system was less than five, both figures low by international standards (World Bank 2002). This low rate of utilization suggests that the East Timorese either lacked confidence in the health system or faced serious barriers to accessing health services. Some have argued that the fact that the vast majority of doctors and senior health officials in the territory were non-Timorese engendered a lack of trust in the system among the East Timorese.

The dysfunctional nature of the health system during this time was reflected in basic health indicators for the territory. Life expectancy, at 55–58 years, was low. Infant mortality, at 85 per 1,000 births, and under-five mortality, at 124 per 1,000 births, were high compared with Indonesian averages (Joint Assessment Mission 1999). A doctor or midwife attended less than a quarter of all births, contributing to high maternal mortality rates. Outbreaks of preventable and communicable/vector-borne diseases were not uncommon, in part because World Health Organization immunization targets were not achieved. Malaria and tuberculosis were particularly problematic. Malaria accounted for 65 percent of all new outpatient visits to government health facilities in 1998 by school-age children and 50 percent of all visits by the working-age population; tuberculosis accounted for 25 percent of new outpatient visits by the working-age population and 46 percent by people 45 and older (World Bank 2002).

What little the Indonesians achieved with respect to health care in East Timor was destroyed during the massive violence that occurred in

September 1999. As Morris (2001, 873) observed:

> . . . health care was deliberately disrupted and facilities specifically targeted: a third were severely or completely destroyed, and less than 9 percent escaped damage. An assessment by the Joint Working Group on Health Services in January 2000 found that two-thirds still had no main electricity, almost half had no mains water, and 67 percent lacked vital equipment. In the eastern Lautem district, all ten health posts were destroyed, the Los Palos hospital was looted and damaged, and two nurses and one pharmacist were killed. I found one particularly petty reminder of the militia's vindictiveness in the radiology room: an X-ray machine left for the rats to chew any available flex, because the exposure button was deliberately cut off and destroyed. A replacement button is unlikely to be found.

The violence also resulted in the complete loss of all medical equipment and consumable items, such as medicines, and the departure of many skilled health workers and administrators. Of the 160 doctors in the territory under the Indonesians, only 30 remained after the Indonesian withdrawal in 1999 (Joint Assessment Mission 1999). The violence had very serious consequences on the services and the health status of the population (figure 5.1).

Figure 5.1 Basic Health Indicators , 1999 and 2001, in Timor-Leste

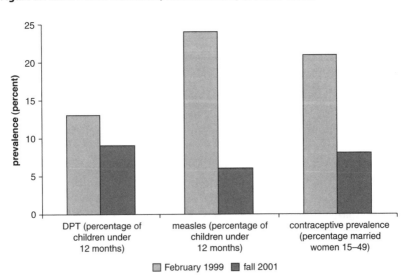

Source: World Bank 2003.

In the immediate aftermath of the Indonesian withdrawal, numerous international NGOs, including the International Committee of the Red Cross, Médecins Sans Frontières, World Vision, and OIKOS, poured into the territory to deliver emergency health services. The Catholic Church and religious charities continued to run clinics and small hospitals as they previously had, and assisted with the humanitarian effort. Among them, these organizations established 71 health facilities at the subdistrict level or higher by February 2000 (before the violence there had been 96). Facilities below the subdistrict level were relatively inactive, however, and services consequently remained scarce there. To ensure that as many districts as possible received at least some health services, each NGO concentrated its efforts within particular areas (World Bank 2000a).

At the same time, rapid progress was made in establishing an authority to run the health system. Initially, the Joint Health Working Group, a body that brought together representatives from UN agencies concerned with health, representatives from the NGO community, and Timorese health professionals in the East Timorese Health Professionals Working Group, played key roles in this respect (Tulloch and others 2003). For the most part, it focused on issues related to humanitarian relief, in particular identifying "the most pressing needs in healthcare service provision, the measures that would rapidly address them, and the minimum short-term requirements for the fulfillment of these needs" (La'o Hamutuk 2000, 3). But it also began preparations for establishing a bureaucratic authority to oversee development of the territory's health system, thereby agreeing at a workshop in February 2000 to a minimum set of standards for doing so (La'o Hamutuk 2000). This agreement led to the establishment the same month of the Interim Health Authority as part of the UNTAET structure. Headed by Jim Tulloch from the United Nations and Dr. Sergio Lobo, East Timor's only qualified surgeon and a member of the East Timorese Health Professionals Working Group, the Interim Health Authority consisted of 16 senior East Timorese health professionals at the central level, another 13 at the district level, and 6 UNTAET health staff who were in East Timor at that time (Tulloch and others 2003).

Overview of the Health Sector Rehabilitation and Development Project

It was in this context that the first joint donor health mission met, in March–April 2000, to plan the rehabilitation and development of the health sector. Led jointly by the World Bank and the Interim Health Authority and consisting of representatives from Australia, Portugal, and the European Commission, it concluded that a sectorwide approach was the most effective way to deliver aid to the health sector. According to the World Bank, this approach "was designed to work at two interrelated levels: (a) to permit the definition of needs across the board—service delivery, rehabilitation of the health infrastructure, health systems and health policy development; and (b) to coordinate donor financing of the sector" (World Bank 2001a, 39). The joint donor mission also concluded that the best option was to focus on constructing a health system that met the needs of the East Timorese people rather than rebuilding the previous health system, whose weaknesses it recognized. On this basis, it prepared a framework for action that led, after a few weeks of negotiation, to the introduction of HSRDP I (Tulloch and others 2003; World Bank 2001a).

The basic purpose of HSRDP I was to "address immediate basic health needs" without constraining future health policy choices while simultaneously developing "appropriate health policies and systems" (World Bank 2000a). To this end, it consisted of two main components: the restoration of access to basic services and the development of a policy and institutional framework for the health system.

The first component was essentially short term in focus. It consisted of several subcomponents:

- implementation of a transitional strategy for service provision centered on accelerated delivery of selected high-priority programs (for example, immunization, tuberculosis, nutrition, and health promotion) as part of a broader program of delivering a basic packages of services to the largest number people
- development of a pharmaceutical logistics system to ensure the timely availability of drugs and medical supplies
- reconstruction, rehabilitation, and re-equipping of a number of health facilities
- rebuilding of an administrative infrastructure at the central and district levels
- strengthening of capacity within the health system through training for the delivery of basic services, management, and administration
- introduction of a small grants scheme and establishment of district and subdistrict health boards to support community and stakeholder participation

The second component had a more medium- to long-term focus. It involved defining and developing an initial set of health policies and regulations appropriate to the country, designing and planning the organizational structure and supporting systems that would characterize the health system, developing a human resources strategy for the health system, and supporting technical assistance, study tours, and the preparation of policy papers on specific health issues, such as health sector financing and private practice (World Bank 2000a, 2000b).

The first component assumed higher priority under the project, reflecting the magnitude of the short-term crisis facing the country's health sector. Out of a total project budget of $12.7 million, $10 million was allocated to the first component, while only $1.8 million was allocated to the second component. The remaining $0.9 million was to be spent on establishing and running a program management unit.

A key feature of HSRDP I was continued reliance on international NGOs to provide basic health services. Although the government, in the form of UNTAET, had the resources to fund these services, it was recognized that it did not have the capacity to provide these services itself and that inviting the NGOs to stay was, therefore, the only strategy "that held out the possibility of restoring access to basic health services" (World Bank 2001a, 4). At the same time, the European Commission's Humanitarian Office, which had been the principal financier of the NGOs since September 1999, agreed to provide additional funding to them to help the country make the transition from the emergency to the rehabilitation phase of health care. The result was an arrangement whereby the NGOs continued to act as the principal service providers but submitted to overall coordination by the government and to conditions outlined in a memorandum of understanding between them and the government (World Bank 2000a; Tulloch and others 2003). Although some NGOs were initially reluctant to submit to this arrangement, they and the government reportedly established a good working relationship, thus facilitating their ability to provide necessary health services (Tulloch and others 2003).

In mid-2001, donors and the Division of Health Services (the successor to the Interim Health Authority) agreed that a second health sector rehabilitation and development project should be funded to continue and extend the work done under HSRDP I. HSRDP I had focused on establishing community health centers and mobile clinics to provide basic health services and to rebuild public health programs in areas such as immunizations and health promotion. HSRDP II, by contrast, was intended to achieve greater utilization of health services and higher-quality care by giving greater attention to hospital care; to certain elements of the basic package of health services delivered through the first project; and to capacity building in areas such as human resources, management, service provision, community mobilization, and communications (World Bank 2001a). In general terms, it gave more attention to medium- to long-term issues related to the health sector, particularly to the development of a policy and institutional framework. Its declared purpose was to "rehabilitate and develop a cost-effective and financially sustainable health system in East Timor to be responsive to the immediate basic health needs of the population and, within a well-integrated and sustainable policy framework, to prepare the health system to meet future needs" (World Bank 2001a, 35).

HSRDP II consisted of three components. The first focused on supporting ongoing service delivery. This component included the provision of technical assistance to district health management teams to help them develop and implement the district health plan and the provision of pharmaceuticals to health facilities. The second component focused on improving the range and quality of health services and developing and implementing supporting systems. Its activities aimed at strengthening referral systems and "rationalizing" the hospital system, rehabilitating the central laboratory, creating a functioning autonomous medical supply entity, and improving the standardization and quality of a basic package of health services. The third component focused on developing and implementing health sector policy and management systems. Activities under this component included a Demographic and Health Survey to provide policy-relevant information and technical assistance to assist the government in formulating and implementing policy, in developing a human resource management strategy, and in strengthening systems management (World Bank 2001a, 2001b).

The second component was budgeted to consume the bulk of the resources: out of a total project budget of $21.4 million, it accounted for $14.8 million, thus reflecting in large part the high cost of rehabilitating and re-equipping the hospitals as well as the cost of purchasing drugs to be stocked at the autonomous medical supply entity. Of the remaining budget, the first component was allocated $3.5 million and the third $2.7 million (World Bank 2001a).

In contrast to HSRDP I, HSRDP II envisaged a shift in service provision from NGOs to the government. This was due in part to growing concern on the part of donors and the government about the relatively high cost of using NGOs as service providers and in part to the emergence of pressure for Timorese managers to assume greater control over the health system as the capacity of the Interim Health Authority and its successors increased over time. In the place of NGOs, new district health management teams would assume responsibility for delivering services at the local level. To replace the Western doctors whom NGOs had employed, donors and the government planned to recruit doctors from other developing countries and to encourage expatriate East Timorese doctors to return home (World Bank 2001a).

The two projects established a set of key performance indicators that acted as a means of assessing the performance of the projects and the country's health sector overall (table 5.1). These indicators, from both HSRDP I and HSRDP II, were specified in the project appraisal document for HSRDP II. They focused mainly on outcomes related to rehabilitation of the health system, the delivery of key health services, and the **formulation and adoption** of key policies.

Development Results

The most dramatic outcome of the HSRDPs has been the re-establishment of a functioning health service. Under HSRDP I dozens of community

Table 5.1 Key Minimum Performance Indicators in the Health Sector
(percent except where otherwise indicated)

Indicator	June 2001	June 2002	June 2003
1. Children under 1 immunized (in each district)			
a. DPT3	20	30	50
b. Measles	20	30	50
2. Births with skilled attendance at birth			
a. Nationally	20	25	35
b. In each district	4	10	20
3. Population with access to			
a. Basic health services within two hours	60	90	95
b. Inpatient services within two hours from source of basic health services	40	70	80
4. Number of outpatient visits per capita per year	1	2	2.5
5. Health facilities reporting no stock-outs of essential drugs lasting more than two weeks the previous quarter	60	90	90
6. Draft health sector policy paper discussed with stakeholders and completed		✓	
7. Revised regulations on pharmaceuticals			
a. Draft prepared		✓	
b. Regulations issued			✓
8. Human resource management and development plan adopted		✓	

Source: World Bank 2001a.

health centers or health posts were either constructed or rehabilitated, and hospitals were rebuilt. By mid-2004, Timor-Leste was estimated to have 6 functioning hospitals, including a national referral hospital in Dili; 65 community health centers; and more than 170 health posts. Health workers were hired, drugs purchased, and services delivered (World Bank 2004). From a state of utter devastation in late 1999, by mid-2004 an estimated 87 percent of the population had a health facility within two hours' walking distance from home, and these facilities were within two hours' driving time of a hospital in 10 out of 12 districts. Partly for this reason, the delivery of health services improved significantly between 1999 and 2004, as data on key performance indicators reveals. By June 2004, an estimated 42 percent of births were being attended by a skilled health worker, an estimated 70 percent of children under the age of 1 had been immunized for DPT3 and measles, and utilization of health facilities had increased from about 0.5 visits per year to more than 2.0 visits a year per capita (Program Management Unit 2004).

These figures overstate the effect of the projects, because they are based on population figures that probably underestimate the size of the population. Nevertheless, it is clear that the projects have contributed significantly to the re-establishment of a functioning health service. In so doing, the project improved basic service delivery to the poor, reduced negative spillover effects from disease, and reduced poverty.

The HSRDPs also improved governance within the territory. Initially, their main contribution in this respect was getting international NGOs to work in conjunction with the Interim Health Authority to prepare district health plans. Involvement of the NGOs "allowed for the simultaneous preparation of district health plans for each of the 12 districts outside Dili, a task beyond the capacity of the Interim Health Authority alone" (Tulloch and others 2003, 10). The purpose of these plans was not to set in place an overall strategy for health system development but to generate valuable data and innovative local ideas and to provide a mechanism for coordinating health sector activity at the local level (Morris 2001). At subsequent stages, the focus of activity in the governance area shifted to the production of a national level health policy framework and a set of key health laws and regulations. The health policy framework, which was approved by the Council of Ministers in 2003, sought to provide a "comprehensive vision of the strategic policy direction of the Ministry of Health" (Ministry of Health 2002). It identified a variety of objectives for the ministry to pursue, including:

> . . . building on the achievements made to date in restoring public health and curative services; recognizing the importance of the [Ministry of Health's] stewardship role; delivering a basic package of affordable, effective interventions through a system of district health services that are able to respond to local needs; ensuring that basic services are provided to the poor, who remain primarily in rural areas; cooperating proactively with the private sector and nongovernmental organizations . . . and exploring the development of contracting-out options for some ancillary and basic services, such as health promotion, which may be better managed by other providers (World Bank 2004, 85).

The set of key health laws and regulations produced by the projects included the Organic Law of the Ministry of Health, the Basic Law for Health, and the law creating the autonomous system for drugs and health equipment.

The creation of the autonomous medical stores in May 2004 to manage the procurement and distribution of pharmaceuticals has improved or very likely will improve the quality of governance in relation to financial management in the health sector. Before the establishment of these stores, individual health facilities were not charged for the drugs they used, giving them little incentive to contain drug costs. With the establishment of autonomous medical stores, charges for drug use are now posted against individual medical facilities, and health facility managers have been required to incorporate drug costs into their budgets. To the extent that autonomous medical stores perform their functions effectively, they should help reduce the incentive to overuse drugs, something that reportedly occurs regularly because of health workers' current tendency to prescribe a range of drugs, many of which are unnecessary, to treat a single condition (World Bank 2004).

Another important contribution of the HRSDPs with respect to governance in the health sector has been the establishment of a functioning and fully Timorese administrative structure. Initially dependent on international NGOs to deliver basic health services, the country has proceeded rapidly to self-administration in this sector, notwithstanding the fact that it went through a lengthy period during which there were delays recruiting personnel (Tulloch and others 2003). By July 2004 the government of Timor-Leste could boast the following in relation to the system's administration:

> The Ministry of Health is now fully staffed and has a relevant structure. The Organic Law for the Ministry of Health has been approved by the Council of Ministers. District Health Management Teams have been recruited in all districts and have the responsibility to manage district health services providing management support to health providers . . . Recruitment of senior staff (level 5, 6, and 7) has been successfully completed. Many important vacancies have been filled, such as Director-General, Inspector of Health and several Heads of District Health Services. This has already contributed to a better organizational stability. Recruitment of level 2, 3, and 4 positions has been concluded. A total of 455 permanent positions were advertised and candidates are now being selected and will take up their positions. . . . The number of civil servants in the health sector is within the recommended range in accordance with the Government staff policy (Ministry of Health 2004, 13).

This administrative structure was characterized by clear backward and forward linkages between the central administration in Dili and local health clinics. As one informed source pointed out, the Ministry of Health is relatively coherent internally—all parts of the health administration make decisions on the basis of the same health indicators and work according to the same planning and budgeting systems and vision. In addition, the ministry has made mobilized local feedback as part of its planning mechanisms. Every year, Ministry of Health officials make field trips to the districts to collect information to be used in the formulation of the ministry's annual action plans. The Ministry of Health is also relatively effective at spending the resources at its disposal, having one of the highest budget execution rates in the government.

While the development results achieved by the government and donors through the two health sector projects have arguably been impressive on the whole, they have been weak in certain respects. First, while the projects have re-established a system for delivering a basic package of health services in the country, demand for these services has remained weak. As the World Bank (2004) has pointed out, at about two per capita the number of average annual outpatient visits is low by international standards—far lower than in Latin America (six), the Caribbean (six), East Asia (five), and Sub-Saharan Africa (four).

Second, while there has been a marked improvement in key performance indicators, several of these indicators appear to have stagnated recently or even fallen slightly (table 5.2). The reasons for this are unknown.

Table 5.2 Key Health Indicators, July 1, 2003–June 30, 2004
(percent, except where otherwise indicated)

Indicator	September 2003	December 2003	March 2004	June 2004
1. At least 60% of children under age 1 fully immunized by project completion				
2. Percentage of children under age 1 immunized in each district by June 30, 2003				
a. DPT3: At least 50%	64	64	74	71
b. Measles: At least 50%	54	62	69	68
3. At least 90% of villages with access to a permanent source of care by completion	87	87	87	87
4. Percentage of population with access to				
a. Basic health services within two hours of home: 95% by completion	87	87	87	87
b. In-patient services within two hours from a source of basic health services: 80% by completion	10 of 12 districts reported (83%)	10 of 12 districts reported (83%)	10 of 12 districts reported (83%)	10 of 12 districts reported (83%)
5. Percentage of health facilities appropriately utilized	Actual 2.00	Actual 2.00	Actual 2.27	Actual 2.21
6. Percentage of health facilities with less than two weeks of stock-out of selected essential drugs over three-month period: at least 90% by completion of both projects	85	85	100	100
7. Percentage of births with skilled attendance by June 30, 2003				
a. At least 35% nationally	47	49	46	42
b. At least 20% in each district	12 of 13 Oecussi 19	13 of 13	13 of 13	13 of 13
8. Options paper on health financing	No	No	No	No
9. Options paper on role of private sector	No	No	No	No
10. Regulations on pharmaceuticals	Plan agreed	Draft regulations for autonomous medical stores completed		Autonomous medical stores, legislation passed by Parliament
11. Number of consultations with stakeholders	—	1	1	1

Source: Program Management Unit 2004.
Note: — = not available.

Third, little progress has been made in rehabilitating the hospital system, in part because of delays in securing funding for HSRDP II from the European Union. Nor has much progress been made in improving hospital management, which is generally regarded as very poor and a serious obstacle to the provision of good health hospital care (Program Management Unit 2004).

Explanation of the Projects' Contribution to Development

What accounts for the HSRDPs' contribution to Timor-Leste's development? Ten factors have been critical, five of which relate to the way in which the program was designed and implemented and five of which relate to the nature of the country's political economy since independence.

Design and Implementation Factors

The first factor that accounts for the HSRDP's contribution to Timor-Leste's development is that the HSRDPs were based on a good understanding of the health problems facing the territory after the Indonesian withdrawal, in large part because the joint donor health mission teams that designed the projects were able to draw on the findings of several detailed studies of the health sector prepared during 1999–2000. The Joint Assessment Mission had examined the territory's health status as part of its broader assessment of the country's development situation in October–November 1999 (Joint Assessment Mission 1999). In December 1999, the East Timorese Health Professionals Working Group conducted a workshop to discuss the country's health issues and undertook a review of its health infrastructure. On the basis of these studies, the Joint Health Working Group "identified the most pressing needs in healthcare service provision, the measures that would rapidly address them, and the minimum short-term requirements for the fulfillment of these needs" (La'o Hamutuk 2000, 3). Finally, after its establishment in February 2000, the Interim Health Authority conducted "team visits to all of the districts to gather information to inform the mission that designed the first HSRDP in early 2000" (Tulloch and others 2003, 9).

The second factor that accounts for the HSRDP's contribution to Timor Leste's development is that the HSRDPs simultaneously conducted health sector rehabilitation work and policy and institutional development. A potential problem with rehabilitation work in any sector is that it can constrain future policy choices: if it serves simply to rebuild the previous (deficient) system, it can be very costly to change it, forcing a country to inherit its deficiencies. The HSRDPs reduced the potential for this sort of outcome by trying to incorporate planning processes with policy and institutional development into the projects' designs.

The third factor was that there was considerable flexibility in the way in which the projects were implemented. As one informed source explained, the projects were designed very quickly—the *i*'s were not dotted and the *t*'s were not crossed. This lack made it possible to respond quickly and effectively to changing circumstances. For instance, the first project was able to take over funding of international NGOs when funding from the European Commission's Humanitarian Office ran out, ensuring that the NGOs could continue to provide emergency health services. The project was able to operate as financier of last resort for medical students studying abroad, covering fees, per diems, airfares, and any other costs related to their education—a role not originally envisaged but that was subsequently seen as necessary in order to address the severe shortage of qualified health personnel.

The fourth factor was that the projects provided a mechanism for donor coordination, one that by most accounts proved successful. Donors employed a sectorwide approach in the health sector, holding joint donor meetings every six months at which strategic decisions were made. This has not prevented individual donors from pursuing health interventions of questionable importance. A number of informants for instance, have been highly critical of the priority the World Health Organization has given to an anti-smoking campaign and that AusAID has given to oral and mental health programs. But in general, the informants were positive about the extent to which these regular meetings provided for effective donor coordination. Tulloch and others (2003, 30) concluded that the sectorwide approach strategy was "the best option for ensuring the coherent development of the health sector."

The fifth factor was that the projects were characterized by a relatively high degree of local ownership on the part of East Timorese senior health professionals and administrators. East Timorese professionals were involved in designing the territory's health system through the East Timorese Health Professionals Working Group. Many of them continued to play a role once the Interim Health Authority was formed, assuming senior positions in that organization. In contrast to other sectors, there was considerable scope for East Timorese to influence the development of the health system, because this was the only sector to have an interim authority and to place East Timorese in key positions in it. In this respect, a useful contrast can be made with the education sector. Millo and Barnett (2004, 14–15) argue that "while there was considerable success in reconstructing East Timor's education system, the opportunity to begin the transformation that civil society and CNRT [National Council of East Timorese Resistance] desired was missed." According to them, this outcome reflected in large part the inability of the World Bank and UNTAET to "construct appropriate partnerships that could have facilitated empowerment of the local community." The CNRT and other East Timorese representatives, Millo and Barnett go onto say, did not trust UNTAET and the World Bank, leading to "the creation of parallel systems instead of real partnership." The situation in health was characterized by a more effective partnership.

It seems likely, however, that the extent of local ownership of the activities carried out through the HSRDPs has been constrained by the lack of institutional capacity within the Ministry of Health and its predecessors. Donors regard the Ministry of Health as one of the more capable ministries within the government. However, like other ministries, it is short on skilled staff, in relation to both policy development and medical issues. With many Timorese health officials lacking adequate expertise and experience, the ministry has had little choice but to rely heavily on foreign advisers to formulate policy ideas as well as draft policy documents. It has become common practice for foreign advisers to leave the room at Ministry of Health meetings when policy decisions are made, so they can maximize the discretion exercised by Timorese officials. But the fact that these decisions are made on the basis of information and analyses provided by foreign advisers and that the capacity of ministry officials to evaluate critically such information and analyses is limited means that foreign advisers continue to exert significant influence over policy. One foreign health consultant who has worked on East Timor's health sector for several years suggested that it was difficult to talk about full ownership of the policy-making process in the health sector when many Ministry of Health officials were unable to explain clearly the rationale underlying policy decisions or to articulate government policies. The Ministry of Health is reportedly able to make more strategic use of international advisors than a number of other government ministries because, notwithstanding its human resource problems, it is better staffed than many other ministries in terms of both quantity and quality. But the fact that it is so dependent on foreigners to handle key parts of its work constrains the extent of local ownership.

Another constraint on local ownership has been the fact that many health sector policies and laws have been formulated through nonparticipatory mechanisms.[2] Indeed, some groups have criticized the government and the World Bank for not taking sufficient account of the views of local communities and international NGOs in designing and implementing health projects (see, for instance, La'o Hamutuk 2000).

Contextual Political Economy Factors

Let us now consider the other five factors that mattered. The first point to note is that the government had at its disposal a relatively large sum of financial resources with which to promote the rehabilitation and development of the health sector, reflecting in large part generous levels of donor financing. East Timor received generous donor funding between 1999 and 2002 across sectors: aid per capita exceeded $300 in 2000, and it was $250–300 in 2001 and 2002, significantly higher than in many other Low-Income Countries Under Stress (figure 5.2). Per capita expenditure on health in Timor-Leste was about $27, much higher than the average of just under $6 for low-income countries as a whole (World Bank 2004).

This level of funding had a downside: it was too much for the country to absorb productively. As Tulloch and others (2003, 29) note, "Some

Figure 5.2 Annual per Capita Donor Assistance in Selected Low-Income Countries Under Stress, 1999–2002

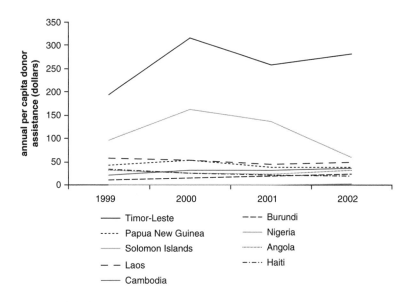

Source: World Bank 2003b.

funded entities, not wanting to be left with unspent funds, [found] creative ways of using them within stipulated guidelines but with little relevance to the true needs."

The high level of funding for the health sector reflected the nature of the country's political economy. Tulloch and others (2003, 29) suggest that donors were able to mobilize relatively large sums of money for East Timor in general and for the health sector in particular because of the "relative political attractiveness of emergencies and the undeniable health needs in such situations." Arguably, however, the high level of funding also reflected public pressure on Western governments to make amends for having effectively abandoned East Timor after the Indonesian invasion in 1975. It is difficult to understand the Australian government's relatively generous aid program for East Timor/Timor-Leste—compared with say, its aid programs for Indonesia, Laos, or Thailand—in any other context.

The high level of funding for the health sector also reflects political decisions made during negotiations between donors and the government over the Transition Support Program (see chapter 3 of this volume). That program, designed to help the government implement the National Development Plan, provided general budgetary support that was funded by various donors. Based on a joint decision by the government and donors, the program allocates at least 35 percent of the government's core budget to health and education.

The second factor is that the Ministry of Health has benefited from relatively good technocratic leadership. Timor-Leste's human resource base is extremely weak. The leaders of Fretilin, the dominant political party, have generally appointed people with strong political connections to top government positions rather than people with good technical skills or senior management experience. In the health sector, however, they have appointed someone with strong technical qualifications to the top job. The Minister of Health, Rui Maria de Araujo, spent many years working as a doctor in East Timor and holds a master's degree in public health from a university in New Zealand. His appointment to the top job has apparently not stopped political appointments from being made within the ministry and, as in other ministries, there is a general dearth of well-qualified and experienced staff. But the personal abilities of the minister and some other senior staff has, according to most informants, given the Ministry of Health greater capacity than most other government departments.

The third, fourth, and fifth factors were discussed in the chapter on the Transition Support Program, so they can be dealt with briefly here.

The third is that there has been a strong imperative for the government to cooperate closely with donors and to make an earnest attempt to produce results because (a) it has lacked access to an alternative source of finance or investment capital besides aid and (b) the country has been vulnerable in security terms, both externally and internally, and hence is dependent on foreign support for the maintenance of political stability and security. The fourth factor is that decision-making authority within the government has been concentrated in the hands of the Council of Ministers, making the policy and institutional development work that has been part of both HSRDPs much easier than it might have been had the political system been more fractured. The fifth factor is that, although Timor-Leste has remained vulnerable in security terms, it has been stable, thus allowing the country's political leaders to focus on development and reducing the prospect of rehabilitated health centers being razed to the ground again.

Conclusion

HSRDP I and II improved basic service delivery to the poor, reduced negative spillover effects from disease, and reduced poverty in Timor-Leste by restoring basic health services and re-establishing a functioning health system. They also improved governance by developing a policy and institutional framework for the health sector. Their success reflected a variety of factors related to the design and implementation of the program, as well as contextual political economy factors.

The HSRDPs serve as models for similar interventions in other contexts in two respects. First, they demonstrate the benefits of conducting the health sector rehabilitation work and policy and the institutional development simultaneously. The projects reduced the potential for a simple recreation of the old dysfunctional health system by incorporating policy and institutional development into the project design. Second, the projects demonstrate the benefits of a sectorwide approach to health sector reform. The sectorwide approach did not prevent individual donors from pursuing their pet interests, but it did help limit duplication of effort and focus donor attention on the same basic set of performance indicators. It also served to reduce pressure on the government of Timor-Leste—an important consideration given its low level of administrative capacity—by concentrating negotiations with donors into a particular time period and a particular forum, the joint donor health mission.

Notes

1. Because Timor-Leste has been officially known as Timor-Leste only since independence, in May 2002, this name is used to refer to the territory only since that time. "East Timor" is used to refer to the territory under the UN administration and Indonesian rule, because that is what they called it—the UN referred to it using the English "East Timor," while the Indonesians called it "Timor Timur," which translates as "East Timor."

2. An important exception is the health policy framework, which was produced through a consultative process involving two large-scale public workshops.

Bibliography

Hill, H. 2001. "Tiny, Poor and War-Torn: Development Policy Challenges for East Timor." *World Development* 29 (7): 1137–56.

Holloway, R. 2004. "NGO Advocacy in Timor-Leste: What is Possible?" In *Aspects of Democracy in Timor-Leste: NGOs Advocating for Social Change*, ed. R. Holloway, 7–15. Dili: Catholic Relief Services.

Joint Assessment Mission. 1999. "Health and Education Background Paper." November, Dili.

La'o Hamutuk. 2000. "Building a National Health System for East Timor." *La'o Hamutuk Bulletin*, November, Dili.

Millo, Y., and J. Barnett. 2004. "Educational Development in East Timor." *International Journal of Educational Development*, 24 (6): 1–17.

Morris, K. 2001. "Growing Pains of East Timor: Health of an Infant Nation." *The Lancet* 357 (9259): 873–77.

Ministry of Health. 2002. "East Timor's Health Policy Framework." Ministry of Health. June.

———. 2004. "Health Care: Priorities and Proposed Sector Investment Program." July 7, Dili.

Program Management Unit. 2004. "Physical Progess Report." June, Dili.

Shoesmith, D. 2003. "Timor-Leste: Divided Leadership in a Semi-Presidential System." *Asian Survey* 43 (2): 231–52.

Suara Timor Lorosae. 2004. "Fretilin Tak Pecah." August 20, 1.

Tulloch, J., F. Saadah, R. de Araujo, R. de Jesus, S. Lobo, I. Hemming, J. Nassim, and I. Morris. 2003. *Initial Steps in Rebuilding the Health Sector in East Timor*. Washington, DC: National Academies Press.

Winters, J. 1996. *Power in Motion: Capital Mobility and the Indonesian State*. Ithaca, NY: Cornell University Press.

World Bank. 2000a. "Project Appraisal Document on a Proposed Grant in the Amount of $12.7 Million Equivalent to East Timor for a Health Sector Rehabilitation and Development Project." May 24, Human Development Sector Unit, East Asia and the Pacific Region, World Bank, Washington, DC.

———. 2000b. "Project Information Document." May 5, East Asia and Pacific Region, World Bank, Washington, DC.

———. 2001a. "Project Appraisal Document on a Proposed Grant in the Amount of $12.6 Million Equivalent to East Timor for a Second Health Sector Rehabilitation and Development Project." Human Development Sector Unit, East Asia and the Pacific Region, World Bank, Washington, DC.

———. 2001b. "Project Information Document." June 28, East Asia and Pacific Region, World Bank, Washington, DC.

———. 2002. "East Timor: Policy Challenges for a New Nation." Poverty Reduction and Economic Management Sector Unit and East Timor Country Unit, East Asia and the Pacific Region, World Bank, Washington, DC.

———. 2003a. "Timor-Leste: Poverty in a New Nation: Analysis for Action." Poverty Reduction and Economic Management Sector Unit, East Asia and the Pacific Region, World Bank, Washington, DC.

———. 2003b. World Development Indicators CD-ROM, World Bank, Washington, DC.

———. 2004. "The Democratic Republic of Timor-Leste: Public Expenditure Review." Poverty Reduction and Economic Management Sector Unit, East Asia and the Pacific Region, World Bank, Washington, DC.

CHAPTER 6

The Direct Support to Schools Program in Mozambique

In 1997 Mozambique's Ministry of Education adopted a comprehensive Education Sector Strategic Plan aimed at increasing access to better-quality education by decentralizing education management and budget allocations. The plan addressed the following problems: the low quality of primary and secondary education, limited and inequitable access to primary and secondary education, low institutional capacity for education system management, nonresponsive technical and vocational education, inefficient higher education, and inadequate funding and inefficient allocation of resources (Ministry of Education 1998). By decentralizing education management and budget allocations, the ministry aimed to improve the learning conditions of students; enhance students' pedagogical achievements; bring education closer to students, teachers, and parents; widen access to education; improve the quality of education; close the educational gender gap; and involve the community in the management of schools. Several donors have committed substantial resources to support the Education Sector Strategic Plan, in the hope that its implementation will lead to long-term growth and accelerate socioeconomic development in Mozambique.

This chapter was written by Fidelx Pius Kulipossa and James Manor.

This chapter examines the extent to which the World Bank–funded Direct Support to Schools program has fulfilled its intended objectives, exerted influence on national policy, and provided insights on best practice. It examines the program's delivered outcomes against its design, wider political impacts and contribution to improved governance, and implications for poverty reduction. It considers key assumptions underlying the reform policies, the domestic ownership, the scaling up of successful development interventions, and the program's sustainability and appropriateness. It also assesses how implementing institutions (including civil society and local institutions) mediate (a) program impacts; (b) institutions' capacity, incentive structures, and performance; (c) complex relationships and processes within and between those institutions; (d) main impact transmission channels; (e) the main stakeholders involved in policy design and implementation, their stated interests, and their degree of influence; and (f) the program's impact on various stakeholders.

The chapter is predicated on the assumption that the reduction of absolute poverty and inequality in societies is the raison d'être of development, as captured by the Millennium Development Goals (MDGs). The acquisition of knowledge and skills through formal education reveals much about the character and pace of a country's economic and social development (Todaro 2000; UNDP 1999; World Bank 1999b; Harbison 1973). Using this rationale, this chapter assesses the impact of the program on various stakeholders, using six criteria:

- principal program objectives
- principal methods employed by the program to operationalize interventions
- types of activities (people oriented or public infrastructure oriented)
- principal beneficiaries of the program
- location of initiatives or activities and intended beneficiaries (rural versus urban)
- assessment of the program's transmission channels, types of impact (direct or indirect, short or long term), degree of access and use of services and public infrastructure by intended beneficiaries, and other development results.

Program Description

Mozambique's education system, like that in other developing countries, is in deep crisis. The crisis is characterized by low achievement rates, high dropout rates, high educational costs, low enrollments, pervasive teacher and student disengagement from teaching and learning, inefficient bureaucracies, collapsing school facilities, and declining parent involvement in school management.

Faced with demands by communities for substantive changes in the ways that schools are run, the Ministry of Education has embarked on decentralization by moving decision making and accountability closer to children, principals, teachers, and parents in order to make schooling more responsive to their needs. In 1997, it adopted a comprehensive Education Sector Strategic Plan aimed at addressing the problems in the sector.

The Direct Support to Schools Program (DSS) is one of the seven subcomponent programs of the quality of education component of Mozambique's Education Sector Strategic Plan. The objectives of the DSS are to promote the decentralization of decision making and resource management to the school level and to improve the quality of education by supplying basic learning and teaching materials and by involving communities in running schools. To attain these objectives, the program has created a School Quality Fund, which is allocated to individual lower and upper primary schools (EP1 and EP2) in the form of annual grants that are spent on the most pressing educational needs. At the school level, grants are managed by the school council, which is composed of teachers, the school principal, community members, and the district education director.

The first phase of the program began in April 2003, the second phase was launched in December 2003, and the third one began in July 2004. It is expected that the program will end in June 2006.

To date the program has reached 8,400 primary schools (EP1 and EP2) and more than 3 million children in all provinces of Mozambique. Per capita funding in the third phase of the program was about $0.73 per student (table 6.1).

Table 6.1 Coverage and Costs of Direct Support to Schools Program

Phase	Number of schools	Number of students	Total funding (thousands of dollars)	Unit cost (dollars)
1	8,137	3,005,963	1,700	0.56
2	8,071	3,005,963	2,117	0.70
3a	8,399	3,071,564	2,243	0.73

Source: Data collected from unpublished sources at the Ministry of Education and the World Bank, Maputo, Mozambique, January 2005.
Note: Phase 3a includes EP1, EP2, and complete primary schools (EPC).

The program is funded by the World Bank. Funds are disbursed to schools through hierarchical chains in the education sector: from the Ministry of Education to provincial directorates of education, district directorates of education, and schools. At each of these levels, structures have clear-cut, well-defined functions and responsibilities in implementing the program.

Two preliminary evaluations carried out by the Proformação Consultores, Lda, in 2003 and 2004 reported progress. The consultants observed higher rates of students passing key lower and upper primary school examinations, substantial reduction in dropout and repetition rates, increases in gross enrollment rates, improvement in educational achievement, and higher rates of girls' enrollment and retention.

Although the evolving nature of the program and its interconnectedness with other Education Sector Strategic Plan components and subcomponents caution against firm conclusions on its impacts, ground observations during fieldwork in Nampula appear to support the two preliminary evaluations. They also suggest that the program has had wider political effects and has contributed to improved governance and reduced poverty. Other plan components are also yielding positive results in all provinces: 138 primary schools have been built, providing 630 classrooms; 266 teachers' houses have been completed; 1,250 latrines and 85 potable water points have been supplied; 6 of Mozambique's 10 provinces have been supplied with classroom furniture; 32 tutors' houses at the teacher training institutes in Pemba and Vilankulo have been completed; and rehabilitation of secondary schools is progressing in all provinces (World Bank 2004, 2).

To implement the Education Sector Strategic Plan's objectives, $717 million has been mobilized, $71 million by the World Bank. Total project costs are estimated at $13.6 million, of which the World Bank contributed $4.95 million. These resources have been put at the disposal of the Ministry of Education's Education Sector Strategic Plan. Since implementation of the plan, its components, and its subcomponents began, the World Bank has disbursed $42.1 million, $6.5 million of which was earmarked for implementation of the DSS (World Bank 2004) (table 6.2). These resources have been reviewed regularly to suit the priorities of the Ministry of Education and adjusted to the rapidly changing financial environment in Mozambique.

Field Work Methods and Sources

Assessment of the DSS began with a desk review of numerous government policy documents, independent evaluations, and a mass of secondary

Table 6.2 Education Sector Strategic Plan Cost, by Component and Subcomponent

Component and subcomponent	Cost Thousands of dollars	Percent of total cost	IDA funding (thousands of dollars)
Quality of education			
Teacher training	24,701	4	6,000
Pedagogical support for teachers	17,700	3	6,150
Curricula transformation	7,071	1	1,000
Learning materials	39,896	6	6,450
Assessment and examinations	2,369	—	300
Direct support for schools	13,641	2	4,950
Training of school directors	3,126	—	950
Subtotal	108,503	16	25,800
Access to education			
School construction and rehabilitation	177,225	27	31,800
Girls education initiatives	8,939	1	4,350
Nonformal education	5,511	1	250
Special education	1,639	—	—
Subtotal	193,314	29	36,400
Ministry of Education institutional capacity			
Organizational structure and decentralization	318,533	49	4,100
Policy and planning	1,619	—	1,000
Financial management	3,086	—	2,200
Monitoring and evaluation	2,200	—	1,000
Subtotal	325,438	49	8,300
Vocational/technical education strategy			
Vocational/technical education	42,111	6	500
Subtotal	42,111	6	500
Total baseline costs	669,366	100	
Physical contingencies	20,721		
Price contingencies	27,082		
Total	**717,169**		**71,000**

Source: World Bank 1999a, 11.

Note: In the table above — signifies less than one percent. Blank cells indicate that the data are not available.

materials. Other sources included interviews with key stakeholders and direct observation of four primary schools in Nampula city.[1] Three main criteria were used to select independent evaluations and program reports or studies: coverage of a wide array of subjects; balanced coverage of the program's performance, combined with the required rigor; and up-to-date, accurate, and relevant evidence. On the basis of these criteria, two independent evaluations by Proformação Consultores, Lda, were selected and used extensively. They were selected in part because they are relevant to debates over development results, design considerations, and implementation processes (Greeley 2004).[2]

The assessment focuses on the main stakeholders and their interests, their degree of influence, and the extent of government ownership of the program. It seeks to determine the program's impact on various stakeholders, to assess how impacts are channeled, and to identify the most appropriate methods to analyze the distributional consequences of the program and types of impacts.

The study also examines (a) the degree of access and use of public infrastructure by intended beneficiaries, (b) the factors influencing access, (c) the nature of benefits from improved access, (d) the unintended negative impacts, and (e) the extent of satisfaction of intended beneficiaries with educational services and infrastructure. It seeks to understand how institutions affect outcomes by addressing roles, knowledge of and access to information, incentive structures, receptivity to policy change, capacity, resources or financial clout, and scope to adapt to the new reform agenda (World Bank 2002a, 2002b, 2003c; Taylor 2001; Baker 2000; Morris, Fitz-Gibbon, and Freeman 1987).

Development Results

In the interests of clarity, this study uses the concept of capital assets to assess development results of the DSS. Capital assets include natural resources (access to private and common property, land, water, housing); human resources (household labor, health, nutrition, education, skills/knowledge); on- and off-farm resources (cattle, real estate, financial); community-owned resources (roads, schools, commons); and social and political capital (claims to social networks, quality of household relations, or access to political power and state institutions). Poverty can be understood in terms of capital assets, because the assets determine "the capabilities and the range of escape strategies from poverty open to the individual or household, along with other 'conditioning factors'" (Cox, Farrington, and Gilling 1998, 3).

This multidimensional vision of poverty allows the use of multiple indicators and different interventions to tackle different dimensions of poverty. It also affects the way that progress in reducing poverty is assessed (White 1999). The mechanisms currently used to reduce poverty fall into three broad categories:

- enabling actions that underpin policies for poverty reduction and lead to social, environmental, or economic benefits for poor people

- inclusive actions, such as sector programs, that aim to benefit various groups and that address issues of equity and barriers to participation or access by poor people
- actions focused predominantly on the rights, interests, and needs of poor people (Cox, Farrington, and Gilling 1998)

These cross-cutting mechanisms establish direct or indirect relationships between poverty reduction and governance issues at the national and local levels. They can thus be used to assess the development results of the DSS.

Assessment of Delivered Outcomes against Design

The DSS has been achieving its stated objectives. From the outset the program focused on mitigating school liquidity problems by channeling grants to individual schools; improving teaching and learning conditions; delivering teaching and learning materials; and improving community participation in education, school governance, and efficient financial management.[3] As a result, the program has been relatively successful in increasing the proportion of students that successfully complete the first cycle of primary school (EP1); reducing the rates of repetition at EP1, EP2, and lower secondary school (ESG1); increasing gross enrollment rates in EP1 and EP2; increasing the proportion of girls registered in comparison with boys at EP1, EP2, and ESG1; improving completion rates at EP1, EP2, and ESG1; and improving the teacher-student ratio at EP1, EP2, and ESG1. In addition to these achievements, the program has

- increased student motivation and reduced absenteeism and dropout rates
- improved pedagogical results
- enhanced student participation in the learning process: students go to the blackboard more often, they make good oral contributions, and a greater number of them do homework
- forged closer links between schools and the community, parents, and families
- increased access to schools and learning materials for the poorest students and families
- increased awareness among teachers, parents, and the community of the need to maximize the use of existing scarce resources
- increased community participation in education in identifying and solving some school problems, promoting girls' education, creating

community partnerships, transparently managing school resources, and promoting civic education in schools

- massively increased enrollments and education benefits
- improved morale of school staff students' regular attendance and completion, and monitoring and follow-up of teacher attendance and performance
- increased parents' attendance at school meetings to learn about their children's learning progress and classroom behavior
- identified factors contributing to education problems
- increased children's readiness for schooling by providing them with adequate meals and stimulating their cognitive development
- increased two-way flows of information between the government and the community, thus bolstering the legitimacy of the government and the entire political system
- improved coordination and complementarity among the Ministry of Education, provincial directorates of education, district directorate of education, and schools in the management of education
- improved decision making about curriculum, instructional practice, and resource use
- created strong ownership of the schools' mission and greater commitment of the staff
- increased accountability for outcomes
- improved student achievement, attendance, and motivation
- engaged parents and other community members in the schooling process
- sustained integration of schools with community resources
- improved school-community relations

These positive results are being achieved because community participation in the DSS is implicitly based on a relatively open and democratic environment; a decentralized policy with greater emphasis on the balance between national and local initiatives, that is, between top-down and bottom-up initiatives; the democratization of professional experts and officials; the formation of self-managing organizations of the poor and excluded; the training for community activism and leadership; the involvement of NGOs; and the creation of collective decision-making structures at various levels that extend from the micro to the meso and macro levels, linking participatory activities with policy frameworks (criteria taken from Campfens 1997).

These results are also consistent with those from other countries where similar objectives have been accomplished (UNICEF 1992; Shaeffer 1992, 1994; Bray 1996, 1999; Heneveld and Craig 1996; OECD 1997; Campfens 1997; McDonough and Wheeler 1998; Uemura 1999; Woessmann 2000). But improvements brought about by the DSS do not end with those listed above. The assessment by Proformação Consultores, Lda, of the impact of the program focused on four areas in which impacts have been particularly positive: procedures, decision making, purchase schemes, and materials distribution.

Procedures. Procedures for implementing the program were kept simple to facilitate positive turnaround at the school level. The manual of procedures produced by the Ministry of Education sets out the criteria that schools must follow to implement the program; the list of eligible materials; the mechanisms of control and accountability; the responsibilities of central, provincial, and district education directorates and schools in program implementation; and the number of primary schools to be involved in each program phase. To increase knowledge about the program at the local level, these procedures were backed up by program publicity aimed at intended beneficiaries through the media (radio, television, newspapers), brochures, and posters. This publicity enhanced the financial and managerial skills of school staff, their knowledge about implementation mechanisms, their positive reaction to increased financial and administrative autonomy at the school level, the revitalization of school-community relations, and the acquisition of operational capacity and skills for the execution of program tasks and objectives.

Decision-Making Process. Although the Ministry of Education makes decisions regarding the overall strategy and management of the program, decisions are channeled in a way that leaves the meso and micro levels with the leverage to adjust them to local contexts and the changing environment. As a result, the program has been able to involve communities in the way schools are run and managed. Indeed, Proformação, Lda, (2003) found only five cases in which decisions regarding the use of funds and the purchase and distribution of teaching and learning materials had been made without community involvement.

Purchase Scheme. The majority of schools have complied with the list of eligible materials for purchase. Most of these materials are purchased at district headquarters or in nearby towns, but the staff of schools in remote areas and without such shops had to travel long distances to buy materials, forcing their schools to spend about 50 percent of their funds on transport and accommodations. In the second phase of the program, local people turned this problem into an opportunity by bringing materials to remote areas: the informal sector is now booming in remote areas. This turn of events can be viewed as a positive spillover of the DSS, because the informal sector is crucial to local economic development and poverty reduction.

Materials Distribution. The list of eligible teaching and learning materials elaborated by the Ministry of Education reflects the most pressing needs of schools. The distribution of such materials is transparent, and all schools comply with the criteria set up by the Ministry of Education. The collective management and accountability mechanisms established under the program make misuse largely impossible. The contrast with the dismal record of previous years is striking.

Wider Political Impacts and Contribution to Improved Governance

The DSS program's wider political impacts and its contribution to improved governance in Mozambique can be analyzed at three levels: school, district and provincial, and national. Various impacts establish direct or indirect relationships between poverty reduction and governance issues. The program's impacts are transmitted through two main channels: improved access to public infrastructure (schools), and assets—both human (knowledge and skills) and social (community participation in school management).

School Level. The DSS program had an impact at the school level in various ways. First, the program has empowered schools and expanded opportunities by improving reach and increasing access to basic school services. School empowerment entailed establishment of representative institutions in schools (school councils composed of school principals, teachers, and representatives of parents and the community) and institutionalization of community participation in school management to revitalize school-community relations. School councils now make decisions about managing grants and resources, and they oversee the functioning of schools. Educational opportunities include institutionalization of downward accountability (publication of accounts of school activities, dissemination of basic data on performance, and mechanisms for students' feedback); flexible delivery of teaching and learning materials (opportunities for community involvement and partnerships between schools, parents, and the community in the improvement of education); and development of school capacity (incentives to deploy teaching staff to remote areas and greater school autonomy).

Second, if schools, family, and the media are viewed as key elements of political socialization, the changes in primary schools since the introduction of the DSS have had great political importance. They are enhancing political, social, and cultural values, as well as cognitive, affective, and evaluative orientations of students toward the political world and their role in it. The improvement in teaching and learning conditions that the program is bringing about is contributing to better training, instructing, and learning. The improved quality of the school staff, teaching, facilities, and school curricula shapes students' understanding of the political world, the society, and the relevance of education for society.

Third, the provision of civic education to students by community leaders has raised students' political awareness not only of their community but also of their national identity, African culture, and global human values. Schools are functioning as training grounds for local democracy in that they are developing students' political skills and stimulating political participation at the local level. This impact extends widely as a result of community participation in school governance and is reflected in joint decision making concerning resource mobilization; experimentation with ideas; self-help; and collaboration among teachers, students, and parents.

Fourth, some schools are addressing social exclusion. For example, the 7 de Abril primary school, in partnership with Caritas (a religious NGO), has used DSS funds to help 40 abandoned children and 6 orphans whose parents died of HIV/AIDS. The school provided them with learning materials and school uniforms, while Caritas provided accommodations, food, and shelter. This assistance is important, because widespread, abject poverty and the lack of financial resources have limited the government's capacity to provide basic social services to tackle the problems of social exclusion and the HIV/AIDS epidemic.

District and Provincial Level. DSS has affected performance at the district and provincial level in three ways. First, district and provincial education staff are learning to adapt to the decentralization of education. Ministry of Education central units and provincial and district directorates are responsible for regularly compiling information on implementation, as well as data on monitoring and evaluation indicators. District and provincial education staff are receiving training in management, budgeting, accounting, procurement, and use of management information systems (MIS) and their school performance is being evaluated.

Second, the involvement of district and provincial directorates of education in the implementation of the DSS has strengthened rather than eroded their powers, because some funds from the program are used to build their capacity. Although schools are now more autonomous, they are, nevertheless, accountable to district and provincial directorates of education. This accountability explains their strong support of the program. Implementation of the DSS has enhanced powers and legitimacy at the school and community levels, because district and provincial directorates of education are seen as astute coordinators and skillful facilitators.

Third, the improvement in the quality of teaching, school facilities, and curricula induced by the DSS is encouraging citizens across Mozambique to view public schools as relevant institutions for promoting socioeconomic development. As a consequence, citizens are willing to support schools, both financially and through participation in school meetings. This support legitimates government institutions in the eyes of ordinary citizens. At the Limoeiros primary school in Nampula city, four classrooms were built with money donated by parents of students. Parents and other community members attend meetings to discuss school problems, acquaint themselves with the way schooling is delivered, and provide civic education to students.

National Level. The central government is enthusiastic about the achievements of DSS and is working out strategies to use the DSS model in allocating the education sector budget. The DSS will inform national policy for decentralizing resources directly to schools to induce further positive effects. The central government now recognizes that local, provincial, and central levels of government can jointly provide education. In effect, primary education is a public service, the provision of which is tailored to local needs, entails economies of scale, and involves national responsibility—a point that has been emphasized by various decentralization theorists (Prud'homme 1995).

Donors are also enthusiastic about the progress made, and they are willing to support the DSS with capital development grants to make it a channel for providing funds to primary schools. The program's achievements have also inspired the central government to undertake decentralization reforms across the public sector to improve its performance and capacity to deliver services.

Implications for Poverty Reduction and Economic Growth

The DSS has direct and indirect implications for poverty reduction and economic growth. It is making the education system more relevant to citizens' development needs in two ways. First, it is changing economic and social incentives outside the educational system that determine the magnitude, structure, and orientation of aggregate private demand for education and the political response in the form of public supply of school places. Second, it is improving the internal effectiveness and equity of the education system by changing the course content and the ways schools structure the teaching and learning environment, deliver educational services, govern themselves, and are held accountable. Attainment of these two policy objectives makes education more relevant to the development needs of a nation (Todaro 2000).

By concentrating exclusively on primary education, the DSS is contributing to the promotion of self-education and rural work-related learning experiences that will help students function later on. The DSS is making parents aware that educating children may create better opportunities for them to obtain secure and well-paying jobs, thereby escaping poverty.

By expanding educational opportunities for girls, the DSS is contributing to the closing of the educational gender gap. Doing so provides economic benefits, because the rate of return on girls' education is higher than the return on boys' education in most developing countries (Haddad and others, cited in Todaro 2000, 1990):

- Increasing women's education not only increases their productivity on the farm and in the factory, but also results in greater labor force participation, later marriage, lower fertility, and greatly improved child health and nutrition.
- Improved child health and nutrition and better educated mothers lead to multiplier effects on the quality of a nation's human resources for many generations to come.
- Because women carry a disproportionate share of the burden of poverty and landlessness, any significant improvements in their role and status as a result of education can have an important impact on breaking the vicious cycle of poverty and inadequate schooling.

Data on the direct impacts of the DSS on poverty variables are not yet available, but given the two-way relationship between education and development, the DSS may contribute directly or indirectly to economic growth and rural development; may reduce inequality, poverty, and fertility; and may lower the incidence of HIV infection.[4] The DSS may indirectly contribute to economic growth, because in the long run, expanding educational opportunities in primary schools will create a more productive labor force. Education provides employment and income-earning opportunities for teachers, school and construction workers, textbook and paper printers, school uniform manufacturers, and related workers; creates a class of educated leaders to fill vacancies in public and private institutions and professions; and provides the kind of training and education that promotes literacy and basic skills while encouraging "modern" attitudes on the part of diverse segments of the population (Psacharopoulos, cited in Todaro 2000).[5]

By linking education to the real needs of rural communities, the DSS may contribute to rural development in the long term, because the needs of rural students are given special attention. Curricula are being tailored to the working environment of rural students, implicitly along the lines proposed by Coombs and Ahmed (1974):

- general or basic education (literacy, arithmetic, an elementary understanding of science and the immediate environment, and so forth)
- family improvement education, designed primarily to impart knowledge, skills, and attitudes that improve the quality of family life (subjects include health and nutrition, homemaking and childcare, home repairs and improvements, and family planning)
- community improvement education, designed to strengthen local and national institutions and processes through instruction in such matters as local and national government, cooperatives, and community projects
- occupational education, designed to develop knowledge and skills associated with various income-earning activities

The DSS aims to change the design of educational programs to cater to diverse occupational groups, so that education is more relevant to rural development.

Discrimination against girls and women in school attendance has negative economic consequences, whereas expanding educational opportunities for them has social and economic benefits. Haddad and others (1990) (cited in

Todaro 2000) and UNICEF (1992) show that educating women reduces infant mortality rates and fertility, raises income and the educational performance of children, and is associated with healthier children. Educating girls and women also helps reduce the HIV infection by informing them about infection prevention, empowering them to defend themselves, and instilling a sense of hope for the future (UNICEF 2004).

Scaling Up the Program

The initial scaling up of the DSS across Mozambique was based on subjective and strategic judgments reflecting World Bank experience and local knowledge. Four considerations guided the DSS scale-up:

- By the program's going nationwide right from the outset, it was thought that public knowledge about the program would spread immediately, ensuring transparency and mobilizing local communities to pressure the district directorates of education to deliver funds.
- The design team wanted to build capacity that could deliver services and, in the future, address other issues, such as equity.
- Simple instructional guidelines were developed to accelerate the development of public awareness and the pace of implementation.
- A careful study of logistics was required in order to set up the incentives and accountability structures at all levels, always balancing transaction costs and overheads against the need to make headway.

Several requirements identified in the literature on scaling up informed this approach:

- fostering a culture of continuous learning
- investing in building the capacity of staff, whether in government, NGO, or private institutions
- spreading lessons on what works
- supporting good learning processes
- stimulating competition to encourage adaptation, innovation, and better service delivery (Malhotra 2004)

The design team envisaged the DSS being implemented through a learning-by-doing approach and through innovative interventions in education, including the flexible delivery of teaching and learning materials; downward accountability (publication of accounts for schools' activities, dissemination of basic information on performance and best practices, and mechanisms for students feedback); and development of schools' capacity. Implementation of the program in phases implied a strong awareness of the need to ensure continuous learning.

Long-Term Sustained Impacts

The DSS is contributing to the gradual attainment of some MDGs (UNDP 2003). It is helping reduce poverty, achieve universal primary education by ensuring that girls and boys are able to complete a full cycle of primary schooling, and promoting gender equality and the empowerment of women by closing the educational gender gap at the primary level.

Although the DSS has made progress toward meeting its objectives, some problems have hindered attainment of more sustained effects, especially at the school level:

- The amounts of money given to schools are meager, given their pressing needs: poor school physical facilities; overcrowded classes; and a lack of desks, chairs, and supplies.
- The criteria for distributing funds do not take into account the diversity of schools in terms of numbers of students, specific school problems, and their geographical location.
- The distribution of funds is irregular and takes a long time. The problem has been attributed to delays in informing schools of the availability of DSS funds. Schools located in remote and isolated areas learn about the availability of funds only slowly, which causes delays in the delivery of learning and teaching materials (manuals, posters, calendars, pencils, pens, and so forth).
- Principals, teachers, and representatives of communities view the list of eligible materials as very restrictive. Some schools need funds to carry out small-scale infrastructure upgrading (roofing, doors, water and sanitation facilities), which is not permitted under the program.

The provision of free primary education has boosted the number of students, especially girls. But the increase in demand has made it impossible for some schools to enroll additional students because of poor physical facilities. Enrolled students study in overcrowded classes, often in the open air.

An increasing number of primary school graduates want to continue their studies at the secondary and university levels. Given enrollment restrictions at these levels, this demand cannot be met.

Principals, teachers, students, and communities are concerned about delays in addressing cross-cutting issues, such as HIV/AIDS, health, gender, social exclusion, and orphans and vulnerable children. Schools play a pivotal role in the political socialization of children and in targeting at-risk youth. They also play "a decisive role in fostering positive social attitudes, civic values, and in fighting against drug abuse and diseases such as HIV/AIDS and malaria" (Govender and Gruzd 2004, 33). These cross-cutting issues are crucial to ensuring the long-term sustainability of the program, because they offer an opportunity for raising children's awareness and education about HIV/AIDS, thereby reducing the spread of HIV/AIDS and other sexually transmitted diseases, and addressing gender discrimination and social exclusion. Currently, no schoolhealth or HIV/AIDS manuals target primary schoolchildren. These delays are likely to have negative impacts, because these cross-cutting issues are crucial to meeting the MDGs.

Long-term sustainability of the program will be in doubt unless progress is made on other components of the Education Sector Strategic Plan. Therefore, expansion of primary education needs to be accompanied by measures and policies geared to improving all levels of education (especially secondary and higher levels), lest the achievements at primary level be jeopardized.

Design Considerations
The design of the DSS was preceded by an analysis of the nature of the Mozambican state and its underlying governance problems. The main governance problems are overcentralization of political and economic power at the central and provincial levels and weaknesses of the Mozambican education system, which is characterized by limited access, poor quality, high costs, and questionable sustainability. The design was also informed by analysis of the role of donors and their impact on the policy process. Various aid agencies have created parallel structures to bypass the Mozambican government and to negotiate projects with line ministries that do not have adequate coordination with other donor agencies. Their reluctance to integrate their resources into the government planning and budgeting process and their preference for sectoral financing represent constraints to progress.

The design of the program was also based on the following theories (Nellemann 2004):

- Providing resources will improve the quality of the environment, forging "social contracting" and mutual dependency between parents and schools will create a power balance (between the traditional role of the teacher as the literate authority and the community), and giving the community assets (and thus influence) and increasing community participation will increase attendance and have a positive impact on factors influencing the success of the system.

- Incentives can increase accountability and transparency. (Thus under DSS schools that use grants effectively receive more funds the following year. Schools that fail to use grants effectively are excluded from the program.)
- Subsidizing the cost of education and reducing the opportunity costs of attending school can increase attendance on average (and not at the margin) and can free up household resources for local consumption of other goods and services. This freeing up of resources can lead to growth spillover effects.

Markets and the delivery of materials are not perfect, but they will—to some degree—work themselves out. The design was based on the assumption that stakeholders would find a way to connect and that the government should not micromanage every aspect of the program.

The design team decided that DSS should be broadly strategic rather than detailed and comprehensive:

- District directorates of education received monetary rewards: overheads, partly to cover travel costs, were sufficiently generous to create a surplus for each program (providing a strong incentive to perform).
- DSS went nationwide right away to increase pressure on district directorates of education to deliver funds and enhance accountability.
- Timing and credibility were crucial to accelerate the implementation pace.
- Grant manuals were made short (one page each) and provided step-by-step instructions (Nellemann 2004).

According to Nellemann, the DSS design emphasized performance incentives, accountability and transparency, and simplicity. The goal was to build a system on which more sophisticated initiatives, such as initiatives to address equity, could later be undertaken. This goal influenced the program's short- and long-term objectives, scale and geographical coverage, choice of implementing agency, ownership considerations, implementation mechanisms, coordination considerations, and revenue and budget management.

By embarking on decentralized financing of schools, the Ministry of Education aimed to address financial problems; to increase efficiency and effectiveness of education; to redistribute political power among central, provincial, and district institutions and individual schools; to improve the quality of education; and to change the way schools structure the learning environment, deliver educational services, govern themselves, and are held accountable. The ministry, therefore, wished to

- Use existing government institutions to implement the program. Funds released by the World Bank were channeled to the Ministry of Education, which in turn disbursed them to provincial and district directorates of education and then to individual schools.[6]
- Strengthen the government's ownership of the program through training of Mozambican staff at the central, provincial, district, and school levels.
- Adopt a learning approach and maintain flexibility in confronting the many challenges in implementing the program.
- Stimulate community participation by involving representatives of the community in the management of school grants in order to enhance transparency, responsiveness, legitimacy, and accountability at the school level.
- Anchor support to schools in the Education Sector Strategic Plan.
- Strengthening coordination of the program and exchange of information between the World Bank and other donors.
- Promote long-term sustainability by introducing cost recovery for some education inputs and reducing duplication of technical assistance by establishing a more integrated system within the sectorwide approach.

Implementation Processes

The DSS was implemented largely through existing Ministry of Education institutions, but the emphasis was on power sharing among the Ministry of Education, provincial and district directorates of education, schools, teachers, principals, and parents. Power sharing can help avoid conflicts. As Manor (1999) notes, most decentralization experiments fail because power holders at higher levels fear the loss of power and influence over national policies. This fear has delayed substantial devolution of political and economic powers to local institutions in Mozambique. Implementation arrangements were also designed to use a sectorwide approach to accommodate donor agencies.

Each level in the system was assigned responsibilities, as follows:

- The Ministry of Education prepares and distributes implementation materials to provincial directorates of education, trains staff at the provincial and district levels, and transfers funds to the provincial directorates of education. The ministry's line directorates and agencies are responsible for day-to-day coordination and implementation of activities for which they have a primary responsibility. Performing these tasks strengthens their ability to plan, monitor, and supervise program implementation and to provide technical support to provinces and districts as they monitor and supervise community and NGO classroom construction or rehabilitation and provide learning and teaching materials. Line directorates and agencies also ensure that line departments and provincial and district directorates receive the necessary guidance and resources to implement the program, and that they meet reporting, financing, and auditing requirements.
- The provincial directorates of education distribute DSS implementation materials to the district directorates of education and sign authorization letters in conjunction with representatives of schools and communities.
- School councils decide which program-eligible materials to buy. The school director and a community representative go first to the district directorate to receive the check and then to the bank to withdraw the money. They fill in two copies of the order note, leave one copy and invoices from purchases with the district directorate, and keep the other copy for the school. Then they deliver the materials (Ministry of Education 2004).

These implementation mechanisms ensure responsiveness, accountability, quality, community participation, and effective school governance.

Summary of Program Achievements and Challenges

Assessing the lasting impacts of the DSS on learning conditions and pedagogical achievements across Mozambique is premature at this point, but preliminary assessment of the program's performance is cautiously positive. The DSS has led to the higher rates of students passing key lower and upper primary school examinations, a substantial reduction in dropout and repetition rates, an increase in gross enrollment rates, and the higher rates of girls' enrollment and retention. These achievements are leading to improved governance, poverty reduction, and civic education for children.

By changing economic and social incentives outside the educational system, the program is making that system more relevant to the development needs of citizens. It is encouraging them to believe that schools are relevant institutions in which knowledge is transmitted for Mozambique's socioeconomic development.

By encouraging community participation in the management of schools, the DSS is engaging the community in identifying and solving some school problems, promoting girls' education, creating and revitalizing community partnerships, making management of school resources transparent, promoting civic education in schools to inculcate democratic values and political culture in students, and fostering accountability. All of these effects have salutary effects on state–society relations in Mozambique.

However, the massive expansion of formal primary education has meant that schools are too few to accommodate all students and that classrooms are overcrowded. The number of primary school graduates who want to continue their education has also risen significantly, but there are too few places to accommodate demand. These problems raise questions about the long-term sustainability of the DSS.

The availability of funds in remote primary schools is stimulating development of the informal sector, which can contribute to reducing absolute poverty there. The program is highly poverty oriented: greater equity in educational opportunities will result in a reduction of imbalances in economic opportunities across regions of the country. Human resource development is a key to the poverty reduction strategy for Mozambique.

The focus on girls' education is aimed at closing the educational gender gap and mitigating the problems of inequality, poverty, and high fertility rates. The DSS should also, in the long term, have positive spillovers in the economy as the skills base improves and as labor productivity increases in all economic sectors. In addition to promoting economic growth—a prerequisite for poverty reduction—expansion of basic education is likely to help poor families by providing them with the knowledge to take advantage of expanding economic opportunities, thereby improving social and human development indicators, such as child mortality rates, maternal mortality, and malnutrition levels.

These direct and positive spillover effects are contributing to the gradual achievement of five of the eight targets set out in the MDGs: eradicating extreme poverty and hunger, achieving universal primary education, promoting gender equality and empowering women, reducing child mortality, and improving maternal health. The DSS is contributing directly to achieving universal primary education, promoting gender equality, empowering women. It is contributing indirectly (through spillover effects) to the other three targets.

The central government has concluded that the DSS enhances its legitimacy, because it is making ordinary citizens believe that public schools are relevant institutions in which political, social, and cultural values—as well as cognitive, affective, and evaluative orientations of students—are forged. This legitimates the Mozambican political system and improves state–society relations. Implementation of the DSS is contributing to mutual empowerment between the state and society.

Challenges remain. In particular, the Ministry of Education needs to pursue cautious but forward-looking and steady decentralization, devolve responsibilities to schools by increasing DSS resources to enable schools to purchase teaching and learning materials, train teachers, and undertake small-scale infrastructure upgrading.

The Ministry of Education needs to examine institutional reform, human resource development, decentralization, creation of relevant and flexible curricula, gender and HIV/AIDS issues, post–primary education, teacher training and management, decentralized and efficient financial systems, efficient school management policies, and school construction and community participation. If changes on these fronts do not take place, the prospects for further improvements in the way the Mozambican education system is run will be constrained.

Lesson for Aid Provision in LICUS

The evidence on the performance of the DSS yields important insights into provision of aid in low-income countries under stress (LICUS). First, it confirms that—when appropriately designed—aid can achieve effective results within a poor governance environment. Despite 16 years of civil war, a history of autocracy, and an overcentralized government even after democratic processes were introduced, the DSS produced positive results. One key factor in its success is that unlike many donor-supported education programs, the DSS is owned by the Ministry of Education. The World Bank assisted the ministry in designing the program and provides funds, but it has little influence on the way the DSS is implemented.

To ensure successful implementation of the DSS, the Ministry of Education took a strong leadership role, providing training and improving working conditions for government officials. These changes raised the morale of officials, enhanced the officials' retention rate, and helped foster confidence in the program's efficacy. Hence, building national institutional capacity is crucial to success.

Second, programs based on thorough analyses of local dynamics are more likely to be effective.

Third, the program had positive spillover effects. Its success with participatory approaches and its promotion of coordination among schools and district, provincial, and central levels of government appealed to policymakers in other sectors. Other ministries are learning that joint provision of some public services may improve outcomes, because having such services draws in local interests, produces economies of scale, and encourages a sense of national responsibility. The ministries are also learning that programs like the DSS may be used to address other problems, such as social exclusion.

Fourth, most development interventions are scalable, but there are no blueprints for expanding successful programs.

Notes

1. Fidelx Kulipossa interviewed key stakeholders and observed DSS efforts in Nampula city, October 14–22, 2004. He visited two primary schools with rural characteristics (Namicopo-Sede and Napipine) and two schools located in the urban part of Nampula city (7 de Abril and Limoeiros).

2. These documents used stakeholder analyses, institutional analyses, social impact analyses, beneficiary analyses, social capital assessment tools, poverty mapping, the services matrix, the gendered services matrix, social risk assessment, and monitoring and evaluation of the project's impacts (World Bank 2003a). The two evaluations fully or partially satisfy the three criteria and use some of these methods, warranting their use in this study.

3. These activities are also consistent with Mozambique's Poverty Reduction Strategy Paper, which focuses on enhancing expenditure programs (education, health, infrastructure, construction, or rehabilitation); institutional reforms (devolution and deconcentration and public sector reforms); and structural reforms (efficient financial management and land reform).

4. Todaro (2000, 342) contends that educational systems reflect the nature of a given society and determine the character and pace of its social and economic development: "[I]f the society is inegalitarian in economic and social structure, the educational system will probably reflect that bias in

terms of who is able to proceed through the system. At the same time, education can influence the future shape and direction of society in a number of ways. Thus the link between education and development goes both ways."

5. To achieve these goals, Al-Samarrai and Bennell (2003) propose an efficient and effective recruitment of school leavers and university graduates; making curricula more practical and vocational; providing basic prevocational training in business, management, and information technology; improving educational quality and relevance (teaching and learning materials and school facilities); and providing training that imparts knowledge and skills relevant to the challenges facing developing countries.

6. This process curbed donors' tendency to set up parallel structures and to bypass the government. For more detailed and critical studies on donors' work in Mozambique, see Hanlon (1991, 1996); Abrahamsson and Nilsson (1995); Wuyts (1996); and Acharya, de Lima, and Moore (2004).

Bibliography

Abrahamsson, Hans, and Anders Nilsson. 1995. *Mozambique: The Troubled Transition from Socialism Construction to Free Market Capitalism.* London: Zed Books.

Acharya, Arnab, Ana Fuzzo de Lima, and Mick Moore. 2004. "Aid Proliferation: How Responsible Are the Donors?" Working Paper 214, Institute for Development Studies, Brighton, United Kingdom.

Al-Samarrai, Samer, and Paul Bennell. 2003. "Where Has All the Education Gone in Africa? Employment Outcomes among Secondary School and University Leavers." Institute for Development Studies, Brighton, United Kingdom.

Baker, Judy L. 2000. *Evaluating the Impact of Development Projects on Poverty: A Handbook for Practitioners.* Washington, DC: World Bank.

Bray, Mark. 1996. *Decentralization of Education: Community Financing.* Washington, DC: World Bank.

———. 1999. "Community Partnership in Education: Dimensions, Variations, and Implications." World Bank, Washington, DC.

Campfens, Hubert, ed. 1997. *Community Participation around the World: Practice, Theory, Research, and Training.* Toronto: University of Toronto Press.

Coombs, Philip H., and Manzoor Ahmed. 1974. *Attacking Rural Poverty: How Nonformal Education Can Help.* Baltimore, MD: Johns Hopkins University Press.

Cox, Aidan, John Farrington, and Jim Gilling. 1998. "Developing a Framework to Assess the Poverty Impact of NR Research. Final Report." Overseas Development Institute, London.

Golias, Manuel. 1996. "Democracy and Education in *Mozambique.*" In *Mozambique: Elections, Democracy and Development,* ed. Brazão Mazula, 289–326. Maputo, Mozambique: Inter-Africa Group.

Govender, Peroshni, and Steven Gruzd, eds. 2004. *Back to the Blackboard: Looking beyond Universal Primary Education in Africa.* Johannesburg: South African Institute of International Affairs.

Greeley, Martin. 2004. "A Framework for Assessing Program and Project Aid in LICUS Countries." Final Draft (September 2004). Institute for Development Studies, Brighton, United Kingdom.

Haddad, Wadi D., and others. 1990. *Education and Development: Evidence for New Priorities.* Washington, DC: World Bank.

Haddad, Wadi D., and others, cited in Todaro, 2000: 334–35. 1990. "Education and Development: Evidence for New Priorities." World Bank Discussion Paper 95, World Bank, Washington, DC.

Hanlon, Joseph. 1991. *Mozambique: Who Calls the Shots?* London: James Currey.

———. 1996. *Peace Without Profit: How the IMF Blocks Rebuilding in Mozambique.* Oxford: James Currey.

Harbison, Fredrick H. 1973. *Human Resources as the Wealth of Nations.* New York: Oxford University Press.

Heneveld, Ward, and Helen Craig. 1996. *Schools Count: World Bank Project Designs and the Quality of Primary Education in Sub-Saharan Africa.* Washington, DC: World Bank.

Jiminez, Emmanuel. 1986. "The Public Subsidization of Education and Health in Developing Countries: A Review of Equity and Efficiency." *World Bank Research Observer* 1(1): 111–29.

Kulipossa, Fidelx Pius. 2004. "Decentralization and Democracy in Developing Countries: An Overview." *Development in Practice* 14 (6): 768–79.

Manor, James. 1999. *The Political Economy of Democratic Decentralization.* Washington, DC: World Bank.

Malhotra, Mohini. 2004. "Lessons: Scaling Up Successful Efforts to Reduce Poverty." http://www.worldbank.org/reducingpoverty/docs/conceptual.pdf.

McDonough, Maureen H., and Christopher W. Wheeler. 1998. *Toward School and Community Collaboration in School Forestry: Lessons Learned from Thai Experiences.* Washington, DC: Advancing Basic Education and Literacy Project.

Ministry of Education. 1998. *Education Sector Strategic Plan 1999–2003: Reviving Schools and Expanding Opportunities–Mozambique.* Maputo, Mozambique: Ministry of Education.

———. 2004. "Manual de procedimentos do Programa de Apoio Directo às Escola: Fases 1, 2, e 3." Maputo, Mozambique.

Ministry of Education and the World Bank, Maputo. 2002. Unpublished sources. Ministry of Education, Maputo, Mozambique, and World Bank, Maputo, Mozambique.

Morris, Lynn Lyons, Carol Taylor Fitz-Gibbon, and Marie E. Freeman. 1987. *How to Communicate Evaluation Findings*. Newbury Park, CA: Sage Publications.

Nellemann, Soren. 2004. "Mozambique: Direct Support to Schools." Comments provided privately to the authors of the present paper on their first draft, November.

OECD (Organisation for Economic Co-operation and Development). 1997. *Parents as Partners in Schooling*. Center for Education Research and Innovation. Paris: OECD.

————. 1998. *Education at Glance: OECD Indicators*. Center for Education Research and Innovation. Paris: OECD.

Proformação Consultores, Lda 2003. "Monitoring of Direct Support to Schools Program. Phase 1." Final Report. Maputo.

————. 2004. "Monitoring of Direct Support to Schools Pprogram. Phase 2." Final Report. Maputo.

Prud'homme, Remy. 1995. "The Dangers of Decentralization." *World Bank Research Observer* 10 (2): 201–20.

Psacharopoulos, George, cited in Todaro, 2000. 1988. "Education and Development: A Review." *World Bank Research Observer* 3 (1): 99–116.

Psacharopoulos, George, and Maureen Woodhall. 1987. *Education for Development: An Analysis of Investment Choices*. New York: Oxford University Press.

Shaeffer, Sheldon, ed. 1992. *Collaborating for Educational Change: The Role of Teachers, Parents and the Community in School Improvement*. Paris: UNESCO.

————. 1994. *Partnerships and Participation in Basic Education: A Series of Training Modules and Case Study Abstracts for Educational Planners and Managers*. Paris: UNESCO.

Taylor, Laurence. 2001. "Good Monitoring and Evaluation Practice: Guidance Notes." Performance Assessment Resource Center, Birmingham, UK. http://www.parcinfo.org.

Todaro, Michael P. 2000. *Economic Development*. 7th ed. New York: Addison Wesley Longman.

Uemura, Mitsue. 1999. "Community Participation in Education: What Do We Know?" World Bank, Washington, DC.

UNDP (United Nations Development Programme). 1999. "New Technologies and the Global Race for Knowledge." In *Human Development Report 1999: Globalization with a Human Face*, 57–76. New York: Oxford University Press.

————. 2003. *Human Development Report 2003. Millennium Development Goals: A Compact among Nations to End Human Poverty*. New York: Oxford University Press.

UNICEF. 1992. *Strategies to Promote Girls' Education: Policies and Programs that Work*. Paris: UNICEF.

————. 2004. *Educating Girls: The Big Picture*. Paris: UNICEF.

White, Howard. 1999. "Global Poverty Reduction: Are We Heading in the Right Direction?" *Journal of International Development* 11 (4): 503–19.

Woessmann, Ludger. 2000. "Schooling Resources, Educational Institutions, and Student Performance: The International Evidence." Working Paper 983, Kiel Institute of World Economics, Kiel, Germany.

World Bank. 1999a. "Project Appraisal Document on a Proposed Credit in the Amount of 51.1 Million SDR ($71 Million Equivalent) to the Republic of Mozambique for an Education Sector Strategic Program (ESSP)." World Bank, Washington, DC.

————.1999b. *World Development Report 1998/99: Knowledge for Development*. New York: Oxford University Press.

————. 2002a. *Monitoring and Evaluation: Some Tools, Methods, and Approaches*. Washington, DC: World Bank.

————. 2002b. *Social Analysis Sourcebook: Incorporating Social Dimensions into Bank–Supported Projects*. Washington, DC: World Bank.

————. 2003a. "Cost and Financing of Education: Opportunities and Obstacles for Expanding and Improving Education in Mozambique." Working Paper 26699, World Bank, Washington, DC.

————. 2003b. "Mozambique Education Sector Strategic Program (Cr. 31720)." Supervision Mission, Draft Aide Memoire. September 21–October 8. World Bank, Washington, DC.

————. 2003c. *A User's Guide to Poverty and Social Impact Analysis*. Washington, DC: World Bank.

————. 2004. "Mozambique Education Sector Strategic Program (C 31720)." Supervision Mission, Aide Memoire, World Bank, Maputo, Mozambique, November 7–27, 2004.

Wuyts, Marc. 1996. "Foreign Aid, Structural Adjustment, and Public Management: The Mozambican Experience." *Development and Change* 27 (4): 717–49.

CHAPTER 7

Decentralized District Planning and Finance in One Mozambican Province

The colonial legacy and the post-independence socialist experience left Mozambique with a heavily centralized and under-resourced administration and a poorly educated, inexperienced, poorly paid, and unmotivated workforce. More recently, its economy has been largely donor driven in terms of priorities and macroeconomic policies. Centralized planning still operates at the national and provincial levels, but it is poorly defined and coordinated.

The weakness of the state administration is more acute at the district and "administrative post" (subdistrict) levels. At these levels, central government policies are implemented mainly by line ministries, which are deconcentrated and have little influence over budget allocations. The practice of sector-specific budgeting, combined with the separation of planning and budgeting, often results in selection of projects that fit individual ministries' priorities, but undermines coordinated district development planning.

Until recently, planning has been almost nonexistent at the district and subdistrict levels, where staff lack planning skills. In many cases, no specific department has been responsible for project planning, appraisal, and

---

This chapter was written by Fidelx Pius Ku(i)ossa and James Manor.[1]

implementation; no system for updating information about development problems existed. When central government institutions, foreign donors, and NGOs have encouraged local-level planning, they have tended to bypass districts and subdistricts or to involve those districts in meaningless exercises. As a result, absolute poverty, social exclusion, and entrenched social tensions have gone unaddressed in rural areas. Communities have had little help with basic needs, little voice in district affairs, and little access to institutions that allocate services and goods, all of which has undermined their capacity to sustain their livelihoods.

Government institutions and actors at the district and subdistrict levels have thus been largely unaccountable and lacking in legitimacy. They depend heavily on grants and investments from the central government and donor agencies for service delivery and their own institutional sustainability. Their limited statutory powers leave them with limited resources from inelastic tax revenues, and these modest revenues are sometimes siphoned off by dubious means.

To address these problems, between 1998 and 2001, the United Nations Capital Development Fund (UNCDF) and the United Nations Development Programme (UNDP) created a pilot project of decentralized district planning and financing in Nampula Province. The project sought to restore the essential small-scale socioeconomic infrastructure through a district development fund; to strengthen the capacity of provincial and district administrations and of communities to plan, finance, implement, and monitor small-scale rural infrastructure; and to promote popular participation in district planning processes. Its long-term objectives were to achieve sustainable planning and financing of local development programs, to improve local governance, to promote socioeconomic development and poverty reduction in selected rural districts, and to generate insights to inform the national debate on decentralization and democratization.

This study examines the extent to which the UNCDF–supported Decentralized District Planning and Financing Project in Nampula Province fulfilled its intended objectives and to determine whether the project is replicable in other provinces, whether it exerted influence on national policy, and whether it can be considered a source of insight on best practice.

This chapter examines the project's impact on poverty reduction and its implications for gender, growth, natural resource sustainability, and improved governance. It analyzes the project's design and implementation processes. It then considers key assumptions underlying reform policies, questions of domestic ownership, scaling up of successful development interventions, donor coordination, and project's sustainability and appropriateness. It also assesses how implementing institutions (including civil society and local institutions) mediate the impacts of development projects; the institutions' capacity, incentive structures, and performance; the various project components; the complex relationships and processes within and between those institutions; the main impact transmission channels; the main stakeholders involved in policy design and implementation, their stated interests, and their degree of influence; and the project's impact on stakeholders. All of these aspects shed light on the factors that contribute to the success of the project.

Design of This Study

The design was predicated on the assumption that the reduction of absolute poverty and inequality in societies is the raison d'être of development, as captured by the Millennium Development Goals (MDG). Hence, any decentralized planning and financing project must be geared to meeting the needs of the poor and securing their livelihoods. On the basis of this rationale, the study assesses the impact of the project on stakeholders, using eight criteria:

- principal project objectives
- principal sectors or activities from which outputs accrued
- principal methods used by the project to operationalize interventions
- types of projects and activities: mass oriented or elite oriented, development oriented or public infrastructure oriented, and labor intensive or capital intensive
- concentration (or not) on pro-poor priority areas
- principal beneficiaries of the project
- location of projects or activities and intended beneficiaries (rural versus urban)
- types of impacts (direct or indirect, short or long term), degree of access and use of services and public infrastructure by intended beneficiaries, and other results

These criteria are commonly held to be relevant in assessing the design, implementation, and results of decentralized planning and finance projects (Koehn 1989; Conyers and Hills 1984; Chambers 1978).

Project Description

The current project in Nampula Province is a continuation and refine-ment of the 1998–2001 pilot exercise run by UNCDF and UNDP.[2] It was originally intended for 9 districts, but has evolved to cover 14 of the 18 districts in Nampula.

The project has both immediate and long-term objectives. To reach those objectives, the project was designed in a nonprescriptive way. It consisted of a donor-supported district development fund to transfer investment resources to district administrations for small-scale infra-structure, piloting participatory planning processes, and production of manuals and implementation of training programs to build capacity for participatory forms of decentralized planning at the provincial and district levels.

A mid-term evaluation of the project in 2000 revealed considerable progress toward the immediate objectives and outputs and toward pos-itive contributions to long-term goals (UWC and UEM 2000). The evaluation strongly recommended continuation of the project beyond its termination date of June 2001 to ensure its consolidation, embed-dedness, and outreach. It could thus be a model of best practice for other provinces and for national policy. The evaluation urged donors to continue financial and technical support for five years and to link it to development of sustainability and exit strategy and targets (UWC and UEM 2000). In response, UNCDF/UNDP and the Dutch and Norwegian governments funded the project until 2006. UNCDF/UNDP and the World Bank have been working out strategies for replicating the project in a National Program on Decentralized Planning and Finance (NPDPF) (World Bank 2003a).

The current phase of the project consists of three related components: consolidation of the Nampula project and extension to all districts in the province, flexible replication of the project in selected districts of Cabo Delgado Province, and provision of direct technical assistance to the NPDPF.[3] The immediate objective is to improve access by rural communities—especially those most marginalized—to basic infrastructure and public services through sustainable and replicable forms of decentralized participatory planning, financing, and capacity building at the district level. The project's long-term objective is to promote socioeconomic development and poverty reduction through improved governance (UNCDF 2002).

This long-term objective entails six main activities: (a) effective insti-tutionalization of community participation, with special attention to

Table 7.1 Project Budget and Funding Sources

Funding institution	Thousands of dollars
UNCDF/UNDP	7,633
Royal Government of the Netherlands	4,250
Royal Government of Norway	3,500
Government of Mozambique (in kind)	45
Total	**15,429**

Source: UNCDF 2002.

gender mainstreaming; (b) annual production of district economic and social plans and "shadow budgets"; (c) local financing, with an emphasis on improving the collection and recording of district revenues; (d) capacity building for budgeting and financial management; (e) improvement of provincial coordination of the district planning process; and (f) promotion of local economic development (M&E Consultancy 2003).

Donors have mobilized $15.4 million to implement these activities (table 7.1).

Evaluations of this second phase have identified some positive policy changes: increased dialogue on decentralization at the national, provincial, and district levels; progress in piloting the project in Nampula; the government's endorsement of the Nampula model as a national model for district planning and financing; and influence on national legislation (UWC and UEM 2000; Serrano 2002; ECIAfrica 2003; World Bank 2003a).

Methods and Sources

This study began with a desk review of government policy documents, working papers, independent evaluations, and project reports and studies that provided rigorous and balanced coverage of the project's performance and up-to-date, accurate, and relevant evidence. On the basis of these criteria, four independent evaluations/reports were selected and used extensively: ECIAfrica (2003), Serrano (2002), UWC and UEM (2000), and M&E Consultancy (2003). The four reports were selected in part because they are relevant to debates over development results, design considerations, and implementation processes.[3]

The analysis focuses on the main stakeholders and their interests, their degree of influence, and the extent of government ownership of the project. It aims to assess the project's impact on various stakeholders, to understand how impacts are channeled, and to determine the most appropriate methods for analyzing the distributional consequences of the project. The study also examines the degree of access and use of public infrastructure by intended beneficiaries, factors influencing access, nature of benefits from improved access, unintended negative impacts, and extent of satisfaction of local people with services and infrastructure. Finally, it seeks to understand how institutions affect outcomes by examining roles, knowledge, and access to information; incentive structures; receptivity to policy change; capacity, resources, and financial clout; and scope for adapting to the new reform agenda (World Bank 2002a, 2003b; Taylor 2001; Baker 2000; Morris, Fitz-Gibbon, and Freeman 1987).

Project Design

The design was based on an analysis of the nature of the Mozambican state and its underlying governability problems: overcentralization of political and economic power, and weaknesses in districts and administrative posts (lack of skilled human resources, financial resources, basic social and physical infrastructure, accountability, and legitimacy, as well as severe institutional, administrative, and managerial problems). It was also informed by an analysis of donors—specifically, their creation of parallel structures and negotiation of projects with line ministries without adequate coordination with other donor agencies, their reluctance to integrate their resources into the government planning and budgeting process, and their preference for sectoral financing.

The UNCDF embarked on decentralized district planning and financing in recognition of the following:

- Districts are sociopolitical units that are functionally related to provincial and national levels and that can pursue centrally defined development objectives.
- Decentralized planning and financing strengthens the capacity and competence of district institutions by making them more effective, open, and responsive.
- Such planning and financing provides an opportunity for redefinition of the role of the central government, provincial governments, and district governments, as well as the division of labor among them.
- District plans can promote and coordinate development objectives, thus reducing absolute poverty and improving food security.
- Creation of these plans can lead to more open, democratic, and responsive district governments if they require the participation of and dialogue with local citizens.

On the basis of these considerations, the design of the UNCDF project emphasized

- poverty reduction, local socioeconomic development, and improved access to basic public infrastructure and services
- use of the Provincial Directorate of Planning and Finance in Nampula to implement the project, to address the problems of capacity building and skilled staffing at provincial and district levels, and to disburse project funds, as well as to keep other project donors from setting up parallel implementation structures and bypassing the government
- coordination of external financing with the government's budget cycle and simplification of donor procedures to facilitate scaling up
- enhancement of district revenue collection, recording, and retention as a move toward the sustainability of the planning and financing processes
- flexibility in confronting implementation challenges
- promotion of effective forms of gender mainstreaming in planning processes
- creation of consultative councils to address the legitimacy and accountability deficits of districts and administrative posts
- anchorage of district decentralized planning and financing in the national statutory and regulatory framework and use of this planning and financing to inform broader national policy with respect to decentralization
- strengthening of the Mozambican government's ownership of the project by replacing expatriate staff with the trained Mozambican staff
- use of other agencies' best practices of decentralized planning and financing in Nampula and coordination with other donors working in Mozambique

Project Implementation Processes

The UNCDF created a district development fund and tasked district governments with implementing district investment projects on the basis of their budgets. The UNCDF then set up technical teams composed of districts' own local staff, provided technical assistance through provincial staff to these teams, created consultative councils at district and administrative post levels, began the process of resource disbursements, selected construction enterprises through competitive tendering, collaborated with the Provincial Directorate for Public Works and Housing for choosing suppliers for construction works, and introduced independent supervisors to monitor and evaluate these works.

The project has been implemented through government institutions at provincial and district levels to ensure the project's success and long-term sustainability and is designed to strengthen the efficiency, accountability, and transparency of these institutions. According to Fozzard (2002a), all budget lines are executed nationally and are drawn from a local currency account held in Nampula. Payments cover the functioning of the program unit in the Provincial Directorate for Planning and Finance, salaries for locally hired technical assistance, and costs of provincial government staff travel and subsistence. Payments for international technical assistance and equipment are made directly by UNCDF headquarters in New York. Thus both national and UN procedures for financial management are followed. Provincial staff are always involved in the budgeting, day-to-day management of, and accounting for, the project's operational funds and bank account. Financial accountability of the project is ensured through biannual external audits. The 2001 external audit concluded that "the financial management system functions adequately and . . . the accounting registers are accurate" (Fozzard 2002a).

Because provincial discretionary funds never exceed 21 percent of the national investment budget (ECIAfrica 2003), the long-term sustainability of the Nampula experiment is in question. However, public officers' satisfaction with the dialogue stimulated by the project at the community level implies that the project's emphasis on a participatory approach and that dialogue's link to fiscal transfers were excellent design choices.

Development Results

Let us begin with a few broad, general findings. Project implementation has promoted the Mozambican government's ownership of the project. In turn, local communities' participation in the project through their consultative councils has strengthened citizens' sense of project ownership. Project implementation has created a link between local communities and district administrations, thus helping local communities to understand the work of district administrations and their own civic responsibilities in a democratic society, and strengthening district administrations' understanding of people's problems and needs at the local level. The overall result is improved local governance.

To understand this result fully, we must consider the results in more detail. This study uses two main concepts to assess the project's development results: sustainable livelihoods and capital assets. Livelihoods are defined as a set of "capabilities, assets (including both material and social resources), and activities required for a means of living" (Cox, Farrington, and Gilling 1998, 2). A livelihood is sustainable when it can "cope with and recover from stresses and shocks, and maintain or enhance its capabilities and assets, both now and in the future, while not undermining the natural resource base" (Cox, Farrington, and Gilling 1998, 2). Capital assets include natural resources, human resources, on- and off-farm resources, community-owned resources, and social and political capital. From this standpoint, poverty can be understood in terms of capital assets, because they determine "the capabilities and the range of escape strategies from poverty open to individual or household, along with other "conditioning factors" (Cox, Farrington, and Gilling 1998, 3). This multidimensional vision of poverty allows the use of multiple indicators and different interventions to tackle different dimensions of poverty. It also affects the way progress toward reducing poverty is assessed (White 1999).

The mechanisms that are currently used to reduce poverty fall into three broad categories:

- enabling actions that underpin policies for poverty reduction and lead to social, environmental, or economic benefits for poor people
- inclusive actions, such as sector programs, that aim to benefit various groups and address issues of equity and barriers to participation or access by poor people
- actions focused predominantly on the rights, interests, and needs of poor people (Cox, Farrington, and Gilling 1998, 9–10)

These crosscutting mechanisms establish direct or indirect relationships between poverty reduction concerns and governance issues at national and local levels. They can thus be used to assess results.

Poverty Reduction Assessment, including Gender Implications

If poverty is considered along these two dimensions, the results achieved to date are reasonably positive. From the outset the project focused on education, health, infrastructure, good local governance, financial management, agriculture, transport, and communication. These areas were stressed because they are commonly held to be priority areas, they are oriented toward the masses and the poor, and they focus on development and infrastructure. They are also consistent with Mozambique's Poverty Reduction Strategy Paper, which focuses on enhanced expenditure programs (education, health, road construction or rehabilitation); institutional reforms (devolution and deconcentration and public sector reforms); and structural reforms (efficient financial management and land reform). The project has had an impact through three main transmission channels: employment (agricultural labor), improved access to public infrastructure (improved roads and markets), and assets—both human (education and health) and social (community participation).

One case study was selected for detailed analysis, because carrying out such an analysis of case studies of all 18 districts of Nampula Province would be impossible. An especially useful case study of Mecuburi District (ECIAfrica 2003) was selected, because the district is fairly typical and very rural, because the long life-span of the project there allows a full assessment of its impact, and because that report's findings are consistent with several other studies, including Weimer, Cabral, and Jackson (2004); UWC and UEM (2000); Serrano (2002); and Fozzard (2002a). The study is based on interviews with 200 people (86 percent of them men) and 30 focus groups. It examined factors that influence access to services and infrastructure; the nature of benefits from improved access, including unintended negative impacts; and local residents' satisfaction with three local development projects—the market at Namina, the rehabilitation of the Namina-Mecuburi road, and the primary school at Inchua. Because these infrastructure projects were supposed to be delivered through participatory processes, the assessment focused on participatory planning.

Results of the Survey on Participation in Planning Processes

Local residents' perceptions of planning processes—who makes decisions about infrastructure improvement, who is invited to take part in local meetings, whether invitees are appointed or elected—varied significantly. Eighteen percent of respondents stated that decisions were made by head or traditional authorities; 55 percent said that they were made by district or central government officials. Fifty-one percent said that those officials decided who would be permitted to attend meetings, while only 1 percent said that local people did so. Eighty-seven percent of respondents said that household representatives had been invited to attend meetings. The frequency of meetings ranges from once a week to once a year, but most respondents indicated that they took place every three to four months. Generally, respondents indicated that planning meetings yield positive outcomes, including "better local infrastructure" and significant improvement in the lives of children. Only 12 percent of respondents had negative perceptions of planning meetings. Most expressed satisfaction with their participation, because it enhanced their social relationships and networks (improved communication, better relationships, extended collaboration between families, or closeness between people) and improved their quality of life through access to new infrastructure (ECIAfrica 2003).

In certain cases, however, participation by local residents was very limited. Fully 95 percent of respondents said that they were not involved in decisions about a new market in Namina, and 72 percent said that they did not participate in decisions about school improvements in Inchua. Yet more than 90 percent of respondents were satisfied with these projects. Those who were excluded from decision making, and even those who were excluded from benefits still welcomed the projects, because they offered some hope of future benefits.

Use of Local Infrastructure Projects. The Mecuburi District case study assessed use of and satisfaction with infrastructure projects by examining responses by various categories of respondents ("rich," "not-so-poor," "poor," and "very poor"), as defined by the respondents, as well as by age and gender. The picture that emerges is one of considerable diversity.

The study found that improvements in roads have benefited mainly the "rich," government officials, and traders, because only they had means of transportation. Eighty-eight percent of respondents stated that they did not make use of a single improved road. The absence of public transportation prevents the "poor" from benefiting, except in their use of roads to search for work in rich people's homes. Road improvements may eventually benefit them directly if adequate public transportation is provided. They may already enjoy some indirect benefits from a surge in the informal sector that is occurring as a result of some road improvements. In terms of gender and age, young people (both women and men) are the major beneficiaries, because they are the ones "who go searching for goods and services to provide for the family"; the elderly (both women and men) gain least.

Although access to education is viewed as crucial to the poor, improvement of school buildings has not benefited them, because user fees keep poor children from attending schools. The "rich" and "not-so-poor" benefit more. "Very poor" (and possibly "poor") households need to be given free education or government subsidies if they are to gain access to improved schools.

The pattern of market use resembles that of schools. "Rich" households are the greatest beneficiaries, because they are able to purchase stalls in improved markets and goods from them. The "poor" rarely make use of them, and the "very poor" have no access. The nonpoor of all age groups and both genders, especially the young, make use of markets. Improved markets enhance local revenues through fees. District authorities now depend on such revenues.

Health facilities are widely used by all groups except the "very poor," who cannot pay for services or purchase medicines. The "poor" often have to queue for hours for treatment. The "not-so-poor" are better able to pay and thus spend less time waiting. Despite the exclusion of the "very poor," health facilities were viewed as having the greatest pro-poor impact.

Water is considered the most accessible infrastructure provision for all social groups, but the "rich" benefit most, because they have access to water inside their homes and use water most. The "not-so-poor" and the "poor" buy water from wealthier families. The "very poor" have access only to poor-quality traditional sources, because they cannot afford to purchase water. Nevertheless, improvements in water infrastructure were viewed as pro-poor.

Access to and Impact of Local Infrastructure Projects. An assessment of the new market at Namina, the rehabilitation of the road between Namina and Mecuburi, and the new primary school at Inchua reveals many positive outcomes. It also indicates the need for greater local involvement in all phases of such projects.

Construction of the Market at Namina. The new market at Namina has brought about some positive outcomes, but it falls short in terms of local people's involvement in the decision-making process and planning: 95 percent of households report not having been involved. However, the new market has improved working conditions for most users, especially with regard to good hygiene. Previously, products such as fish and meat were sold in the open air, where fly infestation was a problem. In the new market, all products are protected from flies. Informal trade has also increased as a result of the market's construction. The increase in self-employment and informal sector activities can help reduce poverty.

Local communities now have access to almost all basic goods and services, which can be purchased at relatively low prices. Satisfaction with the market is very high: 93 percent of survey respondents report being "very satisfied" or "satisfied" with the market, 88 percent of households report that the quality of life had improved, and 97 percent report that they expect the market to have positive long-term impacts. The market will stimulate local taxation through market fees, which will enable district authorities to provide some welfare-improving services to local communities.

It is worth noting that opportunities now exist for local communities to make suggestions to improve the projects discussed here—and that for them, those opportunities represent a major improvement in governance over the former system in which they had no input. They have made useful suggestions for improving market operations. These suggestions include rotating allocation of and payment for stalls on a daily basis to give access to all traders, creating a cleaning association to provide employment for the poorest, enlarging the market to accommodate more traders, restructuring the market according to the type of products being sold, and establishing new contractual arrangements for renting market stalls.

Rehabilitation of the Namina-Mecuburi Road. The boom in informal trade in Namina can, to some extent, be attributed to the improvement of the Namina-Mecuburi road. Informal traders can now move more easily from Namina to various places in search of tradable goods and services. Dissatisfaction with this infrastructure is high, however; women are much more dissatisfied than men. Men welcomed the rehabilitation of the road, because it reduced the distance between Namina and Mecuburi, but they are concerned about the road's unevenness, which causes frequent accidents. Eighty-eight percent of respondents stated that they do not use the road, although 97 percent said that the improvement made reaching their destinations easier, should they ever use it.

Rehabilitation of the road does not appear to have improved the welfare of the poor. Use of the road is confined to short-distance travel on foot or bicycle. The short-term beneficiaries of road construction are better-off households, traders, and government officials who possess motorized vehicles. If accompanied by other investments (especially in public transport), road rehabilitation is likely to have a long-term impact on the life of local communities. The short-term impact has been minimal, however.

Local communities have made useful suggestions for increasing the short-term impacts on poor people. These suggestions include having the public or private sector create a public transportation system along the Namina-Mecubri, thus maximizing the use of the local labor force in road rehabilitation works, and ensuring effective rehabilitation and maintenance of the road.

Construction of the Primary School at Inchua. Parents, students, and teachers have welcomed construction of this primary school, because it saves time for parents and improves working and learning conditions for teachers and students. Sixty-nine percent of respondents are "very satisfied," 26 percent are "satisfied," and only 5 percent are "dissatisfied." Eighty-six percent of households believe that the quality of their life has improved as a direct result of the building of the school. Satisfaction was high, despite the fact that only 28 percent of households reported having been involved in the project. Women expressed their dissatisfaction with the neglect of complementary services, such as water, which are crucial to making the school work well. They noted that students have to go to the river to get water during school hours. This problem would not have arisen if local communities had been more fully involved in all phases of the project.

Suggestions by local residents for improving school operations included using local rather than nonlocal labor (carpenters, masons, and mechanics), involving the local community in all project phases, providing water at the school, setting up a first aid center at the school, rehabilitating the wooden bridges over the Catamasi River, and building additional classrooms.

Human and Institutional Capacity Building in Provincial and District Administrations

To increase the management skills and competency of district and provincial staff, the decentralized district planning and financing project set up technical teams at provincial and district levels. Provincial teams are responsible for supporting district technical teams, which mobilize local communities and district consultative council representatives for planning meetings. Provincial and district technical teams are composed of officials from specific sectors. The multidisciplinary nature of their skills makes it possible for experience, knowledge, and information about participatory district planning to be channeled back to these sectors and integrated into their development policies and strategies. It also promotes collaboration between sectors.

Headway has been made in building human and institutional capacity at the provincial and district levels. Innovations have occurred in community participation, district planning and financing, elaboration of instruction manuals, and commissioning of studies on difficult problems specific to certain sectors. These innovations were due in part to the actions of donors that have been implementing similar projects in Nampula Province. In one region, for example, NGOs and donors have been training local communities in lobbying, collective action, and other skills. The ECIAfrica study notes the following outcomes of participatory planning in the province:

- It creates opportunities for dialogue among district governments, local communities, and civil society organizations.
- It allows local communities to influence decision-making processes affecting their lives.
- It allows local communities to identify their development priorities and ways of overcoming their problems.
- It raises the awareness of provincial and district authorities and local communities about the relevance of participatory planning.
- It makes local governance more transparent, responsive, democratic, and open.
- It allows donor-funded projects to be incorporated into overall district development plans and development activities by public, private, and third-sector actors and to take into account the functional and spatial complementarities of local economies and development interventions, thus increasing the overall efficiency and effectiveness of resource allocation in some districts.
- It allows district development plans to be integrated on the basis of one framework. Districts are gradually introducing the four elements of a comprehensive district development plan emphasized by some researchers: base-line planning data, project planning at the district level, integrated district development planning, and strategic development planning (Kulipossa 2003).
- It permits district governments to collect information about local communities' needs and to organize dialogue with communities through district consultative councils.

The sustainability of participatory planning is a major concern for local authorities, for several reasons. First, the costs of implementing the project are covered by UNCDF, raising the question of who will cover these costs when UNCDF funds dry up. Second, because of their ad hoc character, provincial and district technical teams are vulnerable to turnover, which leads to loss of expertise; the costs of technical teams are not budgeted in the provincial budget. Third, a close relationship between community participation in the planning process and the improvement of people's living conditions is needed. The process is likely to fail in the absence of sufficient resources. Fourth, communities view district consultative councils, CCPAs (Administrative Posts Consultative Councils), and municipal assemblies as miniature local parliaments. But members of municipal assemblies are entitled to attendance allowances, while district consultative council and CCPA representatives are not. These representatives may eventually demand allowances.

Community participation in district planning must be sustained by some material incentives. Mozambique's high dependence on foreign aid undermines the recommendation that the government provide contributions to participatory institutions. Any donor-funded project or program in Mozambique must help the central government and district governments build public revenue systems to enable them to tax their citizens more effectively and fairly.

Impact on Growth and Natural Resource Sustainability

The effect of the project on economic growth is difficult to determine, because no reliable figures on recent growth in the district or provincial economy are available. The evidence presented earlier suggests that growth resulting from the infrastructure project may largely benefit non-poor groups and may not gather momentum unless other changes with economic and social multiplier effects (such as the introduction of public transportation) occur.

The project failed to take stock of environmental sustainability issues. ECIAfrica's assessment reported problems with natural resource use and management; use of firewood and charcoal gathered from the natural forest and bush contributed to deforestation. The project should, therefore, undertake a thorough environment assessment.

Political Impact and Contribution to Improved Governance

The project's contribution to improved governance and its wider political impact in Mozambique must be analyzed at the district, provincial, and national levels.

District Level. Despite some limitations, the project's impact on governance has been substantial and constructive in terms of building capacity, promoting participatory mechanisms, and changing attitudes. Training and capacity-building efforts have enabled district governments to make effective use of three planning tools: District Development Plans (DDPs), portfolios, and district economic and social plans, as demanded by the national planning program. These governments have also been involved in budgeting for and implementing district economic and social plans, thereby demonstrating to themselves, to higher authorities, and to ordinary people that they can plan and manage local development in a somewhat participatory manner.

The project has changed attitudes in two crucial ways. First, district staff now recognize that the public sector can and should be more open and responsive. This recognition helps them in consulting with citizens on development strategies and plans, in negotiating funding with donors, and in coordinating and responding to the activities of stakeholders in the implementation of strategies. Second, these changes plus the establishment of consultative councils at the district- and administrative-post levels have enhanced the legitimacy of district-level institutions in the eyes of citizens.

In addition, the project has promoted coordination among various line ministry representatives at the district level. Higher-level officials in the various ministries recognized that such coordination improved development outcomes and began pursuing it in all districts—in consultation with people's representatives. As a result, multisector plans that were forged consultatively in the districts are no longer contradicted by the uncoordinated activities of individual line ministries. This is a fundamental change, for the better, in the way that the public sector works in Mozambique.

Weaknesses remain, however. Consultative councils need to be strengthened and their composition broadened. District plans have not been fully integrated into the general planning and financing process, and opponents use weaknesses in provincial plans as an excuse to disregard them. Activities funded by the district development fund have not been defined on the basis of poor people's concerns, as expressed in the consultative councils. These problems notwithstanding, the change from the heavily centralized, unresponsive system has been remarkable.

Provincial Level. The project contributed to the training and strengthening of provincial staff in decentralized planning, in strategic and participatory planning, and in public accounting. However, the provincial resource base has not been broadened sufficiently to guarantee the sustainability and continuation of the program once UNCDF funds dry up.

National Level. The short-term impacts of the project—improving infrastructure, strengthening public institutions, and promoting good governance—have made immense contributions at the national level. They have persuaded new donors to extend the experiment to other provinces. And crucially, they have persuaded powerful officials at the national level that more open, decentralized government can work and can substantially enhance both developmental outcomes and the government's own legitimacy. Evidence from the project was instrumental in enabling the passage of three key laws that are making governance more open, effective, and responsive[3] and in inspiring several other substantial changes that have a similar effect.[4]

Project Scale Up

The project was extended first to all 18 districts within Nampula Province and then to seven additional provinces, including four (Manica, Sofala, Tete, and Zambézia) in which the World Bank is involved.[5] In these provinces, the project has produced similarly constructive outcomes. The government intends to expand it to the whole of Mozambique (Kulipossa 2004b). Before it does, it will have to deal with several constraints to achievements in extension of the project throughout Nampula Province (table 7.2).

Table 7.2 Achievements and Constraints in Expanding the Project in Nampula Province

Achievements	Constraints
All 18 districts in Nampula have an institutionalized participatory planning cycle and a district development plan	Lack of self-sustainability
Elaboration and establishment of systems for register and control of income; transparent financial management system established in some districts; substantial increase in some district governments' income	Lack of qualified personnel, basic financial skills, tax-tracking potential, accountancy, and local public finance skills
Progress in establishing participatory planning process and building capacity in the construction industry	None
Comparatively highly qualified technical teams in areas where participatory planning has taken place; improvements of institutional capacity in some districts	Lack of institutional capacity and sustainability of the participatory planning cycle in some districts
Some gender training; some gender-relevant materials elaborated and distributed to technical teams at provincial and district levels	Absence of explicit gender strategy
Project staff's growing awareness of the need to include local development issues into decentralized planning methodology	Lack of expertise in local economic development and natural resource management; lack of district-municipality integrated planning
Elaboration of guidelines for community participation in district planning and of manuals for district planning and district annual socio-economic plans	Poor dissemination of project's best practices

Source: Authors' interpretation of the main findings from the Mid-Term Evaluation of the program carried out in September and October 2004 (UNCDF/UNDP 2004).

As the Ministry of Health in Malhotra (2004) points out, the main constraint on scaling up development interventions is lack of human and institutional capacity, not lack of financial resources. The implication is that the Nampula Project needs to incorporate technical assistance; capacity building of staff; dissemination of lessons; and competition to promote adaptation, innovation, and better service delivery. Moreover, as the project expands nationwide, it must address the wider problems of fragile institutional and legal frameworks, dubious political will to undertake comprehensive public sector reforms (especially for democratic decentralization and local economic development), and lack of capacity within district administrations and administrative posts (Weimer 2004). Unless these problems are tackled, the prospects for obtaining sustained payoffs will be severely diminished.

Donor Coordination in Project Implementation
UNDCF coordinated project implementation with the Swiss Agency for Development and Cooperation, CONCERN, Care International, SNV (Dutch Development Agency), and other donors. The donors' cooperation is manifested in cofinancing, cross-fertilization of decentralized planning and financing experiences within Nampula Province, learning from the successes and failures of previous projects, and agreement on the most appropriate ways to engage with the Mozambican government.

Lessons for Development Interventions in LICUS

In many respects, the UNCDF–supported Decentralized District Planning and Financing Project in Nampula Province represents best practice with respect to fostering constructive forms of democratic governance. In this and other regards, the project suggests several lessons for development interventions in low-income countries under stress (LICUS).

In general, the project suggests the efficacy of designing interventions on the bases of strong analyses of local dynamics and of implementing them in a learning-by-doing approach.

More specifically, the project in Nampula confirms that aid can achieve positive results within a poor governance environment when it works through government institutions. The UNCDF provided funds, technical assistance, and capacity building (which improved working conditions for government officials, raising their morale and engendering confidence in the project), but it was not responsible for implementing the project. As project implementer, the government gained project ownership. The project's positive results persuaded the government to scale up the project (which persuaded donors to provide additional external financial support) and to embody decentralized planning in new laws that fundamentally reorient its approach to development.

Notes

1. We are grateful to Anselmo Zimba, Bernhard Weimer, and Miguel de Brito in Mozambique for providing us the relevant literature and information on DDPFP in Nampula Province and to Kathryn Casson and David Potten in Washington, DC for critical and constructive comments on the first draft of this study.

2. The mid-term evaluation mission by the University of the Western Cape (UWC) and Eduardo Mondlane University states, "MOZ/98/C01 represents much more than a continuation and extension of the earlier UNCDF project. Its aims, rationale, and scope and activities were quite different in a number of important respects. This reflected changed country conditions, the Mozambican government's commitment to experimenting with district-level planning, new UNCDF policy orientations with respect to participation and monitoring and evaluation, and the substantial financial participation of the Dutch government, which, as the province's largest bilateral donor, has long supported a range of developmental programs and initiatives in Nampula. There was also a need to change the project leadership to acquire the necessary technical profile" (UWC and UEM 2000, 24). The project has as its core objectives the training and capacity building of district governments and local communities in identifying, planning, and evaluating projects for the rehabilitation of social infrastructure; the setting up of a local development fund for decentralized investments in social infrastructure at the district level; and the introduction of more effective local planning processes that are based on popular participation, with the aim of increasing the long-term sustainability of such investments. In 1998, the Ministry of Planning and Finance and the Ministry of State Administration approved the Guidelines for District Development Planning. Shortly thereafter, the province of Nampula began piloting the district decentralized planning and financing program, with the aim of promoting more effective district development planning and community participation by deconcentrating administrative and financial responsibilities to the district level and by establishing a district development fund (Ministry of Planning and Finance 1998). As part of their development objectives, UNCDF and the Dutch government have been providing budget support to the provincial capital investment budget to enable direct fiscal transfers to the district level, as well as technical assistance for capacity building and the creation of conditions for the permanent continuation of such transfers (UWC and UEM 2000).

3. This phase of the project is co-funded by the Dutch government (in Nampula), the Norwegian government (in Cabo Delgado), and the government of Mozambique. In Cabo Delgado Province, the project will have a phased approach and will focus on five areas: development of long-term strategic and multisectoral district development plans and planning processes; establishment of criteria and methodologies for the efficient allocation, programming, and disbursement of Local Development Fund/District Development Fund funds through the annual project cycle; promotion of community dialogue and participation in the district planning processes, in particular through the establishment of consultative councils at the district and subdistrict levels; provision of a strong capacity-building element (for provincial and district technicians, communities, and small-scale contractors) that runs through all of these processes; and generation of lessons and best practices to inform policy debates and initiatives on decentralization at the national level (M&E Consultancy 2003). The differences in the configuration of technical assistance and the institutional arrangements in Cabo Delgado reflect the need to apply the Nampula model in a creative and critical way, adjusting it to local contexts.

   These laws are Law 9/2002 on the State Financial Administration System (SISTAFE); Law 8/2003 on Local State Bodies (LOLE), which enshrines district planning and investment financing nationwide; and the 2003 Guidelines for Community Participation. Evidence from Nampula also facilitated creation of the National Steering Committee to develop the National Strategy for a Decentralized Planning and Finance Program.

4. The project has also contributed to institutionalization of transparent and efficient financial and public expenditure management at the national level. It has helped to inspire other public sector reforms such as analyses of all ministries's functions, implementation of the national system of training in public administration (SIFAP), approval of a comprehensive national anticorruption strategy, establishment of anticorruption units in the Attorney General's Office, ongoing national research on public perceptions on corruption, and adoption of a national strategy for promoting good governance and combating corruption.

5. Replication is also under way in Niassa Province with support from the German and Irish embassies; in Manica Province with support from an Irish NGO (CONCERN); and in Cabo Delgado Province with UNCDF, Norwegian, and Mozambican government support.

Bibliography

Baker, Judy L. 2000. *Evaluating the Impact of Development Projects on Poverty: A Handbook for Practitioners.* Washington, DC: World Bank.

Chambers, Robert. 1978. "Project Selection for Poverty-Focused Rural Development: Simple Is Optimal." *World Development* 6 (2): 209–19.

Conyers, Diana, and P. Hills. 1984. *An Introduction of Development Planning in the Third World*. New York: John Wiley and Sons.

Cox, Aidan, John Farrington, and Jim Gilling. 1998. "Developing a Framework to Assess the Poverty Impact of NR Research." Final Report. Overseas Development Institute, London.

Devereux, Stephen, and Alessandro Palmero. 1999. "Creating a Framework for Reducing Poverty: Institutional and Process Issues in National Poverty Policy. Mozambique Country Report." Institute of Development Studies, Brighton, United Kingdom.

ECIAfrica Consulting International. 2003. "Companion Report: Mozambique. Independent Program Impact Assessment (PIA) of the UNCDF Local Development Program." Woodmead, South Africa.

Fozzard, Adrian. 2002a. "Mozambique Decentralized Planning and Financing Program: Financing Flows and Financial Management Systems for Provincial and District Administrations." Overseas Development Institute, London.

———. 2002b. "How, When, and Why Does Poverty Get Budget Priority? Poverty Reduction Strategy and Public Expenditure in Mozambique." Working Paper 167, Overseas Development Institute, London.

Government of Mozambique. 2001. "Action Plan for the Reduction of Absolute Poverty (2001–2005) (PARPA): Strategy Document for the Reduction of Poverty and Promotion of Economic Growth." Maputo.

———. 2003. "Country Paper: Mozambique." Paper prepared for the Fifth Africa Governance Forum, Maputo, May 23–25.

Grindle, Merilee S., and John W. Thomas. 1991. *Public Choices and Policy Changes: The Political Economy of Reform in Developing Countries*. Baltimore, MD: Johns Hopkins University Press.

Hanlon, Joseph. 1991. *Mozambique: Who Calls the Shots?* London: James Currey.

———. 1996. *Peace Without Profit: How the IMF Blocks Rebuilding in Mozambique*. Oxford: James Currey.

Holmes, M., S. Knack, N. Manning, R. Messick, and J. Rinne. 2000. "Governance and Poverty Reduction." http://www.worldbank.org/publicsector/toolkits.htm.

Hulme, David, Karen Moore, and Andrew Shepherd. 2001. "Chronic Poverty: Meanings and Analytical Frameworks." CPRC Working Paper 1, IDPM, Manchester, UK.

IDS (Institute of Development Studies). 1998. "Participatory Monitoring and Evaluation: Learning from Change." Policy Briefing 12, Brighton, UK.

———. 2000. "Poverty Reduction Strategies: A Part for the Poor?" Policy Briefing 13, Brighton, UK.

————. 2001. "The New Dynamics of Aid: Power, Procedures and Relationships." Policy Briefing 15, Brighton, UK.

International Monetary Fund (IMF). 2003. "Republic of Mozambique: Poverty Reduction Strategy Paper." IMF Country Report No. 03/98, Washington, DC. www.imf.org/external/pubs.

Kabeer, Naila. 2003. *Gender Mainstreaming in Poverty Eradication and the Millennium Development Goals: A Handbook for Policy-Makers and Other Stakeholders*. London: Commonwealth Secretariat.

Kent, George. 1981. "Community-Based Development Planning." *Third World Planning Review* 3 (3): 313–26.

Koehn, Peter. 1989. "Local Government Involvement in National Development Planning: Guidelines for Project Selection Based Upon Nigeria's Fourth Plan Experience." *Public Administration and Development* 9 (4): 417–36.

Kulipossa, Fidelx Pius. 2003. "Democratic Decentralization and Local Development in Mozambique: Lessons from Vilankulo Municipality." Ph.D. thesis, University of Sussex, Brighton, United Kingdom.

————. 2004a. "Participação Local e Descentralização em Moçambique: Uma Análize do Quadro Legal e Institucional para a sua Promoção e Implementação." Comunicação Apresentada no Workshop dos Gestores de Projectos da Acção Agrária Alemã, 6 de Abril 2004. Maputo, Mozambique.

————. 2004b. "Progress Towards the Implementation of Decentralization Policies in Mozambique: A Progress Summary Written as an Input to the Government-Donor Joint Review of the Public Sector Reform (PSR)." Maputo, April 12.

————. 2004c. "Decentralization and Democracy in Developing Countries: An Overview." *Development in Practice* 14 (6): 768–79.

Malhotra, Mohini. 2004. "Lessons: Scaling Up Successful Efforts to Reduce Poverty." http://www.worldbank.org/reducingpoverty/docs/conceptual.pdf.

M&E Consultancy. 2003. "Decentralized Planning and Financing Program (DPFP): Monitoring and Evaluation." Report for the Ministry of Planning and Finance. Maputo.

Ministry of Planning and Finance (MPF). 1998. "Plano Distrital de Desenvolvimento: Orientações para Elaboração e Implementação." Maputo, Mozambique.

————. 2003a. "Participação e Consulta Communitária na Planificação Distrital: Guião para Organização e Funcionamento." MPF/MAE/MADER, Maputo, Mozambique.

————. 2003b. "Guidelines for Sectoral Coordination of Small-Scale Rural Development." Discussion draft. Maputo, Mozambique.

Morris, Lynn Lyons, Carol Taylor Fitz-Gibbon and Marie E. Freeman. 1987. *How to Communicate Evaluation Findings*. Newbury Park, CA: Sage Publications.

Morrissey, Janice. 2000. "Indicators of Citizen Participation: Lessons from Learning Teams in Rural EZ/EC Communities." *Community Development Journal* 35 (1): 59–74.

Moore, Mick. 2004. "Revenues, State Formation, and the Quality of Governance in Developing Countries." *International Political Science Review* 25 (3): 297–319.

Olowu, Dele, and Soumana Sako, eds. 2003. *Better Governance and Public Policy: Capacity Building for Democratic Renewal in Africa*. Bloomfield, CT: Kumarian Press.

Oxfam. n.d. *Influencing Poverty Reduction Strategies: A Guide*. Oxford: Oxfam UK and Ireland.

Pavignani, Enrico, and Volker Hauck. 2002. "Pooling of Technical Assistance in Mozambique: Innovative Practices and Challenges." European Center for Development Policy Management, Maastricht, Netherlands.

Pearse, Andrew, and Mathias Stiefel. 1979. *Inquiry into Participation: A Research Approach*. New York: United Nations Research Institute for Social Development.

Plummer, Jannelle. 2001. *Municipalities and Community Participation: A Sourcebook for Capacity Building*. London: Earthscan Publications.

Randall, Vicky, and Lars Svasand. 2002. "Introduction: The Contribution of Parties to Democracy and Democratic Consolidation." *Democratization* 9 (3): 1–10.

Rasheed, Sadig. 1995. "The Democratization Process and Popular Participation in Africa: Emerging Realties and Challenges Ahead." *Development and Change* 26 (2): 333–54.

Robinson, Mark. 1998. "Democracy, Participation, and Public Policy: The Politics of Institutional Design." In *The Democratic Developmental State: Politics and Institutional Design*, ed. Mark Robinson and Gordon White, 150–86. Oxford, UK: Oxford University Press.

Romeo, Leonardo. 2004. *Decentralized Development Planning: Issues and Early Lessons from UNCDF-Supported Local Development Fund Programs*. New York: United Nations Capital Development Fund. http://www.uncdf.org/english/local_governance/thematic_papers/risks_decentralized_deve.

Serrano, Rodrigo. 2002. "Participation, Transparency, and Downward Accountability in District Planning in Mozambique." Final Report. August 2003. Washington, DC: World Bank. Report prepared as an input for the design of the Decentralized Planning and Finance Project, commissioned by the Water and Urban Group 1, Eastern and Southern Africa, World Bank.

Shepherd, Andrew. 2000. "Governance, Good Government and Poverty Reduction." *International Review of Administrative Sciences* 66 (2): 269–84.

Taylor, Laurence. 2001. "Good Monitoring and Evaluation Practice: Guidance Notes." http://www.parcinfo.org.

Therkildsen, Ole. 2000. "Public Sector Reform in a Poor, Aid-Dependent Country, Tanzania." *Public Administration and Development* 20 (1): 61–71.

UNCDF (United Nations Capital Development Fund). 2002. "Project Formulation Document: Support to Decentralized Planning and Financing in the Provinces of Nampula and Cabo Delgado." Maputo, Mozambique. http://www.uncdf.org/english/local_governance/thematic_papers/risks_dece ntralized_deve.

UNCDF/UNDP (United Nations Development Programme). 2004. "Mid-Term Evaluation of the Program 'Support to Decentralized Planning and Financing in the Provinces of Nampula and Cabo Delgado/Mozambique—PPFD.'" Aide Memoire September 22–October, Maputo, Mozambique.

UNDP (United Nations Development Programme). 1993. *Human Development Report 1993: People's Participation*. New York: Oxford University Press.

———. 2002. *Human Development Report 2002: Deepening Democracy in a Fragmented World*. New York: Oxford University Press.

———. 2003. *Human Development Report 2003. Millennium Development Goals: A Compact among Nations to End Human Poverty*. New York: Oxford University Press.

UWC and UEM (University of the Western Cape and Eduardo Mondlane University). 2000. "Report of the Mid-Term Evaluation Mission June–July 2000: Project of the Government of Mozambique Support to Decentralized Planning and Financing in Nampula Province." Maputo, Mozambique.

Weimer, Bernhard. 2004. "Capacity Building for Participatory District Planning and Financing in Manica Province, Mozambique: Framework, Elements and Options for Concern's Engagement in Participatory District Planning in Manica Province." Final Report. Leloba and Madeira Lda, Maputo, Mozambique.

Weimer, Bernhard, Lidia Cabral, and David Jackson. 2004. *Aid Modalities, Flow of Funds and Partner Structures: Experiences and Recommendations for ASPS II. Final Report*. Maputo, Mozambique: Leloba & Madeira, Lda.

Werlin, Herbert. 1989. "The Community: Master or Client? A Review of the Literature." *Public Administration and Development* 9 (4): 447–57.

White, Howard. 1999. "Global Poverty Reduction: Are We Heading in the Right Direction?" *Journal of International Development* 11(4): 503–19.

World Bank. 2000. "Memorandum of the President of the International Development Association and the International Finance Corporation to the Executive Directors on a Country Assistance Strategy of the World Bank Group for the Republic of Mozambique." World Bank, Washington, DC.

————. 2001. *World Development Report 2000/2001: Attacking Poverty*. New York: Oxford University Press.

————. 2002a. *Monitoring and Evaluation: Some Tools, Methods, and Approaches*. Washington, DC: World Bank.

————. 2002b. *Social Analysis Sourcebook: Incorporating Social Dimensions into Bank-Supported Projects*. Washington, DC: World Bank.

————. 2002c. *Education and Health in Sub-Saharan Africa: A Review of Sectorwide Approaches*. Washington, DC: World Bank.

————. 2003a. "Mozambique Decentralized Planning and Financing Project: Project Appraisal Document." World Bank, Maputo, Mozambique.

————. 2003b. *A User's Guide to Poverty and Social Impact Analysis*. Washington, DC: World Bank.

————. 2004. "Local Development Discussion Paper." Prepared for the International Conference on Local Development, World Bank, Washington, DC, June 16–18. http://www1.worldbank.org/sp/ldconference/background/asp.

Wuyts, Marc. 1996. "Foreign Aid, Structural Adjustment, and Public Management: The Mozambican Experience." *Development and Change* 27 (4): 717–49.

CHAPTER 8

The Community Fora Process in Mazar-e-Sharif, Afghanistan

A network of community-based institutions provides political, social, and economic benefits to people in the city of Mazar-e-Sharif in northern Afghanistan. The community fora (CF) were established through the intervention of UN-Habitat in a process that began in 1995. This process not only continued through turbulent political changes—civil war, the rise and fall of the Taliban, and the establishment of a new transitional government—but also grew and expanded in size, mandate, coverage, and influence. The CF "program"[1] illustrates how development processes can be established, even in extremely difficult circumstances, and can be built on once the political environment becomes more stable.

This chapter was written by Sarah Lister.

I am grateful to those who facilitated this study: Eng Sayed Sawayz in Habitat Mazar and Eng Islamuddin Amaki in the Community Forum Development Organisation. I am also grateful to Samantha Reynolds, former regional program manager of Habitat Mazar, for her comments on a draft and subsequent discussions.

Background and Context

This study of the CF was conducted in September and October 2004. Key informants from CF committees, Habitat, and municipal government in Mazar were interviewed. Attempts were made to interview individuals no longer involved in the program.

Extensive use was made of four key reviews of the program: "Building Trust: An Evolving Approach to Resettlement: Some Lessons from Afghanistan," a 1995 report for the United Nations Development Programme (UNDP) and United Nations Center for Human Settlements (UNCHS); "Origins of the Community Fora Program: Innovative Community Development in Mazar-e-Sharif, Afghanistan, 1995–1998," a 1998 report for UNCHS; "Quantum Leap: A Framework for Peace and Development in Conflict and Postconflict Afghanistan: A Socioeconomic Evaluation of the Community Forum Program," a 2000 report for UNCHS; and "Rebuilding Communities in the Urban Areas of Afghanistan," a paper prepared for the Symposium and Round Table on Operational Activities in June 1999. Interviewees stated that these reviews were accurate in their portrayal and analysis of the process.

Although the CF program was implemented in five cities and two rural areas in Afghanistan, this case study concentrates on the experience of the program in Mazar. Time constraints did not allow for an assessment of the nationwide program, which has not been as well documented. The experience of different cities with the program appears to vary and is referred to in relation to the general applicability of approaches and the possibilities for program expansion.

Historical and Social Context of the CF Program

Throughout Afghanistan's history, centralized state structures have coexisted uneasily with fragmented, decentralized power structures and have resisted rule by outsiders (Evans, Manning, Osmani, Tully, and Wilder 2004). When Russia invaded Afghanistan in 1979, the response was a resistance movement formed of about one million fighters (Mujahideen) in 1,200 units across the country. After 1989, when the Russians finally abandoned Afghanistan, a minority of armed Afghans, estimated at about 50,000, formed militias that vied for political and military control. These militias became associated with the four main ethnic groups in the country (Uzbek, Tajik, Hazara, and Pashtun) and explicitly exploited ethnic divisions to consolidate their own positions.

In 1992, when the Soviet-backed regime of Najibullah collapsed, a coalition of anti-Soviet, Peshawar-based Mujahideen groups took power. However, these groups suffered from weak leadership and factionalism, and the coalition gradually disintegrated into warring factions on ethnic, clan, religious, and personality lines. The state largely ceased to exist, and the economy was ruined. The various Mujahideen parties battled among themselves for control of Kabul, and anarchy reigned in much of the rest of the country. Militia leaders and regional warlords extracted various taxes from local populations, and engaged in numerous forms of extortion, including kidnapping. In 1996, UNDP's *Human Development Report* placed Afghanistan 169th out of 175 in the Human Development Index.

Order was largely restored and authority centralized with the emergence of the Pakistani-backed Pashtun Taliban, who gained control city by city until they captured Kabul in 1996. They imposed strict uncompromising notions of Islam on the country but showed little interest in governing. They appointed relatively few people to the administration, except in the areas of law enforcement and security. Women generally could neither work outside the home nor be educated in formal schools, and in public they had to be covered with the traditional burqa. Nonetheless, the Taliban did bring order of a kind to Afghanistan, putting an end to the violence and chaos brought by factional squabbles. However, poverty and political oppression led to refugee outflows. Formal data on poverty levels from this period are scarce. However, a 1997 UNDP document described the situation in the country thus:

> Afghanistan remains a country in crisis, with its infrastructure and social capital mostly destroyed and its governance systems ruptured. The national economy has been crippled through loss of export earnings, loss of jobs, lack of national economic management and revenue generation capacities. . . . the urban areas have seen widespread destruction of their physical, economic and social infrastructures. This has severely disrupted the delivery of basic services, as well as eroded the capacity of urban residents to cope with the war. It has also had a devastating effect on municipal administration. Urban areas have become the final destination for many internally displaced persons and returnees . . .[2]

The Taliban were ousted in November 2001 by an international military campaign, after the September 11 attacks on New York and Washington by Al-Qaeda.

Following the signing of the Bonn Agreement in December 2001, an interim US-backed administration was established in Afghanistan under

Hamid Karzai. After the Emergency *Loya Jirga* (Grand Council) of June 2002, this administration was replaced by a transitional authority, and Hamid Karzai was appointed president. A new constitution was developed and presidential elections were held in October 2004, followed by National Assembly and provincial council elections in September 2005. Despite some recovery, social indicators are very poor. The estimated rates of infant mortality at 115 per 1,000 live births, and maternal mortality at 1,600 per 100,000 live births are among the highest in the world. Access to clean drinking water and health services is very low. Illiteracy is extremely high; provincial and gender disparities in this area are stark (World Bank 2004).

Mazar-e-Sharif

Mazar-e-Sharif is a city with a population of about 700,000, in Balkh province, 270 kilometers from Kabul and about 90 kilometers from the border with Uzbekistan.[3] Since the 1930s, the town has been the major commercial center for northern Afghanistan, drawing agricultural products and carpets from surrounding provinces and exporting them to Kabul and, from 1979, northward into the former Soviet territories. It was also a major industrial town with fertilizer and textile production.

With the withdrawal of the Soviet army in 1989, Mazar became a stronghold of the various parties that made up the different factional alliances that held Kabul, until it was taken by the Taliban in 1996. During the early and mid-1990s, Mazar was under the shifting control of different Mujahideen alliances and was subject to sporadic fighting and the constant threat of war. There was virtually no relationship with Kabul, and different ministries responded to local rather than national power holders.

In 1997, the Taliban made their first assault on Mazar and, with the help of various alliances, succeeded in entering the city. However, they failed to maintain the support they had negotiated, and an uprising drove them out; a massacre of 2,000–4,000 Taliban soldiers followed. The following year, the Taliban finally took the city and exacted revenge, most notably against the Hazara people. When resistance to the Taliban in Mazar crumbled in August 1998, they imposed their severe interpretation of Islamic law on that city, as had gradually occurred across most of the rest of Afghanistan. Tensions in the city remained high throughout the Taliban period, and some of the fiercest fighting in October 2001 was in and around Mazar.

Since November 2001, the city has been the center of power struggles between two of the northern warlords: General Dostum, an Uzbek, and the provincial governor, Ustad Atta, a Tajik. Skirmishes regularly break out as they fight over control of customs revenues from border crossings, local gas and oil fields, and profits from the fertilizer factory in Mazar.

Development of the Community Fora

Since 1986 the United Nations Center for Human Settlements (UN-Habitat[4]) has been involved in Afghanistan, mainly in sanitation and urban infrastructure projects. Development of the CF marked a shift in Habitat in Afghanistan from a technology-focused infrastructure approach to a community-focused process approach. Changing political circumstances have considerably affected the way the CF have developed and operated.

Phase 1: 1995–98, from Project Inception to the Taliban Takeover in Mazar[5]

The activities that eventually became known as the Community Fora Program began within several sequential UNCHS programs, in particular, the Urban Rehabilitation Program (1995–97) and Rebuilding Communities in Urban Afghanistan (1997 onward).[6] The former had its origins in several other UNCHS programs, in particular, the Housing for Resettlement Program (1991–95), which was viewed primarily as a construction and infrastructure project in which institution-building was a relatively minor component. As one review of it notes: "the culturally appropriate institution-building community development process . . . was mentioned infrequently as a minor element . . . (and) over 90 percent of the text in the project's 1994 document relates to physical aspects of reconstruction" (Tamas 1998, 14–15).

By 1995 a review of the program concentrated entirely on the process and noted Habitat's

> progressive expansion of scope and a steady shift from technology-oriented projects to a process-oriented program. [The Housing for Resettlement program] was crucial in making this transition. While many of the elements in the project document reflect a technology-oriented approach, in its execution it rapidly became focused on the process (Dudley 1995, 16).

This change of focus was partly driven by the international regional program manager (RPM), Samantha Reynolds. On arrival in Mazar in 1995, she began extensive consultations with community leaders, male community members, and municipal officers on technical issues of infrastructure repair.[7] In a symposium paper (Reynolds 1999, 6–7), she identified three interrelated needs:

- The program needed to take an integrated approach to addressing interrelated human settlement issues. Drainage issues were linked to solid waste systems, which were linked to health and education, and thus to people's ability to pay, and hence to livelihood issues. In attempting to address all of these issues, the program had to avoid spreading itself so thinly that it adequately tackled none of them.
- The program needed to form partnerships with other aid organizations so that they might coordinate efforts. Although many such organizations were working in the area, "each had its own diagnosis, and set of prescriptions and often operated with total disregard for other actors treating the same symptoms in the same sector and area." In the context of an emergency and with rapid turnover of expatriate staff members, aid programs tended to be short term and poorly designed and to lead to a culture of dependency (box 8.1).
- The program needed to facilitate and support indigenous processes. Consultations emphasized the lack of local unity, which led to factionalism, discrimination, and prejudice, as well as competition over access to assistance. Although people were organizing through extended family and other traditional structures, these structures were neither linked to one another nor to the assistance community.

Box 8.1

Lack of Aid Coordination

Aid organizations operating in Afghanistan in the 1990s did not agree on prescriptions for ills, or even the ills themselves, and rarely consulted the patient. According to Habitat international Regional Program Manager Samantha Reynolds, "Too often prescriptions in the form of project documents were like screenplays for the assistance actors to perform before donors to raise more funds for the next script." Funding awarded performance "perpetuating what were fast becoming iatrogenic illnesses; the very treatment was exacerbating the illness."

One example of this phenomenon was attempts to clear rubbish. Aid organizations would pay the municipality to collect it, but as soon as the funding stopped, the service would collapse. This approach not only made citizens dependent on an unsustainable system but also allowed the authorities to divert municipal funds to the conflict.

Aid for water supply was also ineptly managed. A central water department with suboffices in each city was responsible for management and maintenance of water systems and collection of water tariffs. With the breakup of the state, no central funds were available for tariff collection, and people refused to pay for services they did not receive. The aid community addressed these problems in an ad hoc manner, funding various rehabilitation projects but without consulting the water department or developing means to recover recurrent costs. When the system broke down, people complained to the water department, but the department knew nothing about the repair schemes and had collected no tariffs to cover maintenance and repair costs.

Source: Reynolds 1999.

As Habitat began to build trust with community leaders, a local mullah was persuaded to allow a meeting of women in the mosque. The women argued that they needed to be included in consultation processes and to receive some relief items immediately. Thus before addressing longer-term development issues, Habitat helped facilitate the involvement of relief agencies and helped women to organize and identify beneficiaries. During this process, the need for a meeting place more accessible than the mosque emerged. Habitat was initially reluctant to provide such a place because of ownership and cost recovery issues, and because it feared that the building could be taken over for political or military uses or looted. Eventually, however, the idea of a community forum—a space where women and men could gather to discuss their problems and decide on the best ways to solve them—was born.

The first community forum was established in District 5 in Mazar. Habitat provided seed funding to cover establishment costs, and income-generating projects were created to cover recurrent costs. These projects would build on an indigenous system of profit sharing (described next).

After the CF in District 5 had been functioning for about four months, it began to attract attention. Tamas (1998) notes requests to establish fora elsewhere in the city:

- In District 7 a women's cooperative was having marketing problems, and in that district the forum essentially absorbed the cooperative. The head of the co-op became the manager and drew on existing networks of displaced women living in a nearby camp. At one point, more than 1,000 women were registered with this forum for embroidery work, which was outsourced and done in homes.

- Women from District 4 approached Habitat, which did not have the time to help them. With some guidance and with their own capital, the women began establishing a forum. Habitat later assisted the process.
- In District 2 Habitat was given a large building with land by an NGO that had received funding to build a clinic but could not run it.

By July 1998, at least one forum was operating in each of the city's districts (11 in total). Expansion continued with establishment of branches of fora in two districts (Tamas 1998).

Soon afterward Habitat formalized ad hoc coordination among CF management teams as the Community Fora Development Organisation (CFDO), which it also funded. CFDO was designed to operate on the same consultative and value-driven basis as the CFs (Tamas 1998).

Recognizing that neighborhood-driven initiatives would not be productive unless citywide systems were made operable, the Habitat program also undertook some larger-scale interventions in different sectors. In addition, Habitat provided education courses and health care, as well as training in vocational skills, on a cost-recovery basis, with exemptions for the poorest.

These activities—and others—were managed by a three-member management team that answered to a consultative board. This board initially consisted of members of the *shura* (traditional council), but over time people began to select other members on the basis of different capacities, such as honesty. All major decisions were discussed at community meetings every three weeks. These meetings had three distinct parts: devotional, administrative, and social.

When the United Nations evacuated international staff members in 1997, the Habitat program not only continued to function but also expanded its operations. Regular radio contact revealed that the program was making progress, even in the midst of heavy fighting.

Funding for Community Fora. Each forum began with $9,900 in seed capital from Habitat to cover establishment costs (facilities rental, fixtures, and fittings), provision of tools and facilities for the different production activities, and employees' salaries for a six-month period. This capital was used to set up income-generating activities. In theory, education and health services paid for themselves, and production facilities made a profit. Services were made available to the poor for free or at a level they could afford.

Employees received base salaries at the going rate for their professions, and administrators were paid at levels comparable to government rates. Profit percentages were calculated on the basis of the going rates for the services or goods provided. A profit-sharing system distributed 20 percent of the profit to the worker and 80 percent to the Community Fund, which paid for center operations, the CFDO, or expansion activities (such as establishing a branch of the community forum in another neighborhood or expanding or providing additional services).

Full transparency of the financial aspects of forum operations was a central operating principle. At each third-week meeting, a complete financial report was provided, and it showed all income and expenditures.

Partnerships. Fora and aid agencies began to form partnerships. The agencies used the fora to interact with communities. Communities used the fora to compare the agencies' assistance strategies and to reject those that offered assistance only to a minority and not necessarily the poorest.

Partnerships with municipalities were also established and strengthened. Officials were invited to attend community meetings and to coordinate strategies and logistics. Communities attempted to establish working relationships with whoever was in control and to remain nonpartisan.

The emphasis, however, was on community organization to solve problems. As one evaluator commented:

> . . . [the program] is as much about re-building the social dynamics of urban life as it is about repairing damaged buildings and services. As such the most visible results of a program like this—clean drinking water, passable streets and lane ways, a regular system of waste disposal—only provide a partial picture of change. Behind the scenes, citizens and their institutions are organising to overcome the scourges of war and poverty . . . (interim project evaluation, 1996, cited in Tamas 1998, 18).

Phase 2: 1998–2001, under the Taliban

Even in the absence of Habitat international staff, the fora continued operating and even expanded under the Taliban. In interviews, fora staff and participants attributed their ability to keep functioning to their careful cultivation of key Taliban officials in the city and to the program's willingness to be flexible in its approach. In particular, a relationship was cultivated with the young Talib in charge of the Ministry of Labour and Social Affairs. He was frightened that his seniors would disapprove of the program but would be basically supportive of its aims. A senior Habitat official spent almost a month with him, showing him the work and explaining, using Quranic verses, what the program was trying to do. As a result, in 2000, Habitat signed a contract with the ministry and was able to establish separate women's forums, increasing women's involvement. Habitat also cultivated a relationship with the mullah in charge of sanitation by drawing on Islamic arguments about the importance of cleanliness.

Habitat adapted its approach to external constraints. Women continued to educate women at the fora, under the cover of embroidery and other income-generating projects (box 8.2). In surprising ways, women were also able to engage in advocacy for their own needs. When the Taliban stopped a pasta-producing project on which many widows depended for their livelihoods, the women demonstrated outside the official's house until he relented. Much organizing continued underground, at considerable risk to those who participated.

By the end of the Taliban period, many institutional issues had arisen. These issues included the level of community involvement in decision making, the representativeness of boards, the extent to which fora were reaching wider communities, and the level of dependency of the CFDO and fora on Habitat. Moreover, in September 2001, Habitat funding for the CF program came to an end, largely because of shifting agency structures and priorities.

Box 8.2

Girls' Right to Education

When Kabul District 3 Community Forum was established in 1997, the Taliban allowed only boys to attend courses. But fathers also wanted their daughters to learn. Habitat suggested that they approach the authorities. On further consultation, the men asked a *mullah* (religious leader) who sat on the Consultative Board to meet with the Taliban. With the Quran in hand, he approached the Office of Vice and Virtue and argued that nothing in Islam prevented girls from being educated. As a result, the Taliban gave written permission for girls up to age 12 to attend classes. For a period, hundreds of girls filled Kabul's community fora.

Source: Adapted from Rodey 2000.

Phase 3: 2001–04, After the Taliban: Crisis and Restructuring

Community fora and the CFDO were supposed to be financially self-sustaining, but the extremely difficult political and social context of their operation made this impossible. Termination of funding from Habitat forced a rethinking of strategy. The fora and CFDO began to approach other donors (the International Organization for Migration is currently funding the salary of CFDO managers) and to develop new relationships, for example with the mayor of Mazar (box 8.3) and new officials in various ministries. They also decided to restructure, bringing back together the men and women's fora, which had been separated under the Taliban. Finally, they improved financial systems and began addressing their legal status and the legalization of property ownership. The CFDO is being made more efficient and accountable.

To some, the fora might look less impressive today than when they were involved with large relief assistance programs and helped implement many projects. Researchers at the Afghanistan Research and Evaluation Unit and elsewhere have questioned the extent to which the fora are really engaged with communities and have the capacity to facilitate activities other than income-generating projects. However, the CFDO program manager (who has a long involvement in the program) argues that recent changes have made the program fundamentally healthier than at any time in the past. More rigorous accounting and accountability systems have been established, elections of management committees and boards have been instituted, and a new system of smaller-scale neighborhood fora is being implemented to enable people to participate at a more local level. Nonetheless, other interviewees argue that continued technical assistance is needed to ensure both checks and balances within the developing structures and continuation of capacity building.

Box 8.3

Partnership with Municipal Government: Linking Citywide and Community Solutions for Solid Waste Removal

In 1994–95 solid waste was one of the most visible problems confronting Mazar. The tariff collection system had broken down, and municipal sanitation services operated only in the most visible areas of the city. Aid for sanitation was uncoordinated and unsustainable, and proposed projects were often inappropriate.

(Continued)

Habitat began consulting with the Sanitation Department, which eventually agreed that both a citywide and a neighborhood-level system were needed. Habitat facilitated meetings with neighborhood representatives in each district to discuss local sanitation issues. One district began using local donkey carts (*karachi*) to collect garbage, a known system that could be paid for at a local level. Habitat supported the municipal system by providing fuel so that trucks could clear accumulated waste. It hoped the local tariff system would eventually support the municipal costs. People in nearby neighborhoods noticed the improvements and began to start *karachi* systems in their own areas. With help from the Habitat staff, the *karachi* system gradually spread across the city. Habitat purchased a tractor and two trailers for the city and supported the costs of taking waste from the collection points to the city.

Each year during the *Nau-Rooz* (new year) holiday, thousands of pilgrims come to Mazur to pay homage at the Blue Mosque, an event of great religious and cultural significance. In 2002, the mayor had an emergency budget of $90,000 to clean up the city before *Nau-Rooz*, but only 10 days to do it. The CFDO suggested that the mayor discuss the cleanup with community representatives. The mayor agreed. Each district decided on its own work plan and need for vehicle use, and before the end of the fifth day the city was clean. As a result, the mayor pledged his support for the fora process and told all municipal officials that they should collaborate with the fora. Indeed, he threatened to remove from their posts certain individuals who had been causing problems for the fora.

Source: Tamas 1998 and interviews.

Establishment of Community Fora in Other Cities

Between 1995 and 1999, the Habitat project established fora, each with the same principles (box 8.4), in five cities and two rural areas, Bamyan and Panjshir, as shown on figure 8.1. (Panjshir, where the initiative was smallest and occurred latest, does not appear on the map.)

Fora participants in Mazar and those in other cities have learned from one another. In 1999 a key Habitat official from Farah moved to Mazar and was instrumental in instituting the election of board officials. But lack of knowledge exchange was identified as a key problem in an evaluation in 1998 (Standley 1998). Moreover, interviewees for this study suggested that establishment of fora in other cities had been less "organic" than in Mazar, where fora grew out of consultation that

Box 8.4

Principles of Community Fora

Justice—Honor the dignity and capacities of every individual. Give everyone the freedom to speak and be heard.

Equity—Include everyone in decision making and in distribution of benefits.

Unity and solidarity—Work together to identify and solve problems.

Consultation—Arrive at a consensus about the truth of a given situation and the wisest choice of action among the options open at any given moment.

Ownership—Allow individuals and communities to "own" projects and be responsible for their own development and progress.

Service—Establish a new work ethic based on a spirit of service.

Partnership—Build a community on partnerships between individuals and groups, between men and women, and between civil society and authorities.

Sustainability—Establish long-term capacity to manage and sustain one's own affairs without external support.

Capacity building—Identify capacities within the community and allow them to flourish. Build the capacity of community members to work together.

Source: Rodey 2000.

occurred in Mazar and spread by word of mouth through the city, creating a sense of local ownership. By contrast, fora outside Mazar were not as strongly rooted in local communities, and they retained characteristics of donor-promoted processes. In other cities, establishment of fora proceeded more quickly than in Mazar and with a shortage of staff with community development experience (Reynolds 1999 and interviews).

The less successful outcomes in other cities may also be the result of differing experiences of conflict. Social structures may have been differently affected, and ongoing active conflict makes it difficult to establish a program. The CF program in Mazar, unlike that elsewhere, was developed during a period of almost two and half years of relative stability.

The differing experiences of the community fora raise questions about the replicability of the fora, as well as warn against attempts to short-cut processes, either in terms of time taken or staff resources allocated.

Figure 8.1 Community Fora Established in Six Provinces of Afghanistan

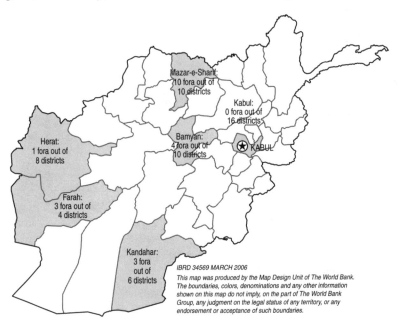

Mazar-e-Sharif:
10 fora out of
10 districts

Kabul:
0 fora out of
16 districts

Herat:
1 fora out of
8 districts

Bamyan:
4 fora out of
10 districts

KABUL

Farah:
3 fora out of
4 districts

Kandahar:
3 fora
out of
6 districts

IBRD 34569 MARCH 2006

This map was produced by the Map Design Unit of The World Bank.
The boundaries, colors, denominations and any other information
shown on this map do not imply, on the part of The World Bank
Group, any judgment on the legal status of any territory, or any
endorsement or acceptance of such boundaries.

Development Results

Community fora have brought about many positive development results,
as noted by Reynolds (1999, 18):

> People now have a local institution at the neighbourhood level where a
> number of different activities take place, where there are services, infor-
> mation and an increasingly familiar system of governance that they have
> recourse to on a regular basis through the community meetings. People
> have a common place where they feel they can access the assistance
> community or different technical departments as appropriate. There are
> local systems of cost recovery in place and systems of legislation and
> enforcement through community action. In addition, people are both
> able to exercise their rights and practice their obligations to society.

Development results are summarized in the annex to this chapter.
Quantitatively assessing these results is difficult, because reliable cumulative
figures since 1999 are not available. Moreover, verifying the figures given
next was impossible, but interviewees in Mazar did not contradict them.

Project and Service Delivery Outcomes

Assessing program outputs across 11 fora over 10 years is difficult. The necessary documentation simply does not exist, and the figures that do exist do not always break down outcomes by city. The following statistics (Rodey 2000) reflect the situation in 2000 (the height of Taliban control) in the 37 fora across Afghanistan:

- Overall, 78.5 percent of families surveyed in Mazar-e-Sharif reported that they had participated in some way in their Community Forum, even though meetings were often irregular and attendance was quite limited because of the political environment.
- Programwide, 235 men and 187 women were serving voluntarily on consultative boards.
- Some 2,300 girls and 3,150 boys were receiving educational courses.
- The Youth and Children Development Program (YCDP) in Mazar had a membership of 740, including 200 girls.
- Across the program, 300 women and 500 men were regularly employed in community-owned enterprises and in management and education sectors.
- In Mazar, the Ministry of Foreign Affairs (Taliban) gave one-month work permits to 674 resource-poor women in September 1999 to undertake a house-to-house survey to identify the most vulnerable population for winter relief.
- The fora provided organized training and resources to facilitate emergency relief for more than 200,000 people over three years. The fora not only distributed aid but employed vulnerable community women and men to do so.
- As a network, they had partnered with at least 28 UN agencies and NGOs between 1995 and 1999. In 1997 and 1999, these partnerships provided assistance to more than 100, 000 people.

Many of these outcomes, especially the emergency assistance elements, were poverty sensitive. The fora, founded on principles of transparency and fairness, provided a vehicle for assistance agencies and the public sector to reach into communities and to allocate aid with fairness to those most needy. On many occasions the fora decided who would be beneficiaries, and lists were made public so all could see the decisions. Although many of the services operated on a cost-recovery basis, exemptions were usually available for those who were unable to pay.

There were few formal assessments of beneficiary satisfaction. The meetings every three weeks provided opportunities for input by beneficiaries.

Institutional and Capacity-Building Outcomes

Institutional and capacity-building outcomes are particularly difficult to gauge. Although fora function in each of Mazar's 11 districts, assessing the extent to which they have become local institutions and serve the community empowerment objects of the CF program is problematic—particularly during each phase of the project. One indication that the fora became local institutions is that—when the international Habitat manager left Mazar in September 1997 because of security problems—they maintained their services to the community. The national Habitat staff and CFDO personnel managed the CF program but with the involvement of many individuals from communities. Indeed, the CF program was the only UN program to maintain operations in that part of northern Afghanistan at that time. Moreover, unlike most other private and public facilities, the fora buildings were not vandalized or looted during the general lawlessness and chaos.

As well as building the capacity of those who were involved with the fora, the CF program also strengthened the municipality's service capacity. It worked on a one-to-one basis with individuals to help them understand how to engage with communities, and it conducted training courses for officials. It also created greater partnership and cooperation among aid agencies. By 1999, 28 aid agencies had worked through the network to identify the most vulnerable families (Rodey 2000).

Governance Outcomes

The fora provided a model of representative governance that, until recently, was unique in Afghanistan. Although drawing on traditional methods of organization, such as the *shura* (which is almost always made up entirely of male elders), the fora went beyond such structures to increase representation, participation, and accountability. Everybody was also allowed a voice at the public meetings.

The fora linked civil society with the public sector in a new and productive way, organizing fair systems of tariff collection for services after the public taxation system had collapsed.

The CF program played a significant role in local reduction of ethnic tensions at a time when issues of ethnicity were heavy politicized in Afghanistan and when conflict was increasingly conducted along ethnic lines. People from different ethnicities have worked together in the fora and defended each other in quite extraordinary ways (box 8.5).

The fora have worked to preserve human rights, not only under a political regime in which they were under severe attack, but also to this day in a context in which discrimination on the basis of ethnicity and gender

Box 8.5

Promoting Cross-Ethnic Collaboration and Understanding

The Taliban were Pashtun from the South, but the population of Mazar is primarily Uzbek, Tajik, and Hazara. The conflict between the Taliban and Hazaras was particularly brutal. During the late 1990s, the Taliban brought 25 Pashtun families to live in District 5 in Mazar, which could have caused great local conflict. However, after discussion, the community decided this group could elect one representative to the CF board. The chosen man proved of great assistance to the community, providing information and a channel of communication with the Taliban. When the Taliban fell, and the Pashtuns fled from the North while fearing for their lives, nine members of the forum brought the man and his family to the CF building for their safety. The members told him he was free to leave whenever he wished, but until then they would do their best to protect him. They told local leaders not to harm him or his family.

Source: Interviews.

continues. The fight to provide education and health care for women and girls is the most notable example.

Spillover Effects

As noted in chapter 2, there are serious problems of attribution in identifying spillover effects. Moreover, in a program with such broad and somewhat undefined objectives, drawing a line between designed outcomes and spillovers is difficult. Nevertheless, the CF program can reasonably be assumed to have had two spillovers.

First, it reduced displacement and cross-border migration. In a context where there were already between 2.7 million and 3.5 million Afghan refugees between 1995 and 2001 (UNHCR 2001), as well as uncounted internally displaced persons, it is reasonable to suppose—but impossible to quantify or verify—that the provision of livelihood opportunities, some basic services, and emergency assistance helped reduce emigration from the cities in which fora were functioning.

Second, the CF program made a broad—and perhaps unquantifiable—contribution to peace building by providing stability and a model of negotiation and cooperation. A review argued that the program had "demonstrated its potential to achieve a positive impact on the peace process by providing a greater sense of normalcy, by providing opportunities for expressing ideas, and by providing incentives which motivate people to dis-engage from conflict" (UNDP 1999, quoted in Tamas 1998, 19). Many young people of Mazar, who have grown up with permanent conflict, have had involvement with the youth movement associated with the fora. The impact of such involvement is hard to assess but is unlikely to be negligible.

Design Considerations' Contribution to Development Results

A rigid assessment of outcomes against design is not possible, because the CF program evolved from many different programs in which design was left relatively flexible. In fact, program interventions were remarkably undesigned. They emerged from the program's fundamental method-ology: consultation, action, reflection. As Reynolds (1999, 20) has noted, "The project's progress and evolution was also very much facilitated by the style in which the original project document was written in that it stated principles, but left much room for the genuine development of an implementation strategy on the ground through consultation with peo-ple." This flexibility enabled the process to incorporate lessons and adapt to changing external circumstances.

Domestic Ownership

Domestic ownership of the foras was always in the program's design and was intimately linked with financial self-sufficiency in the program's conceptualization. Habitat planned to withdraw support early, but the extremely difficult political and economic context under the Taliban made that impossible. Rodey (2000) concluded that the initial capital-ization of $9,900 per forum was sufficient to create viable community organizations but that sustaining income-generating projects with that level of capitalization would be challenging.

When Habitat withdrew financial and other support in 2001, the program experienced difficulties, suggesting that it had not reached self-sufficiency. Furthermore, at the time the program was dependent on funding from other international donors. However, this new funding was sought and gained without the intervention of Habitat. Moreover, Afghans managed the program, although municipal officials and others continued to view the fora as a Habitat project.

Civil Society and Local Institutions

The objective of the CF program was to build a local institution through which individuals could organize, access assistance, and mobilize local resources. Although dependent on the help and good will of traditional local institutions, such as the *shura*, the program recognized that such institutions in Afghanistan are often dominated by those with economic, military, or other powers and consist entirely of men. It thus sought to draw on the strengths of traditional institutions but to move beyond them to establish a more representative and participatory form of self-governance.

The extent to which this goal was achieved is open to question. Individuals who are able to dominate one institution are often able to "capture" another. However, those who have been involved in the fora report that participants have felt increasingly free to appoint to positions of influence those community members who display desirable characteristics. These characteristics are discussed at the third-week meetings. The recent institution of secret elections to the management committee is a further step in this process. Moreover, women continue to be involved in the running of the fora. Since the men's and women's fora were rejoined after the collapse of the Taliban, female members have become active in a way that is somewhat unusual in other organizations in Afghanistan.

Implementation Processes

Flexibility is one of the key characteristics of the CF program's implementation. This flexibility has both facilitated and hindered resource acquisition.

Resource Mix and Adequacy

The CF program was developed with the understanding that it must find a means to address many interlinked problems without spreading scarce resources so thinly that nothing would be achieved. It also was developed in recognition that resources from other agencies were being used in an unsustainable way but that community resources—financial and non-financial—were available. People were already paying for the services they received (for example, trash collection and water delivery), but often the services were poor, expensive, or unreliable.

For these reasons, the original Habitat project under which the fora were developed, the Urban Rehabilitation Programme, had two distinct components: the Neighbourhood Action Programme and the Municipal Infrastructure Programme. The umbrella program's $2.4 million fund was split 2:1 in favor of the community-based work, which made infrastructure development sustainable (Dudley 1995). Aside from the allocation of $9,900 to start each forum, direct expenditure on the CF program is difficult to identify for various reasons:

- The fora were developed as part of Habitat's broader urban rehabilitation activities and did not constitute a specific program.
- In the early years money was not allocated within Habitat's financial management system for community development in the way that other project activities were funded. Therefore, assessing allocations for "soft" activities such as capacity building and facilitation, as opposed to infrastructure or construction, is impossible.
- Joint operations by different UN agencies during the years of conflict meant that budgets were often combined by or shared between agencies. Thus tracking allocations to particular activities is especially difficult.
- The fora's community development work was often funded through relief programs, which were administered through the fora.
- Fora staff members acknowledge that the program's paper trail is poor.

However, the program Rebuilding Urban Communities in Afghanistan, 1997–99, within which the CF program was embedded, had a core UNDP budget of $6.9 million plus additional funds (raised as either parallel funding or part of the joint effort with other agencies) for a total working budget of around $10 million. Approximately half the core budget was devoted to direct capital expenditure; the remainder was allocated to personnel, equipment, and miscellaneous support items. Standley (1998, 17) notes that UN personnel and other support inputs accounted for approximately 50 percent of the overall UNDP budget (although a much smaller percentage of the overall budget):

> Whether this ratio of direct investment to the overheads allocated for delivering the outputs is justified is an issue that cannot be resolved without reference to evaluated experience elsewhere and the use of some sophisticated and probably wholly academic assumptions on social values. However, the P.E.A.C.E. Initiative [UNDP] is not the normal post-war rehabilitation program and the strategic thrust towards community development at the grassroots level explicitly involves human resource inputs for capacity-building without immediate measurable gains and, in any event, requires highly creative approaches to tracking and quantifying benefits.

This discussion parallels discussion of Afghanistan's National Solidarity Program (NSP) in which partners are being castigated for their high delivery costs. Under the current NSP budget, training and capacity building are classified as overheads, thus producing very high and visible project delivery costs. However, those implementing the program argue that training and capacity building are integral to the program.

In general, the Habitat program was expensive to run, not only because of high staff costs but also because of poor security and poor infrastructure. Because of security concerns, the project helped pay the cost of running two UN airplanes and installing a radio network throughout the country to maintain communications between field offices and the support office. These types of costs must be factored into the budgets of programs in insecure environments.

Shortages of funds in the late 1990s meant that Habitat had to put a great deal of effort into raising funds for the fora and had to portray their activities as relief-focused to attract donor funding that was humanitarian in orientation. Use of such funding meant that fora were required to participate in citywide relief efforts when they had neither the structures nor capacity to do so.[8] Those involved in the program questioned the donor consensus that development activities were not feasible during conflict. They argued that seeds during conflict would bear fruit when the external environment and broader political economy became conducive to reform.

Habitat recognized that funding was not the only important resource. Technical assistance was also critical. Habitat had strong technical engineering skills but weak understanding of how to facilitate community development. Its engineers had to learn that decisions were not always taken in accordance with their advice. Adapting to the community consultation process was difficult for many of them.[9] Tamas (1998, 83–84) reported on the problem thus:

> The process of helping to mobilize a community around issues of common interest moves at its own pace: ensuring collective ownership of the process is more important than rapidly achieving a tangible result. . . . Most technical professionals become impatient with the ambiguous and seemingly directionless process. Few have been exposed to the concepts that would enable them to recognize and support the subtle dynamics of an emerging consensus resulting from an evolving expression of a community's interests. Few recognize the need for collective ownership as a prerequisite for sustainable development. Because they have not been trained in these matters, it is not fair to expect them to demonstrate competence in this complex area of professional practice.

This difficult process of mixing the technical skills of engineers with the "softer" skills of community development was mostly achieved through the leadership and example of Habitat's international Regional Program Manager Samantha Reynolds. She encouraged the development of a more consultative environment in the office, for example, by having regular cross-departmental meetings and spent much time in the field with engineers, where, as she notes, she tried to set a good example: "If the international manager was prepared to listen to people then . . . it was not beneath their [engineers'] dignity to do so either."[10]

Remarkably, an engineering project was transformed into a community development process. But Habitat found it difficult to convince the principal donor, UNDP, which pushed for "hardware delivery," of the value of this transformation.

Revenue and Budget Management

Habitat developed effective systems to release funding. These systems reflected the good relationship between the regional program manager and her manager in Kabul. Tamas (1998, 82) identified the productive relationship between the Habitat office in Mazar and the country office in Kabul as a key factor in the success of the project:

> In Mazar the Regional Program Manager [RPM] operated in a broader organizational context that provided . . . support from her Program Manager (and other parts of the Habitat system) to do the work that resulted in the CF. This included establishing an atmosphere of trust and confidence in the RPM's abilities and making financial and other resources available as required. Guidance was provided as needed to keep work on a productive track. An example of this high quality interaction was the question of releasing funds for community projects in a timely and effective manner. . . . The manager in Kabul did what he could to make these funds readily available, providing the RPM in Mazar with the tools she needed to maintain credibility with the community and her own colleagues. Success with this task function (making funds readily available) contributed to an effective *process.*

On the negative side, fora had little capacity to formulate and track budgets. This limited capacity not only constrained project implementation but also led to opportunities for corruption. Better budget tracking systems are being established.

Implementation Process and Activities

Important implementation activities of the CF program not discussed earlier are policy dialogue, coordination, learning and sharing, and public relations.

Policy Dialogue. In all phases of the project, Habitat staff interacted with authorities and facilitated the interaction of community members, particularly on service provision issues. In phase one, when the state was very weak or nonexistent, Habitat convinced the city of Mazar that it should set up a systematic operation in which people would pay for services, thereby ensuring that the services would be more equitable and sustainable. Through this policy engagement, Habitat was able to link small-scale community initiatives with larger citywide processes. In phase two, staff and community members engaged in remarkable ways with Taliban authorities, even convincing them to allow girls to attend classes in Kabul. More recently, the program has influenced development of the National Solidarity Program (NSP).

While senior program staff maintain dialogue with policy makers, community members have little engagement in policy processes. Moreover, many community members appear to have little desire to have such engagement, perhaps because mechanisms for it are few and because the current government is not very open to their creation. However, now that Afghanistan has an interim poverty reduction strategy paper, the CF program could provide one means for community consultation about the strategy to take place.

Coordination. In the 1990s UN agencies recognized the seriousness of the lack of agency coordination in Afghanistan. In 1998 UNDP developed a strategic framework to address this problem (UNDP 1998) but results were mixed.

In Mazar, failure of agency coordination, as well as its negative effects on development outcomes, was one of the factors that influenced the design of the Habitat program. Habitat established a city commission to provide a forum for coordination among aid agencies, various city departments, and formal and informal leaders. In this forum the municipality asked UN agency staff to describe and explain their activities. Although some agencies resisted this request, the forum strengthened the role of local departments in influencing aid agency activities. It also increased Habitat's credibility with municipal and other authorities.

The CF process also contributed to greater agency coordination by providing a mechanism through which agencies could interact with communities. To some extent, the coordination function was passed to the fora, which gained greater influence over implementation of programs that affected them. Reynolds (1999, 17) commented that "increasingly, antagonistic sister agencies and departments have become less hostile and more inquisitive about the process."

The CF program has at times been stymied by aid agencies. In the early days of the program, for example, Habitat's efforts to establish cost recovery systems were undermined by other agencies that were promoting welfare-oriented interventions. When the CF program established training courses on a fee basis proportional to income, other agencies not only established free courses but also paid people to attend training. This pattern was replicated in other sectors. The situation was exacerbated by Habitat's limited links with other UN programs (Reynolds 1999).

More recently, the CF program has created links with some government agencies whereby the agencies are drawing on CF facilities and its organization to expand services—particularly in the areas of adult literacy and establishment of kindergartens—to more people and in a wider geographic area. Many of the links are based on personal relationships and officials' involvement with fora over the years. However, interviewees for this study have commented that in some ways coordination with municipal authorities is harder now that the fora are unable to pay salaries, benefits, and other inducements to municipal officials.

Learning and Sharing. Learning has been critical to the success of the CF program:

> There are no easy formulas for this kind of work. There are broad principles and approaches but in the end it is trial and error. A successful program learns from its experience and that of others. Program managers and field staff take time to reflect on their errors and achievements, and draw lessons for future practice . . . (interim project evaluation, 1996, cited in Tamas 1998, 18).

As noted above, the program's methodology is consultation, action, and reflection. This methodology is reflected in the program design, which allows implementation to accommodate learning from reflection and which is articulated, somewhat as a mantra, by those involved in fora management today.

But the program has not kept track of its learning, which makes sharing it with fora in cities outside Mazar difficult. Some lessons are reflected in the few reviews and evaluations of the program, but most are held by the individuals involved in the processes. Often those who are most involved in the processes and who have learned the most valuable lessons are too busy to document those lessons. Agencies and donors should attempt to provide resources for this task.

Public Relations. Throughout the CF program, Habitat has invested considerable time and energy in identifying and working with individuals of authority. Habitat has improved relationships with these individuals not only by its willingness to listen to them and its capability to deliver results but also by its attempts to increase municipal influence in coordinating the activities of other agencies.

In LICUS, where institutional capacity is low, focusing efforts on one or two individuals who are receptive to change and who have some measure of influence in bringing it about is particularly important.

Conclusions

The CF program demonstrates that aid can achieve effective results within a poor governance environment and can deliver sustainable benefits. It emphasizes the importance of a flexible and consultation-driven process of design and implementation. Furthermore, it reveals the importance of program personnel's understanding of local power dynamics—both within communities and between communities and government agencies. In the absence of such understanding, projects would have continued to fail or would have succeeded only for a short time.

The CF program also demonstrates that links can be forged between different processes and between groups that are often separated in development efforts in LICUS, particularly those emerging from conflict:

- *Technical engineering and community processes*: Simultaneous repair of physical infrastructure and the social fabric occurred in an engineering project that became a community empowerment program. This shift involved considerable reorientation of staff and agency expectations.
- *Small-scale community development efforts and larger-scale infrastructure processes:* The success and sustainability of the individual projects and activities hinged on the CF program's capacity to link community efforts with citywide processes.
- *Local authorities and civil society:* Even under one of the most repressive regimes, women and others were able to advocate for their rights.

The CF program moved beyond oppressive traditional structures in helping citizens establish a more equitable and inclusive form of self-governance, even in conditions of extreme instability and conflict.

Some have argued that the CF process may illustrate that widespread political instability actually creates conditions that make development initiatives *easier* to implement. When old systems and relationships of power are not entrenched, the destruction of a system of governance can contribute to the emergence of alternative structures (Tamas 1998). In the absence of a strong state, innovation and freedom can sometimes flourish, access to communities can be more direct, and people may be more willing to organize because they have no alternative way of meeting their immediate needs. As the CF program demonstrates, even in very oppressive environments, it can be possible to negotiate with power holders to permit development activity to take place. But as the CF program also illustrates, success in such negotiation requires outstanding program leadership. Even though the Habitat international regional program manager was forced to evacuate in the late 1990s, those she had trained were able to carry on the program's work.

The transition from activity during a period of a weak or collapsed state to participation in processes of state reconstruction or formation is critical and needs to be supported. One of the biggest lessons learned by those involved in the CF program is that periods of conflict or state collapse should be viewed as transient and as an opportunity to pilot programs and to establish skills, trust, ownership, and systems that can be built on when conflict ceases. When the political context changes, an explicit shift in approach and support is needed.

One of the biggest challenges facing the fora today is how they can become integrated into broader development and state-building agendas in Afghanistan. What is a legitimate role for the fora in current efforts to establish representative and participatory forms of governance? Can the fora be "legalized" in some way so that they become a legitimate form of lower-level governance? At present, there is little clarity about how the fora, or indeed the community development committees being formed under NSP, can be integrated into the elected lower-level bodies mandated in the new constitution, and how such "experiments" in community development can fit into broader subnational reform agendas.

Annex

	Description
Program or project outcomes	
Service provision	Health and education (literacy, vocational training, Quran) classes provided on cost-recovery basis. By 1999, 33 health posts established (Reynolds 1999). In 1998 the Mazar program provided education and vocational training to 10,480 people (Tamas 1998). Emergency assistance channeled through CFs to numerous beneficiaries. Beneficiary identification citywide for distribution of relief items.
Capacity building	Training to staff, both vocational and organizational. Strengthening of capacity of community members to participate and organize.
Natural resource management	Community decision making on issues of NRM strengthened, particularly on use of water and sanitation. Rehabilitation of green spaces. By 1999, 500 kitchen gardens had been established, 84,800 trees planted, and 10 parks reestablished (Reynolds 1999). Families trained in composting.
Infrastructure development	Strong links with Habitat's municipal infrastructure program. Local initiatives through CFs linked into wider municipal initiatives. By 1999, Habitat installed 700 hand pumps, which communities maintain and repair. By 1999, 100 neighborhood solid waste collection schemes were established and linked to municipal waste collection systems.
Policy reform and economic management	Municipal officials advocacy on policy around service provision. Considerable policy advocacy with the Taliban both directly by Habitat and communities about allowing women to associate and continue working. Significant policy advocacy following Bonn with senior UN officials, new administration, and World Bank, which led to the development of the National Solidarity Program.
Private sector development	Numerous small income-generating projects were established. Full-time employment was provided for 250 people in Mazar by 1998 (Tamas 1998).
Governance outcomes	
Political stability	Local levels of factionalism and conflict diminished. Practical working relationships were established between "the state" and citizenry.
Domestic leadership	Valuable training was given. Many officials currently working in municipal government in Mazar were involved with the fora under the Taliban.
Ethnic tensions	Ethnic tensions were reduced.
Security	Local-level tensions diminished.
Human rights	Women's education and participation was strengthened.

Source: Author.

Notes

1. There was no program called Community Fora Program. Community fora developed from several programs. Here Community Fora Program refers to Habitat interventions and activities that brought about development of the fora.

2. "Poverty Eradication and Community Empowerment: Afghanistan Peace Initiative, 1997–1999" (UNDP 1999) quoted in Tamas (1998, 13).

3. Information on Mazar is drawn partly from Pain (2003).

4. UNCHS became known as UN-Habitat when it became a "program" (the United Nations Human Settlement Program) within the UN system in 2002.

5. This section draws heavily on Reynolds (1999).

6. In 1997, Habitat's activities became part of UNDP's Poverty Eradication and Community Empowerment (P.E.A.C.E.) Initiative 1997–99, which coordinated activities of UN agencies in Afghanistan at that time.

7. This process is described in detail in Tamas (1998).

8. Source: personal communication with Habitat's international Regional Program Manager Samantha Reynolds.

9. Source: interviews with Habitat engineers and others.

10. Source: personal communication with Habitat's international Regional Program Manager Samantha Reynolds.

References

Boesen, I. 2004. "From Subjects to Citizens: Local Participation in the National Solidarity Program." Working Paper, Afghanistan Research and Evaluation Unit, Kabul, Afghanistan. http://www.areu.org.af.

Dudley, E. 1995. "Building Trust: An Evolving Approach to Resettlement: Some Lessons from Afghanistan." Report for United Nations Development Programme/ United Nations Center for Human Settlements.

Evans, A., N. Manning, Y. Osmani, A. Tully, and A. Wilder. 2004. *How Government Works in Afghanistan.* Kabul and Washington, DC: World Bank.

Misra, A. 2004. *Afghanistan: The Labyrinth of Violence.* Cambridge: Polity Press.

Pain, A. 2003. "Empire Light-State Light: Transforming the Punctuated Equilibrium or a Pathway to Extinction?" Paper presented at Symposium on State Reconstruction and International Engagement in Afghanistan, London School of Economics and University of Bonn, Bonn, Germany, June.

Rasanayagam, A. 2003. *Afghanistan: A Modern History.* London and New York: I. B. Taurus.

Reynolds, S. 1999. "Rebuilding Communities in the Urban Areas of Afghanistan." Paper prepared for the Symposium and Round Table on Operational Activities, Japan, June 27–29.

Reynolds, A., and A. Wilder. 2004. "Free, Fair, or Flawed: Challenges for Legitimate Elections in Afghanistan." Briefing Paper, AREU, Kabul, Afghanistan.

Rodey, B. 2000. "Quantum Leap: A Framework for Peace and Development in Conflict and Post-Conflict Afghanistan: A Socioeconomic Evaluation of the Community Forum Program." United Nations Centre for Human Settlements, Afghanistan.

Rubin, B. 1995. *The Fragmentation of Afghanistan*. New Haven, CT: Yale University Press.

Standley, Terry. 1998. "UNDP/UNCHS Rehabilitating Community in Urban Afghanistan" Internal Evaluation Report, United Nations Development Programme/United Nations Centre for Human Settlements, Afghanistan.

Tamas, A. 1998. "Origins of the Community Fora Program: Innovative Community Development in Mazar-e-Sharif, Afghanistan, 1995–1998." United Nations Centre for Human Settlements, Afghanistan.

UNDP (United Nations Development Programme). 1998. "Strategic Framework for Afghanistan: Towards a Principled Approach to Peace and Reconstruction."

———. 1999. "Poverty Eradication and Community Empowerment: Afghanistan Peace Initiative, 1997–1999." Islamabad, Pakistan: UNDP.

UNHCR (United Nations Centre for Human Settlements). 2001. "Afghan Refugee Statistics Database." http://www.un.org.pk/unhcr/Afstats-stat.htm.

World Bank. 2004. "Afghanistan: State-Building, Sustaining Growth, and Reducing Poverty." Country Economic Report, World Bank, Washington, DC.

CHAPTER 9

Aid Effectiveness and Microfinance: Lessons from Afghanistan

When the Taliban lost control of Afghanistan at the end of 2001, aid organizations almost immediately identified microfinance as an important opportunity for providing social protection and promoting employment. Small- and medium-size enterprises, including trade, had become a main source of livelihoods in the economic crisis caused by continuous war and state breakdown. These enterprises—and particularly women as producers—had urgent credit needs.

Microfinance was included in the country's first-ever National Development Framework and became a priority line item in the national budget in 2002. In June 2003 the Microfinance Investment and Support Facility (MISFA) was established through an agreement of the government of Afghanistan and the World Bank and with funding from the Consultative Group to Assist the Poor (CGAP). The facility provides performance-based funds, technical assistance, and training to retail financial intermediaries that serve the poor in Afghanistan. Its overall objective is to help establish a healthy microfinance sector that provides diverse financial services.

This chapter was written by Martin Greeley.[1]

Context

The recent political history of successive state failures in Afghanistan has been well documented, but there had been little attempt at nation building even before the arrival of the Soviet forces in 1979 and the beginning of civil war. The monarchy had retained control by giving local leaders considerable latitude on revenue raising and on law and order enforcement. These conditions of weak central leadership followed by virtual nonstop fighting from 1979 left Afghanistan one of the poorest and least-developed countries in the world (table 9.1). Key indicators, such as maternal mortality, were the worst in the world. Internal displacement (mainly out of the cities) was massive, as was the outflow of refugees—perhaps five million people in all.

In November 2001 U.S.-led international forces took control away from the Taliban. Warlords and commanders with local support, dating from *mujahudeen* fighting the Soviet forces but representing much longer traditions of family, clan, and ethnic affiliations, were important in the military victory and had expectations of political power. Other groups, loyal to the Taliban, had to be reintegrated peacefully—and those elements among them that continued to oppose the new powers in Kabul had to be and still must be contained and defeated in a guerrilla war. The new Afghanistan is an extreme example of quasi-statehood in which political legitimacy and provision of security are both fragile and, in some geographic areas, either or both are absent.

Table 9.1 Afghanistan: Social Indicators

Indicator	Measure
Population (millions; 2002) (underestimate)	21.8
Life expectancy at birth (2001)	42.8
Infant mortality per 1,000 live births (2001)	165
Under-five mortality per 1,000 live births (2001)	257
Children underweight (percentage under age 5; 1995–2001)	48
Undernourished people (percentage of population; 1998–2000)	70
Adult literacy (percentage age 15 and above; 2001)	36
Male	51
Female	21
Primary school enrollment ratio, gross 1995–99 (percent)	
Male	53
Female	5
Population without sustainable access to improved water (percentage; 2000)	87

Sources: Central Statistics Office of Afghanistan; UNDP 2003; UNICEF 2002; and World Bank 2003.

The international community supported the Bonn peace process in 2001 and pledged substantial reconstruction and development support in Tokyo in January 2002. This support followed a twin track: benchmarks established for political progress in the Bonn Agreement became the responsibility of the Afghan Support Group, and an implementation group was established for donor mobilization and harmonization on economic reconstruction. Economic reconstruction plans drew on a preliminary needs assessment by the Asian Development Bank (ADB), the United Nations Development Programme (UNDP), and the World Bank.[2] This assessment identified microfinance as a short-term need, particularly in the context of social protection, and of long-term importance, particularly in the context of employment. Critically, the assessment identified the need to support microfinance services "within a sound policy and institutional framework aimed at ensuring the viability of microfinance institutions and their access to capital" (ADB, UNDP, and World Bank 2002, 27). Three months later the Afghanistan Transitional Authority's (ATA) first budget and National Development Framework was established. Within this framework, microfinance was explicitly identified as a key reconstruction element: "support to micro, small and medium enterprises through the backing of micro-finance schemes and the provision of training in small business management. . . ." (ATA 2002).

Development of a microfinance project concept began with a country sector review by the World Bank–housed CGAP, which promotes sustainable microfinance supported by the donor community, and by a World Bank identification mission in May 2002. In October 2002 a World Bank mission drew up a detailed proposal for sector development. The program falls under the Ministry of Reconstruction and Rural Development (MRRD). An initial grant agreement was signed in June 2003 with $1 million in funding from CGAP. It specified that the Microfinance Investment and Support Facility would be established to provide performance-based institution building and lending funds to retail financial intermediaries that serve the poor. In addition, the facility would provide and facilitate access to technical assistance and training for those intermediaries, as well as establish reporting standards for them. The overall objective of MISFA is to provide flexible and high-quality support to help establish a healthy microfinance sector that provides diverse, sustainable, and appropriately scaled financial services to the poor.

The World Bank was the lead agency for creating MISFA. CGAP is a key advisor. All other donors interested in funding microfinance in Afghanistan join MISFA as cofunders.

Initially within the MRRD, MISFA now has its own offices and supports all the major microfinance institutions (MFIs) the service delivery agents operating in Afghanistan. It provides them with grant funds for capacity building and loan funds for disbursement to clients; the loan funds carry an interest rate of 5 percent. Most funding has been routed through the Afghanistan Reconstruction Trust Fund, a multidonor financing instrument managed by the World Bank. MISFA closely monitors the performance of its partner MFIs; second and subsequent tranche releases are dependent on meeting the strict performance criteria relating to the use of funds and the size and quality of the MFI's loan portfolio.

MISFA has been able to garner donor support and rapidly scale up its activities. Funding totaled nearly $50 million by the end of the pilot phase, March 2005. In that phase, MISFA and MFI capacity-building expenditures were greater than funds disbursed as loans. But, as table 9.2 shows, the percentage share of MISFA and MFI grants is declining, while that of loan funds is increasing.

One reason for MISFA's quick growth is the facility's variety of partnership arrangements, which reflect a diversity of service delivery models. MFI partners have international experience with microfinance service provision and adapt their own proven models to Afghan conditions. By October 2004 MISFA had made loan funds available to 11 partner MFIs (table 9.3), which in turn were working with nearly 60,000 borrowers. The first clients of some of the initial eight MFI partners have received second or third loans.

New growth in Afghanistan's microfinance sector will come first from expansion planned by existing MISFA partners and later from support from additional donors. MISFA partners will seek to attract more commercial money as their operations become profitable.

The performance of one agency has been instrumental to MISFA's success. Bangladesh Rural Advancement Committee (BRAC) Afghanistan

Table 9.2 Growth of MISFA, 2003–08

	June 2003– March 2005 (Pilot)	April 2005– March 2006	April 2006– March 2007	April 2007– March 2008
Total (millions of dollars)	25.	48.5	57.4	57.
MISFA	13.2	6.0	3.5	3.1
Sector technical assistance	5.6	2.0	1.8	1.3
MFI grant	49.2	39.0	34.4	27.0
MFI loan fund	32.0	53.0	60.3	68.6

Source: MISFA presentation to the World Bank supervision mission, December 2004.

Table 9.3 MISFA Client Activity: October 2004

	Number of active loan clients	Loan portfolio outstanding (dollars)	Number of savings clients	Savings outstanding (dollars)
BRAC	46,809	3,034,290	65,777	662,542
AKDN	3,334	1,948,229	0	0
FINCA	3,260	363,684	3,499	31,443
Mercy Corps	1,587	139,815	0	0
CARE	304	90,349	1,832	55,807
WfW	576	81,739	0	0
CHF	304	98,200	0	0
WOCCU	0	0	892	4,651
DACAAR	1,272	89,516	6,480	14,137
MADERA	210	23,136	0	0
Parwaz	560	40,000	560	5,429
Total	58,216	5,908,958	79,040	774,009

Source: MISFA presentation to the World Bank supervision mission, December 2004.
Note: AKDN = Aga Khan Development Network; BRAC = Bangladesh Rural Advancement Committee; CARE = Cooperative for Assistance and Relief Everywhere; CHF = Cooperative Housing Foundation; DACAAR = Danish Committee for Aid to Afghan Refugees; FINCA = Foundation for International Community Assistance; MADERA = Mission d'Aide au Développement des Economies Rurales en Afghanistan; WfW = Work-for-the-World; WOCCU = World Council of Credit Unions.

started operations with a small startup fund from BRAC Bangladesh. It adopted the BRAC Bangladesh model and used the trained Bangladeshi staff. As table 9.4 shows, BRAC Afghanistan grew rapidly in its first two years. Within MISFA it accounted for a high proportion of total borrowers, loans, and provinces covered. By 2006 it accounted for more than 80 percent of total borrowers and 60 percent of total funds loaned.

BRAC Afghanistan has ambitious growth plans and could absorb more funds than are currently available through MISFA. Its success stems from BRAC Bangladesh's vast experience shaping the microfinance sector in another Islamic Asian country. Like its sister organization, BRAC Afghanistan has begun offering small enterprise loans for merchants and small entrepreneurs. These loans are larger than those available through the main BRAC program operating in village centers. Ultimately, as in Bangladesh, BRAC will seek to link microfinance service provision in Afghanistan with its other services—for health, education, agriculture, and community development. This ambition derives from BRAC's appreciation of the diversity of coordinated support required to promote sustainable livelihoods, especially in a context like contemporary rural Afghanistan. BRAC's vision and commitment make it an extraordinarily important contributor to MISFA's current and prospective achievements.

Table 9.4 Overview of BRAC Afghanistan Microfinance Program, 2002–04

Item	December 2002	December 2003	June 2004	November 2004
Provinces covered	3	6	12	12
Districts covered	8	13	41	46
Regional offices	3	4	12	13
Area offices	8	28	70	75
Village organizations	163	1,008	2,171	3,477
Members	3,845	24,571	43,824	67,379
Borrowers	264	15,710	28,958	50,497
Member to borrower ratio (percent)	7	64	66	75
Number of loans disbursed (up to)	64	16,894	37,476	67,690
Amount disbursed (dollars)	18,840	1,509,194	3,441,931	6,699,201
Average loan size (dollars)	71	90	92	100
Value outstanding (dollars)	17,960	786,976	1,727,627	3,211,404
Member savings (dollars)	3,740	121,719	267,304	7,57,225

Source: BRAC Afghanistan 2004.

Development Results

At MISFA's inception, the government of Afghanistan and the World Bank, the two administrators of the Afghanistan Reconstruction Trust Fund, specified progress indicators:

- increased outreach with appropriate geographical coverage and particular emphasis on poverty-stricken areas and women
- qualitative effect on clients' ability to rebuild their lives
- improvements in the types and quality of financial products and services offered to low-income clients
- established systems for microfinance delivery by microfinance institutions and nongovernmental organizations (best practices, trained staff, improved services delivery, and so on)
- appointment of a board of directors

First, MISFA has made progress according to the coverage indicator. MISFA partners now operate in all of Afghanistan's provinces, but security conditions have prevented them from providing services in the south. MISFA is under pressure to extend its operations to the southern provinces, and several MFIs are willing to do so, subject to improvements in security conditions.

Second, assessing progress on MISFA's qualitative impact is difficult. Some case studies by various MISFA partners indicate evidence of success in this area, and this evidence is supported by field trip reports from MISFA. For example, women interviewed during field trips to BRAC program villages talked about the importance of continuing access to loan funds and noted the funds' contribution to household livelihood security. However, more extensive monitoring of loan use and client performance is needed to better assess MISFA's impact.

Third, a range of services is built into MISFA, ensuring progress according to that indicator. MISFA provides support to varied service providers with different targeting methods, market segments, and loan sizes ranging from less than $50 to $3,000.

The fourth indicator, establishment of service delivery systems, can be assessed through the performance of MISFA's MFI partners. They operate according to detailed business plans and have received extensive training on and tailored support for fiduciary standards, reporting, and monitoring, as well as business development when appropriate.

With respect to the fifth indicator of progress, a board of directors for MISFA has been established, and a management plan has been created.

Design Considerations

The defeat of the Taliban in November 2001 triggered a delicate process of state building in Afghanistan. The international brokers and the domestic constituencies grappling with the complexities of the political process were fully aware that progress in their deliberations was the touchstone for a massive development effort financed by the global community. Political progress was the basis for buy-in from aid agencies to the economic reconstruction agenda. Inevitably, the elements of this agenda were being developed before the successful conclusion of the initial political process.

In January 2002 a needs assessment mission of several donors reported stark conditions to a ministerial meeting of donors with the Afghanistan Interim Administration. More than two decades of conflict and three years of drought had led to widespread human suffering and massive displacement of people in Afghanistan. Many parts of the country were vulnerable to famine, the infrastructure base had been destroyed or degraded, and human resources had been depleted. State institutions had become largely nonfunctional and the economy was increasingly fragmented. The social fabric had been weakened considerably, and human rights had been undermined. Women and minorities were the principal sufferers. Before 1979 Afghanistan was among the poorest countries of the world. Since then, its economic and social indicators had deteriorated further.

The work of the joint needs assessment mission was critical in establishing the first National Development Framework (NDF). This framework was important in establishing some sense of domestic ownership of the reconstruction and growth agenda. Visionaries, including the Minister of Finance in the ATA, established in June 2002, had a clear sense of priorities that were in nation-building and were reflected in the evolution of priorities within the NDF.

Budgetary Process

Identifying priorities was not difficult—governance and security, livelihoods, social protection, human development, and infrastructure. Coordinating their achievement was the challenge. Aid agencies, particularly the World Bank, realized that successful aid requires real domestic ownership. In the context of Afghanistan, such ownership was especially critical, because state sovereignty was fragile, and the leadership of the central government needed to be strengthened to avoid insecurity.

In the absence of resources, polices, and people, Afghan ownership of the political and development agendas could, at best, be partial. Donors needed to provide more meaningful domestic ownership of aid as domestic capacity was built. Their approach was to target support to priorities identified in the NDF and to provide that support through the domestic budget. Although a national budget was established in April 2002, main funding that year continued through the UN–coordinated Immediate and Transitional Support Program. A new budget in March 2003 strengthened domestic leadership by reflecting the NDF's 12 priority programs, including 6 priority subprograms, each of which has a consultative group chaired by a minister. The consultative groups were expected to encourage coordination of policy agenda efforts in a way that would allow increasing domestic ownership. The budget process became the vehicle for policy design and resource allocation.

From an implementation perspective, adherence to the budgetary process was a mixed blessing. The process gave credence to MISFA, which under World Bank guidance as an administrator of the Afghanistan Reconstruction Trust Fund has been funded within the government's budget and has aided its subsequent growth. But it also led to political and bureaucratic problems, specifically release of funds that were the price of supporting the budgetary process (see next). Although MISFA was envisioned as an apex organization supporting all the major MFIs operating in Afghanistan, it was expected to evolve into a semiautonomous body. Given that expectation, other apex financing arrangements would have been easier to manage.

Contextual Assessments

MISFA was developed on the basis of four contextual assessments made by the mission of October 2002:

- A strong microfinance sector plays a key role in the livelihoods strategy of poor and low-income households by providing financing that these households can use to invest in enterprise activities, meet emergency needs, reduce vulnerability, and build assets.
- Microfinance is a critical input but not a panacea and should be viewed as an "entitlement."
- The current supply of microfinance services is extremely limited.
- The potential to develop large-scale, sustainable microfinance programs is constrained by lack of funding and technical capacity.

The first of these assessments is self-evidently true. The second is addressed to those who claim that microfinance is not "state building." It underlines the validity of the first assessment without making excessive claims on what microfinance can achieve.

The last two assessments were evidence-based. The earlier CGAP mission had reviewed the 24 existing MFIs in Afghanistan and found that they reached approximately 10,000 clients in selected villages in 10 to 15 provinces in all regions of the country (Forster and Pearce 2002). The mission observed that the programs, though sometimes offering savings services as well as loans, were not directed toward sustainable microfinance provision but were part of broader development programs—for example, support to war widows. These findings strengthened commitment to expand the sector and make financial service provision sustainable.

Design Lessons from Another Apex Microfinance Organization

As noted above, MISFA was envisioned as an apex organization supporting all Afghanistan's MFIs. Its design was informed by the experience of the World Bank and CGAP with a similar organization in Bosnia-Herzegovina.

According to Forster and Pearce (2002), MISFA could replicate that experience in the following ways:

- The Bosnian microfinance-sector apex facility was established early in the country's reconstruction phase so that it could take a lead role in shaping the microfinance sector and could be included in donors' microfinance programming.
- The facility was not viewed as an exclusively World Bank project. Considerable effort and diplomacy were used to involve other donors.
- Access to funding for MFIs was dependent on agreed performance criteria. Funding was withdrawn from MFIs that did not meet these criteria.
- The facility provided a range of technical assistance. This assistance became increasingly demand-responsive through involvement of microfinance providers in the design and prioritization of technical assistance inputs.
- The facility provided institution-building grants as well as funds for lending.
- The facility provided umbrella legal protection and monitoring for MFIs while banking law was being revised and while banking supervisory capacity and a microfinance law were being developed. It subcontracted legal expertise to the government in designing and implementing microfinance regulations. International and local MFIs were increasingly involved in dialogue with the government.
- The facility promoted good microfinance standards for both microfinance institutions and donors.
- By supplying a channel for other donor money, the facility provided a service to donors lacking their own microfinance capacity and helped ensure that donor support to microfinance was well coordinated.
- For the most part, the facility resisted political pressures to work with MFIs associated with ethnic priorities and instead supported MFIs with the capacity to provide large-scale and long-term microfinance to the poor.
- The facility worked only with microcredit NGOs, several of which have reached the stage at which either a conversion to a microfinance bank or a merger with a commercial bank is a realistic option. NGOs are generally not well placed to provide savings, insurance, and payments services. An apex microfinance support facility in Afghanistan should therefore include banks and nonbanks, as well as NGOs, as its clients.

Domestic Ownership

The CGAP mission of May 2002 examined the strength of domestic commitment to microfinance service provision. Some of the widespread support it found for such provision was driven by the government's need to spend in ways that visibly benefited people. An internal CGAP document identified the following government perspectives on microfinance:

- Microfinance operations should be developed as part of the private sector.
- Microfinance institutions should serve large numbers of people on a financially sustainable basis. These institutions should operate according to high performance standards and should be designed to become financially self-sufficient, thereby reducing dependency on donor funding.
- Microfinance approaches should help clients build assets and create wealth that will pull them out of poverty.
- The government is interested in enterprise development, in increasing agricultural and textile exports, and particularly in creating links between microfinance and business development.
- Providing access to finance for women is a government priority. Women play a role in managing the family assets, and they generate income through activities such as animal husbandry, carpet production, and embroidery. The government would like to use microfinance to empower women and support their further involvement in the economy.
- The government will not impose restrictions on the charging of interest for microloans.
- All ministers and other government representatives interviewed are supportive of the concept of a national microfinance support facility that would provide a channel for donor support for microfinance.

Support for an apex microfinance facility did not mask potential obstacles to the facility's successful operation. The NDF noted that these obstacles included "high inflation, lack of infrastructure, security, skilled staff, religious restrictions, and cultural sensitivities" (government of Afghanistan 2002). In practice, the religious and cultural obstacles appear quite manageable, and inflation has not been an issue, but MFIs, like all other institutions, must cope with the national crisis in relation to infrastructure, security, and staffing.

The Afghanistan Transitional Authority wanted to get development resources to communities to secure and extend its legitimacy, and it viewed MISFA as a way to do so quickly. But lack of physical security made an MFI presence difficult to establish in some provinces. MISFA faced pressure from the Ministry of Reconstruction and Rural Development to extend into new provinces. This difficulty was resolved through agreement that a gradual approach to nationwide coverage would have to be adopted. MISFA is actively looking for more partners in the south of the country, where security issues are serious.

Implementation Arrangements

Development of MISFA was driven by the need to create a sustainable microfinance sector; this development meant working with service delivery partners (MFIs) prepared to adopt financial performance standards that would allow them to operate profitably in the long run. The presence of CGAP staff on the design mission meant that global knowledge on the sector could be brought to bear. CGAP has been leading the global development of financial standards and governance arrangements that focus on sustainability.

Successful microfinance efforts have encompassed a range of service delivery models, market segments, and lending arrangements. MISFA drew on this global experience by working with international partners such as BRAC, AKDN, and FINCA. These partners have substantial experience with and a demonstrated commitment to microfinance sector development more or less in accord with the principles supported by CGAP.

A consultant screened MISFA's prospective partners and selected 9 partners from 15 applicants. Although the nominal grounds for selection were knowledge of Afghanistan and institutional capacity, only two of the first nine partners, Mercy Corps and CARE, had worked in Afghanistan before 2002, and they had not worked in the microfinance sector. Selection was primarily influenced by institutional capacity, as eventually reflected in the business plans submitted to MISFA. The development of a business plan has become a basis for interaction between MISFA and its partners before financing is provided. This plan has helped MFIs identify their capacity development needs as well as analyze their market segments, product offerings, and terms of lending. Table 9.5 shows one plan in which growth projections reflect movement toward sustainable service delivery.

A business plan has not guaranteed that managers would deliver on it. MFIs with good global records have not necessarily brought the benefits of their expertise to bear on their Afghanistan operations. Moreover, some partners have continued to work toward their own program goals and found it awkward to focus on the imperatives of microfinance sector development. The disparity between business plans and results suggests

Table 9.5 One MFI's Financial Planning and Growth Projections

Performance variable	Year 1 (2005)	Year 2 (2006)	Year 3 (2007)	Year 4 (2008)	Year 5 (2009)
Subsidy Dependence Index	390.13	141.09	71.71	31.26	−6.15
Operational self-sufficiency (percent)	20.88	43.27	62.07	82.53	121.52
Operating cost ratio (percent)	263.28	85.00	49.55	35.33	21.64
Total costs/average portfolio outstanding (percent)	348.57	112.90	62.86	48.63	29.77
Loan portfolio outstanding (dollars)	312,121	938,367	1,922,354	3,882,138	8,046,935
Number of active clients (all products)	3,388	7174	11,285	16,387	27,046
Number of field workers	12	18	30	48	72
Case load per field worker	282	399	376	341	376
Portfolio per field worker	26,010	52,132	64,078	80,78	111,763
Cumulative loan disbursements (dollars)	438,372	1,737,149	4,442,856	989,8084	2,1595,985

Source: MISFA October 2004.

that in the future MISFA should consider making an initial investment in managers' capacity to develop and execute credible business plans before actually investing in the plans.

Quality of Technical Assistance

MISFA is implemented by a project manager appointed through the World Bank and by a consultancy company providing facilities management and technical expertise. The speed with which MISFA has developed has been the result of high quality from these personnel. The senior-most management has been exemplary in handling difficult negotiations with skill and in energizing the process of sustainable sector development. Stakeholders' satisfaction with the MISFA leadership is evidenced by a successful fundraising effort in 2004. That effort raised most of the needed commitment for the 2005 financial year.

MISFA imposes performance standards that are consistent with good MFI business practice. Maintenance of these standards is crucial for the successful transition from relief (the usual form of external agencies' engagement with communities) to development, in this case development of a substantial and sustainable microfinance sector. MISFA has created a model of service delivery that is intended to endure. It has already led to rapid growth in the sector and can be expected to promote even more rapid growth on the sound institutional foundations that it has laid.

Funding Modalities and Donor Coordination

MISFA is funded through the Afghanistan Reconstruction Trust Fund, which pays for the recurrent costs of the government, the return of Afghans, and the priority investments. Twenty-four donors have contributed more than $900,000, largely for the recurrent budget, to the Afghanistan Reconstruction Trust Fund. Some leading donors contribute a substantial proportion of their Afghanistan development budget through this fund. Canada and the United Kingdom earmarked funds for the Afghanistan Reconstruction Trust Fund for MISFA.

The fund provides two major advantages for MISFA. The first is a mechanism for single reporting of multidonor financing. The second is retention of CGAP—through the World Bank as administrator of the Afghanistan Reconstruction Trust Fund—as mentor on sector development issues.

Procurement and Disbursement

As the support of the recurrent budget, which has been linked to various investments to strengthen public sector finance management, the Afghanistan Reconstruction Trust Fund must be seen to observe high procurement standards. Because MISFA operates through the trust fund, it is required to follow IDA rules for procurement and disbursement. These rules initially caused some delays. For example, MFI partners were identified through a selection process based on their probable operational capabilities. However, IDA procurement rules initially required competition for awards of service delivery contracts. Once this hurdle was overcome, MFIs had to learn IDA procurement rules, which took time. Partner MFIs are now familiar with the operating environment and the required fiduciary standards. To further accelerate progress, the World Bank relaxed rules regarding no objection certificates for expenditures below a certain level and rules regarding statements of expenditure before release of second and subsequent tranches. As the MISFA board becomes fully operational, a further relaxation of IDA monitoring is expected.

Because MISFA funding is channeled through the Afghanistan Reconstruction Trust Fund, its expenditures go through the budget. As a result, requests for fund disbursement move from the MFI through MISFA and the MRRD to the Ministry of Finance, from which they are forwarded to the Afghanistan Reconstruction Trust Fund for approval. The approved requests then go back to the Ministry of Finance, which disburses funds into the MFI's bank account. This process, though cumbersome, means that the government has more direct ownership of the investment in microfinance than would have been the case with an off-budget bilateral arrangement. Integration in the Afghanistan Recons-truction Trust Fund lends authority to MISFA; and though CGAP has driven development of MISFA activities, the government has some voice in development of the microfinance sector.

Institutional Autonomy

MISFA was designed to develop as an independent entity. CGAP viewed its formal separation from the MRRD as an essential good practice. This separation was achieved when the MISFA board (with government and donor members) replaced the steering committee that watched over MISFA on behalf of the MRRD. MISFA has now established its desired legal and institutional status—one that will allow it to promote sound fiduciary standards and to develop the microfinance sector.

The longer-term future of MISFA is unclear, but it is expected to grow as the sector grows and as its training and oversight functions expand. Funding for this growth, at least in the short term, will be primarily through the Afghanistan Reconstruction Trust Fund. As an authority to establish and monitor fiduciary standards of service providers, MISFA is expected to become a conduit for other funds, including commercial funds, for sector expansion. This change may be beneficial, because the Afghanistan Reconstruction Trust Fund has, in a sense, provided an addi-tional layer of control that duplicates MISFA functions. As administrator of the Afghanistan Reconstruction Trust Fund, the World Bank has applied IDA rules, as described above, to direct both MISFA funding and that of its partner MFIs. But MISFA is set up expressly to monitor the performance of these MFIs by developing their capacity and supporting their growth through grants and loans that it monitors. It was for this rea-son that MISFA's senior manager, Steve MacQueen,[3] described MISFA as a success "in spite of the design." However, as discussed earlier, budget support and coordinated funding mobilization were sensible reasons for use of the Afghanistan Reconstruction Trust Fund as MISFA's funding instrument. Moreover, as noted earlier, this use gave MISFA credibility within policy discussions on development of microfinance.

Donor Partnerships

Today MISFA receives direct donor support in addition to funding through the Afghanistan Reconstruction Trust Fund. The International Labour Organization (ILO) and United States Agency for International Develop-ment (USAID) have assigned experts to MISFA to help develop particular aspects of the facility and to link it to ILO and USAID interventions.

ILO has developed its own framework for addressing microfinance needs in postconflict communities and brings valuable expertise to bear. In addition, it has acted as a conduit for the assessment of aspiring local NGOs, often with support from domestic political constituencies that wish to develop or expand their microfinance services. The ILO expert assigned to MISFA has acted as a broker between MISFA and these potential MFI partners and has helped the latter develop work plans for sustainable service delivery.

USAID's support to MISFA comes in the context of support for development of agricultural markets, which has taken the form of support for existing NGOs and strengthening of indigenous capacity. USAID's Rebuilding Agricultural Markets Program (RAMP) has a rural finance component of, which $5 million is earmarked for disbursement through MISFA—$4 million as a loan fund and $1 million for technical assistance directed to development of agricultural markets. The MISFA-USAID partnership started with a pilot agricultural loan product through BRAC and market research to help other service providers identify market niches. As USAID becomes more heavily involved in spending resources on Afghan agriculture, and as political and disbursement pressures grow, it is unclear how its relationship with MISFA will evolve, but its commitment to the MISFA approach is clear.

Local Capacity

Key MFI partners are working hard to promote Afghans within their programs. The introduction of new NGO partners will strengthen the Afghan presence within MFIs. However, given the human resource crisis faced by Afghanistan, it will be sometime before any MFI is fully Afghan-controlled. As for MISFA, the pressure of delivering services has deflected attention from training Afghans to take over the roles of the technical assistance team. In some areas—monitoring, for example—oversight consultants have had to focus on sector development and the strengths of their MFI partners rather than on the strategic plan for MISFA.

Governance

MISFA, in essence, is a development instrument for the financial services sector. It seeks to contribute to governance aims by supporting institutional development of service providers and by establishing performance standards. As an apex organization, MISFA uses financial incentives—access to on-lending funds—to make service provision sustainable, inclusive, and transparent. These incentives come into play in the negotiation of business plans of partner microfinance service providers, typically NGOs. This negotiation allows MISFA to identify the partners' training and institutional strengthening needs. These needs typically relate to accounting standards, product design, portfolio development and management, staff development, information systems, and monitoring.

Coordinated donor support to MISFA through the Afghanistan Reconstruction Trust Fund has lent coherence to MISFA's service delivery standards. Confidence in MISFA and its fiduciary management arrangements has, in turn, been crucial in leveraging additional funds. Key donors such as CGAP and DFID have earmarked funds routed through the trust fund for MISFA and have participated in MISFA supervision missions. Through these means and its role on the steering committee, and now the MISFA board, CGAP has largely been responsible for MISFA becoming a vehicle for sustainable development of the microfinance sector.

MFI partners and donors know that they are supporting a sector development approach focused on sustainable service delivery. In part because of its origins in the MRRD, MISFA has established a degree of sector leadership. This leadership is reflected, for example, in its involvement in the elaboration of new banking laws and their requirements with respect to the microfinance sector.

MISFA supporters hope that the facility will be sufficiently influential on the microfinance sector development agenda so that its standards become industry standards. This aspiration is threatened by pressure to deliver financial services quickly and, therefore, with little regard to the longer-term governance of the sector and its sustainability. The key concern is speed of development as measured by the share of donor grants used for client loans compared with the share for capacity building of service delivery agencies (the MFIs). This conflict between service delivery and capacity development has, at times, resulted in a virtual impasse between government and donors. The share of capacity building has varied from less than 40 percent to nearly 90 percent, depending on the initial capacity and infrastructure of the partner MFI. When MISFA managers checked these shares against global averages, they concluded that, in the circumstances of Afghanistan, their shares were reasonable.

As noted earlier, MFI grants go through a serious negotiation and approval process involving MISFA management and the Steering Committee/MISFA board; approvals from both the government of Afghanistan and the World Bank are required. Approval of some MFI business plans has been delayed because of what the government of Afghanistan regarded as an excessive expenditure on capacity building compared with loan funds. Vehicles for other partners have been held up as the government of Afghanistan expresses its concern about this split between capacity and service delivery. In all cases the differences have been resolved, sometimes with high-level intervention from Washington, but they underline the tensions of marrying the imperative for service delivery from a political legitimacy perspective and the development agenda's focus on capacity and sustainability.

A related concern is the relationship of MISFA to other stakeholders that wish to use microfinance. Microfinance is, for example, viewed as the natural next phase in the evolution of community development committees under the National Solidarity Program, which is housed in the Ministry of Reconstruction and Rural Development. Some stakeholders envision the committees as the host recipient organizations for most public service providers. The more than 6,000 committees have received block grants totaling $60 million for urgent infrastructure and other modest investments. Use of the committees as an organizational home for delivering microfinance services may be feasible but is desirable only if they can sustain service delivery. MISFA's efforts to develop a sustainable microfinance sector could be undermined by rapid extension of microfinance services to community development committees without adequate business plans, capacity to manage financial operations, and strategic purpose beyond short-term resource transfers.

Other entrants in the microfinance sector, including some NGOs, are not linked to MISFA. In addition, aspiring commercial operations such as the First Microfinance Bank—with technical support and assured commercial money from donors—have arisen to address specific market segments, for example, small urban trade and production enterprises. These operations also face pressures to extend service delivery rapidly, particularly to the agriculture sector. One risk is that grants or loans that go bad could undermine sustainable agricultural loan programs.

With these other stakeholders seeking to engage in microfinance, MISFA will be pressed to secure sectoral financial sustainability standards for service delivery. Failure by some stakeholders to maintain standards could undermine the whole sector. Again, the key underlying issue is speed of service delivery; immediate employment and livelihood gains are pitted against investment in service providers' capacity to ensure sustainability of services. This dilemma for MISFA is, in essence, a microcosm of the bigger debate on state reconstruction—buying political legitimacy through delivery of services now versus strengthening capacity and developing sustainable institutions with coherent and strategic business and management plans. At different points—the drought in the summer of 2004 and the lack of power in Kabul in the bitter winter of 2004–05—political pressure on service delivery has been high. This is perhaps the most politically sensitive issue relating to aid effectiveness.[4] The need to build capacity is fairly fundamental and universally recognized, but the time and money it takes are a source of irritation to political leaders expecting substantial resources for the political process of state building.

Horizontal Equity

MISFA promotes inclusivity through selection of partners that address the financial services needs of different market segments: traders, farmers, traditional and cottage industries, and small- and medium-size enterprises. As MISFA expands partnership arrangements, it brings in partners with different types of experience—for example, local NGOs that can cover a particular geographic area. MISFA is already engaged in development of specialist market niches, including services to those crippled during the wars and to semi-nomadic minority populations. In 2005 it had 14 partners delivering financial services.

MISFA services overlap at the top end of the market with those of other providers such as the first Microfinance Bank of Afghanistan. In February 2005 these other providers had about 1,000 borrowers, compared with the over 60,000 that MISFA partners serve.

As noted above, MISFA's geographical coverage is mixed as a result of security concerns. Related to this need to expand geographic coverage is the need to assess how microfinance services can best contribute to a reduction in poppy cultivation. Afghanistan is committed to losing its status as the leading source of opium globally. But developing alternative livelihoods is difficult when farmers are indebted and required by their lenders to grow poppies and when returns to poppy cultivation far outstrip current potential alternative land uses. With support from USAID as well as the Afghanistan Reconstruction Trust Fund, MISFA is taking part in some activities to promote alternative livelihoods already, but a more systematic and integrated approach is needed.

Gender

Key MISFA partners, including BRAC, target women as borrowers. This practice follows from the practice that BRAC used so successfully in Bangladesh, where the debate over the benefits to women of being loan recipients has been extensive. There is more or less a consensus now that even when women have only limited control over the use of loan resources, they have typically benefited through empowerment in their intrafamily and community relationships. Very often their income-generating activity benefits, because their labor has been combined with the loans to produce goods for the market, thus leading to household income gains. Even if they do not control the purse strings, women who receive loans from MFIs tend to gain a greater voice in household decisions on expenditure. For many MFIs, including BRAC, the village center or group that is formed for service management is also a basis for additional program inputs, including health and legal education.

Preliminary assessments indicate that female Afghan loan recipients have performed well. Concerns about female repression restricting participation have been addressed effectively. Similarly, concerns about the charging of interest on loans in a devout Islamic country have been limited, because MISFA has been sensitive to this issue. It is too early to determine whether microfinance will act as a significant vehicle for women's empowerment in Afghanistan, but comparisons with Bangladesh suggest that it is on track to serve that goal.

Social Capital

Recent research suggests that access to microfinance in postwar reconstruction can strengthen social capital (Zohir and Martin 2004). The provision of loans promotes business arrangements and joint production—both of which can help build trust and (re)generate forms of economic interaction damaged by wars. Trust is a key ingredient for economic progress when legal provisions for enforcement of contracts are weak. Loans' stimulation to the local economy and the formation of service delivery groups can promote trust, thereby providing a key ingredient for expansion of the local economy.

MFIs establish contract standards in their loan and savings operations, observance of which is monitored by MISFA. Their good contract practices are advertised and adopted elsewhere. This positive spillover of MISFA is difficult to quantify but may be significant.

Lessons for LICUS

MISFA offers six general lessons for the provision of microfinance in low-income countries under stress (LICUS).

First, microfinance is a valuable tool and a priority for investment in LICUS. However, where heavy investment in capacity is required, microfinance will not provide the instant resource transfers and service delivery that emergency conditions might require. For instance, microfinance does not have the high transfer value and quick-disbursing characteristics of a well-designed emergency employment program. There is a trade-off between urgent delivery of services and development of capacity to ensure the long-term sustainability of service delivery. Inevitably, as was seen in Afghanistan, aid organizations are pressured to disburse faster, to move to new politically sensitive areas, and to work with politically preferred partners. These pressures must be resisted if service delivery is to be made sustainable.

Second, early identification of microfinance investment as a reconstruction need can set the stage for a donor-coordinated, domestically supported sector development strategy by allowing for open discussion of the biggest challenge—managing the joint concerns of service delivery and capacity development. Microfinance funding channeled through the government's budget receives a great deal of scrutiny and ultimately gives an organization like MISFA both credibility in its support for specific approaches to sector development and a voice in policy development for the financial sector.

Third, organizing delivery of microfinance through the national budget, at least initially, ensures attention to sector development by donors and gives the government important opportunities to assert its own perspectives on sector development. True domestic ownership will take time and domestic resources, but delivery of microfinance through the budgetary process allows domestic policy processes to inform sector development.

Fourth, donors and service providers should agree on standards of fiduciary responsibility. In the microfinance sector, a rift has developed between those that emphasize financial sustainability above all else and those that view sustainability as a secondary concern to their social mission. The latter position could embrace sustainability, and those who have adopted it are increasingly recognizing the gains to social missions that derive from financial sustainability. The "trade-off" between the two can be managed through careful attention to social performance management.

Fifth, rapid scaling up of microfinance is possible with an organization such as MISFA, which helps partners develop capacity and which is a credible guarantor to donors that their microfinance grants will be used effectively for poverty reduction.

Sixth, microfinance delivery can set standards for sustainable delivery of other types of services, extending microfinance's strengthening of social capital.

Notes

1. This paper is based on background reading and a 10-day trip to Afghanistan in December 2004. During this visit I was housed by MISFA and am very grateful to Steve MacQueen and Debra Boyer, MISFA managers, and their staff for sharing their experiences so readily. The trip included a visit to the BRAC microfinance program in Mazar-e-Sharif and nearby villages in Balkh Province.
2. This was a key background document for the Tokyo aid-pledging meeting of the Interim Authority of Afghanistan and donors in January 2002. See ADB, UNDP, and World Bank (2002, 45).
3. Steve MacQueen was tragically killed in Kabul on March 7 in a street shooting three days before the end of his MISFA assignment. His personal contribution to the achievements described in this chapter was enormous, and it can only be hoped that MISFA will continue growing into the strong service provider for the poor in Afghanistan that was his goal.
4. Donor coordination is also threatened as donors—with different resource levels and different leverage—respond differently to the political pressure to deliver results quickly.

Bibliography

ADB (Asian Development Bank), UNDP (United Nations Development Programme), and World Bank. 2002. "Transitional Support Strategy, Afghanistan." World Bank, Washington, DC.

ATA (Afghanistan Transitional Authority). 2002. "National Development Framework." Kabul, Afghanistan.

BRAC Afghanistan. 2004. "Informal report." BRAC, Kabul, Afghanistan. December 8.

Forster, Sarah, and Doug Pearce. 2002. "Afghanistan: CGAP Microfinance Review." Consultative Group to Assist the Poor, Washington, DC.

Government of Afghanistan. 2002. "National Development Framework." Kabul, Afghanistan.

IMF (International Monetary Fund). 2003. "Islamic State of Afghanistan: Rebuilding a Macroeconomic Framework for Reconstruction and Growth." Country Report 03/299. IMF, Washington, DC.

MISFA. 2004. "Internal documents." MISFA, Kabul, Afghanistan. October and December.

UNDP (United Nations Development Programme). 2003. *Human Development Indicators, 2003*. Geneva: United Nations.

UNDP, and government of Afghanistan. 2005. "Security with a Human Face: Challenges and Responsibilities." Afghanistan National Human Development Report. Kabul, Afghanistan.

UNICEF (United Nations Children's Fund). 2002. *The State of the World's Children 2003*. New York and Geneva: United Nations.

World Bank. 2003. *World Development Indicators 2003*. Washington, DC: World Bank.

Zohir, Sajjad, and Imran Martin. 2004. "The Wider Impacts of Microfinance." *Journal of International Development* (special issue) (April): 301–30.

CHAPTER 10

Community-Driven Development in Conflict and Postconflict Conditions: The Northern Uganda Social Action Fund Project

Uganda is not classified as a LICUS state because of its success in sustaining high rates of economic growth and poverty reduction since the late 1980s. But the 18 districts that make up northern Uganda have economic conditions and social indicators on par with or worse than many LICUS states elsewhere in Africa. Much of the North has experienced a succession

This chapter was written by Mark Robinson.

This chapter draws on 30 interviews with government officials, donors, and nongovernmental organizations in Kampala, Gulu, and Arua and on visits to communities in two districts in October 2004. The advice and assistance of the World Bank staff in Kampala is gratefully acknowledged. Special thanks go to Harriet Kiwanuka, who greatly assisted in drawing up the appointments schedule and logistical arrangements. The time and patience of the staff in the Northern Uganda Social Action Fund (NUSAF) Management Unit in Gulu and the support of Judith Rukho in making arrangements for meetings and field visits in Arua is greatly appreciated. Finally, the senior government staff in the Office of the Prime Minister and the two district offices in Arua and Gulu provided helpful guidance and orientation, which is gratefully acknowledged.

of violent conflicts, and insurgency continues to afflict the Acholi, Teso, and Karamoja subregions.[1] The war prosecuted by the Lord's Resistance Army (LRA) since 1987 has resulted in considerable loss of life, 1.6 million internally displaced persons (IDPs), and the abduction of an estimated 20,000 to 25,000 children (Lomo and Hovil 2004, 22). In the northeast, cattle rustling by armed gangs has decimated the livestock population and, in turn, destabilized the economy and social fabric of the region.[2] At 66 percent, poverty in the North is almost double the average for Uganda as a whole and three times as high as in the Central Region. Variations in household consumption suggest that districts in the North and East are much worse off than those in the West, center, and South.[3] The economic impact of the conflict is significant: the cost is estimated at 3 percent of GDP and the loss of consumption in the North is at a similar level (Republic of Uganda 2004).

The Uganda People's Defence Forces (UPDF) have sought to defeat the LRA militarily but have not ended the conflict. The intensity of the conflict has escalated since Operation Iron Fist was launched in early 2002 with UPDF incursions into southern Sudan to flush out the LRA. The result was a dramatic increase in the number of IDPs and a spread of the violence eastward to the Teso and Lango subregions. Peace initiatives through traditional and religious leaders and a government-sponsored Amnesty Commission have resulted in the surrender of many abductees and LRA followers, and yet small bands of fighters continue to terrorize the rural population in remote areas of northern and eastern Uganda. Even though peace has returned to many areas, problems of insecurity continue. Infrastructure and communications are rudimentary in much of the region, and health and education facilities are in a poor state of repair. Local governments display attributes of a quasi-state: limited capacity, low revenue base, and restricted service provision.

Over the years, the Ugandan government and aid donors have devised programs to improve local infrastructure and livelihoods in this war-ravaged region. Two programs are of particular significance for this study, because lessons derived from their design and implementation heavily influenced the content of NUSAF. The Northern Uganda Reconstruction Project (NURP-I) was designed to upgrade roads, water supplies, health facilities, and schools with the support of International Development Association (IDA) loan finance. The Community Action Program (CAP) originally formed part of NURP-I in the West Nile subregion but evolved as a separate program funded by the Netherlands government. NURP-I was a large, top-down, supply-driven program that built roads, schools, clinics, and bore-wells across the entire region but with little community involvement. The CAP, by contrast, was a demand-driven local infrastructure program, rooted in local community preferences and characterized by a strong participatory thrust. While NURP-I achieved many of its physical objectives, many investments were not sustainable, and its contribution to institutional development was negligible. By comparison, the CAP is generally acknowledged to have been a great success in terms of community assets and building local capacity. This success is tempered by the limitations of parallel administrative structures operating outside the local government machinery.

This chapter examines lessons from these two programs for the design and implementation of NUSAF. Many of the negative lessons of NURP-I implementation and the positive attributes of the CAP greatly influenced the design of NUSAF, which highlights the value of a demand-driven approach and the need to promote implementation through local government institutions. The chapter also examines the experience of scaling up a community-led approach in NUSAF's implementation. This review includes an assessment of the implementation challenges posed by an environment of conflict, weak capacity, and endemic poverty.

The primary focus of this chapter is on the wider lessons emanating from NUSAF's design and implementation in the LICUS-like context of northern Uganda rather than on project management and microimplementation issues that arise in any large-scale social action fund. Although it is too early to assess the governance and poverty impacts of NUSAF, which was created in 2002, an indication of the project's potential and the limitations can be gleaned from the initial stages of implementation. In particular, insights on the appropriateness of a demand-driven approach in a conflict and postconflict environment highlight the importance of integrating project management into local government planning and administrative systems and of building community-level capacity for microproject planning and monitoring. Another design feature of NUSAF worth highlighting is the importance of undertaking conflict mitigation and reconciliation efforts in recognition of the limitations of traditional approaches to postconflict rehabilitation. The experience of NUSAF offers lessons not only for donors concerned with the development prospects of northern Uganda, but also for donors that are designing and implementing comparable social action funds in postconflict LICUS states.[4]

NUSAF's $133.5 million budget provides the largest source of finance for development purposes in northern Uganda and forms the main component of NURP-II.[5] The IDA loan component is $100 million, to which the government of Uganda contributes $13.3 million and local communities contribute $20.2 million. On average NUSAF resources will provide $1 million per district per year over the project's five-year duration, though district allocations vary in line with poverty, social indicators, and intensity of conflict. This figure exceeds the development budget of most districts in northern Uganda, the bulk of which comes from the consolidated grant under the Local Government Development Program (LGDP-II) funded largely by the World Bank and other donors through budget support. No other donor provides assistance to the North on a comparable scale; most bilateral agencies prefer to support national development interventions either through budget support or direct funding to NGOs working in the region. Only the Acholi and Karamoja programs supported by the European Commission offer resources on a comparable scale: these programs are largely for the rehabilitation of infrastructure in two subregions.

This NUSAF study draws on more than 30 interviews and two field visits to the region over a two-week period in October 2004. Interviews with officials in the Office of the Prime Minister (OPM) and donor representatives in Kampala were complemented by visits to the NUSAF Management Unit (NUMU) in Gulu, interviews with local government staff and politicians in Arua and Gulu districts, and field visits to project sites in the two districts. Project documentation on NURP-I, CAP, and NUSAF and the secondary literature on conflict and development in the region were also reviewed.[6]

Project Antecedents

NUSAF had two antecedents.

The Northern Uganda Reconstruction Project

The Northern Uganda Reconstruction Project (NURP-I) was designed to upgrade infrastructure destroyed by or neglected during successive conflicts and thereby to allow resumption of productive activity and to stimulate growth and poverty reduction. The underlying premise was that development interventions would increase the potential for improved long-term security. The project aimed to upgrade highways, feeder roads, telecommunications, schools, urban development, community investments (the Community Action Program), water supply and sanitation, and agriculture.

It was financed largely by the World Bank through an IDA loan of $71.2 million and bilateral contributions from Belgium, Denmark, and the Netherlands; the government of Uganda made an additional commitment of $20 million over a six-year period from 1992 to 1998. The initial intention was that the Netherlands Embassy would fund the CAP for community-initiated microprojects in the West Nile Subregion to strengthen local government agencies' capacity to plan and manage reconstruction and rehabilitation. The CAP subsequently developed as a separate program in parallel with NURP-I.

Construction of roads and social infrastructure in the form of schools and health centers occurred despite conflict in much of the region (World Bank 2002a, 3).[7] A project completion report rated NURP-I as satisfactory and concluded that "The project has substantially achieved its physical objectives and has realized most of the anticipated benefits" (World Bank 1999, 3). Most of the investments in roads, urban development, and education were achieved with increased rates of utilization and school attendance. A performance audit report the following year was more critical; it rated the project as marginally satisfactory (World Bank 2000). The objectives of the project, with investments in seven sectors during a period of insecurity and weak institutional capacity, were considered to be overly ambitious.

The general perception of NURP-I among government officials, donors, politicians, and local community leaders interviewed for this study is circumspect. Districts had limited administrative and absorptive capacity. Centralized and top-down implementation was ineffective. Many subproject investments were devised and implemented by central government line departments without consulting local communities; the results were that construction quality was poor, the physical location was often inappropriate, costs were higher than envisaged, utilization rates were low, and sustainability was compromised. The lack of community involvement in project identification and implementation was reflected in poor supervision and maintenance; many facilities remained incomplete or unused. Centralized procurement procedures were inefficient and wasteful. Contracts were invariably awarded to firms that were from outside the region and that had little regard for local conditions and community preferences. The performance audit drew attention to problems of corruption resulting from questionable procurement, weak control mechanisms, poor onsite supervision, and inadequate monitoring arrangements (World Bank 2000). Communities viewed the investments negatively, because they saw little tangible benefit.[8]

Although NURP-1 was completed on time, design flaws caused implementation problems. The project was implemented through the OPM before the new decentralization policy was launched in 1997. The NURP head office was located in Kampala, necessitating frequent travel to the region by the management agency staff. The political imperative to invest substantial resources for reconstruction in the North dictated a top-down approach, and violent conflict across much of the region limited community engagement (Republic of Uganda 2003, 31–32).

An in-depth analysis of the political context would have highlighted the potential challenges of an approach centered on reconstruction and capacity building, which would probably require expertise from outside the Bank (World Bank 2000, 8).[9] Rather than rely on development and reconstruction to improve security, future interventions would require greater emphasis on activities designed to promote peace,[10] including attention to the challenges of demobilizing armed forces and reintegrating perpetrators of violence into their host communities and a careful assessment of the risks to project personnel working in conflict-prone areas.

Bank documents acknowledge the limitations of a highly centralized top-down approach and central disbursement of resources.[11] Infrequent field visits by Bank staff highlighted the need for a monitoring system to ensure financial accountability and community oversight to prevent corrupt and wasteful practices. Pervasive weaknesses in institutional capacity highlighted the need to strengthen the capacity of local government, NGOs, and the private sector at an early stage of implementation. The value of hiring local contractors was evidenced by problems arising from use of contractors unfamiliar with local conditions and requirements.

A more sustained focus on the needs of vulnerable groups was evident from the lack of poverty targeting in NURP-I investments. In this respect, focusing on production and income generation in the design of microprojects was imperative for rebuilding the livelihoods of widows, orphans, and the victims of violence. Unsustainability and low rates of use highlighted the need for a participatory approach that would entail consultation with community members and local government. Delayed implementation and differences in approach underscored the importance of a coordinated donor response and agreement on the most appropriate forms of intervention in conflict and postconflict environments.

These lessons informed the design process for NUSAF, which adopted an approach modeled on a community-based social fund. The positive experience of the demand-driven approach that underpinned the CAP played a critical role in developing the institutional parameters of this approach.[12]

The Community Action Program, West Nile

The Community Action Program in the West Nile subregion was originally conceived as part of NURP-I. Grant support from the Royal Netherlands Embassy covered the districts of Arua, Nebbi, and Moyo (later divided into two districts). The principles that informed the design of CAP were the inversion of those underpinning NURP-I even though the focus was mainly on rehabilitation of social infrastructure and, to a lesser extent, income generation. The CAP was separated from NURP-I in 1994 at the instigation of the Dutch government and implemented in the West Nile subregion.

Responsibility for program implementation was vested in a Dutch NGO—the Netherlands Development Organization (SNV)—in conjunction with the OPM (CAP 1996a). Local communities identified and prioritized project activities with the help of community facilitators at the subcounty level. The facilitators initially operated in pairs (a woman and a man), one identified by the community and the other appointed by SNV through open recruitment; in the project's second phase, a single facilitator operated in each subcounty.[13] Community facilitators were given comprehensive training and worked with subcounty authorities to identify groups and areas most in need of support. Projects were subject to approval of a district and subcounty steering committee comprising officials, traditional leaders, and NGO representatives. Funds were disbursed directly by the district authorities once approval was granted; communities typically contributed 25 percent of total investment costs.[14] Community investments centered on schools, health posts, boreholes, sanitation, and small bridges, while the income generation component largely focused on group schemes designed to improve agricultural productivity.

The second phase of CAP implementation (1997 to 1999) devolved greater responsibilities to the program management unit in Arua and the district teams, and it placed more emphasis on income-generating activities to stimulate local economic development. An external evaluation in 1999 recommended that CAP be wound up, that project activities be implemented through local government structures, and that a local NGO (CEFORD) be created to take over CAP's mobilization and facilitation role (SNV 1999a; CDRN 2001). The program ended in early 2000 because of resource constraints and new policy priorities that focused on budget and sectoral support. Total disbursements had amounted to $6.3 million.

Internal and external evaluations of CAP acknowledge its positive impact (CAP 1996b, 1999; SNV 1999a).[15] The investments were generally sound, appropriate to the needs to local communities, and broadly consistent with local government priorities. An estimated 20 percent of the population in the subregion benefited directly from project investments in community infrastructure and income generation.[16] The construction requirements of the program stimulated local private sector development, and increased competition led to an improvement in quality and standards. Project management committees formed at the community level and made significant contributions of materials and unskilled labor for community investments. The CAP also created durable local institutions for the management and maintenance of local infrastructure projects in the form of school management committees and water and sanitation committees. The administrative apparatus established for CAP implementation was effective in building community ownership and strengthening local institutional capacity through district level units, steering committees at district and subcounty levels, and a dense network of field officers and community facilitators (SNV 1999a).

However, several challenges arose during the course of implementation. There were significant delays in getting the project off the ground because the acceptability of a demand-driven approach took time to establish, and staff recruitment and orientation required considerable investment of time and resources. Further delays arose from the time required to mobilize community contributions and to identify appropriate income generation ventures. The technical quality of small-scale infrastructure investments was found to be deficient in a number of cases, particularly in the first phase, because of inadequate technical supervision from both CAP field personnel and local government staff (CAP 1996b, 38–40).

Although district and subcounty steering committees served as the key locus for appraisal, approval, and implementation, an external evaluation found that CAP was not closely integrated with the relevant district line departments. Moreover, delivery costs were high (averaging 50 percent of project expenditures) because of staff costs and operational expenses incurred through intensive interaction with local communities. Concerns were raised about the creation of a parallel structure that was expensive, poorly integrated into the local government machinery, and potentially difficult to sustain. Finally, the activities supported by CAP became increasingly diversified and difficult to coordinate (SNV 1999a).

Lessons from CAP informed the NUSAF design process.[17] The principal lessons were the value of a demand-driven approach, the limitations of parallel administrative structures, and the need for effective integration into the local government machinery (SNV 1999b).

The Northern Uganda Social Action Fund Project

In the two years since project inception, there have been considerable delays in setting up the implementing agency, appointing project staff, and procuring vehicles and equipment. At the time of this study, only six months had elapsed since construction, and the purchase of assets began in April 2004. The first major tranche of funding for nearly 1,500 subprojects approved by NUMU began disbursing in June 2004, after a series of pilot investments earlier in the year. Community demand for subprojects has rapidly escalated; by October 2004, 18 districts had submitted summaries of 3,131 desired subprojects. Many of these subprojects did not fall within NUSAF guidelines and were rejected, but several district administrations have approved many more than can be funded under the NUSAF budget for the first two financial years. Although this expression of interest in NUSAF confirms the appropriateness of the project's demand-driven approach, it is generating enormous implementation challenges.

Design Considerations

The proposal for a social action fund in northern Uganda originated in 1999. The proposal reflected recognition that a substantial investment in community infrastructure and livelihoods projects was required to address poverty and to tackle the root causes of conflict and that a demand-driven approach would be required for successful implementation. This recognition reflected an appreciation of the negative lessons arising from the implementation of NURP-I and the positive design features of the CAP (World Bank 2002a, 15), as well as Bank experience with other social action funds (World Bank 2002b; Bloom, Chilowa, Chirwa, Lucas, Mvula, Schou, and Tsoka 2004).

The design of NUSAF resulted from a highly consultative process involving stakeholders from central government to local communities. The OPM coordinated the core design team, which included representatives of all the major line ministries in Kampala (usually senior officials delegated by their respective permanent secretaries) and NGOs. Ugandans from the region or with work experience there played a lead role in the design process. World Bank specialists, including Ugandan staff who had worked on the highly successful CAP in West Nile, were also closely involved in program design. Senior Bank officials helped cultivate support for a demand-driven approach and for the inclusion of a conflict resolution component. The resultant design is considered by most Ugandan observers to be highly appropriate to the conflict and postconflict conditions pertaining in northern Uganda.

Bilateral donors were consulted on NUSAF's design, and they provided collective suggestions through coordination groups dealing with decentralization and the northern Uganda. While supportive of the need to channel more resources to the region to address problems of poverty and insecurity, they expressed concern over the prospect of parallel disbursement mechanisms and the potential for duplication of existing local government programs.[18] They preferred funds to be disbursed through the government budget to ensure complementarity with the LGDP-II planning process and to avoid undermining accountability provisions in local government financial management systems. Donors also suggested that the project design should take adequate account of prevailing conditions of conflict and insecurity and that NUSAF should not be regarded as a substitute for political action to resolve the underlying causes of conflict in the North. These donor concerns did not convince the design team that NUSAF should be integrated into the existing local government budget and planning process. The team argued that the proposed NUSAF district technical officers (NDTOs) would provide a point of contact for district government and that the appraisal process involving local government officers and planning staff would ensure sectoral integration. Bilateral donors remained skeptical of NUSAF and did not provide additional financial support, which weakened the force of their argument and has ensured that their involvement remains peripheral.

Considerable emphasis was placed on a detailed analysis of conditions in the northern region. Participatory poverty assessments and district profiles were carried out in all the northern districts as part of a nationwide effort to identify poverty determinants and trends. These efforts identified the specific problems faced by vulnerable communities in the northern districts and the types of interventions that would be appropriate to address their needs. Community needs assessments were commissioned by the OPM in all 18 districts during the project preparation phase. These assessments elicited local perceptions of key community priorities, coping mechanisms, and characteristics of the most vulnerable groups and were used to determine NUSAF's potential social impact and the best means to promote equitable and sustainable development at the community level. Stakeholder workshops were held in every district. At these workshops, elected politicians, government officials, traditional leaders, NGOs and faith-based organizations reviewed the assumptions underpinning the proposed project design and helped the design team refine specific features of NUSAF (World Bank 2002a, 20). Pilot projects were implemented to field test the feasibility of the project design, but only after delays in setting up the management agency.

The political and economic conditions in the North were an explicit point of reference for NUSAF's design. Although the design team did not examine the underlying causes of conflict in detail, it recognized that political factors played an important role in galvanizing violent insurgency and that resentment against perceived southern political dominance was a root cause of the problem. Conflict in northern Uganda arises more from violent opposition to ethnic claims to centralized authority than from intercommunal animosities at a more localized level (Lomo and Hovil 2004). Therefore, NUSAF was premised on community reconciliation and conflict mitigation as a basis for sustainable development in the region. It was hoped that communities would identify conflict mitigation measures to overcome the legacy of violence and address its underlying causes. Development interventions would flow out of processes of conflict management and would provide former combatants, abductees, and victims of violence with livelihood opportunities and secure sources of income from labor and contracts for community infrastructure projects. Traditional leaders and religious organizations would be the entry point for these interventions.

The project needed to be guided by community preferences but predicated on local government acceptance of a demand-driven approach. A major challenge was to convince local government officials and elected politicians of the virtue of vesting financial management responsibility directly in communities. In this regard the design team had two main concerns: whether communities had the capacity to manage large-scale financial resources in a responsible manner, and how to ensure that local government remained accountable for government funds without being granted direct financial responsibility. These challenges remain, but politicians and officials have largely accepted the validity of the approach and their early concerns have been partly allayed by communities' considerable demand for subprojects. The concern about financial accountability was reflected in OPM's decision at the end of October 2004 to send out teams of government and external auditors to each district to undertake an independent audit of community investments and accounts.

Project Objectives and Major Components

The stated aim of NUSAF is "to empower communities in Northern Uganda by enhancing capacity to systematically identify, prioritize, and plan for their needs and implement sustainable development to improve socioeceonomic services and opportunities. In so doing, NUSAF will contribute to improved livelihoods by placing money and its management in the hands of the communities" (World Bank 2002a, 2). The project was explicitly intended to complement government efforts to reduce poverty in the 18 districts of the North through a participatory approach that draws on community value systems, which are considered "particularly strong in the family, clan and cattle-raising culture of northern Uganda" (World Bank 2002a, 2). NUSAF is a major element of NURP-II. Although NUSAF is listed as a program under the new security pillar of the Poverty Eradication Action Program (PEAP), it is not integrated into national and local government plans and budgets (Republic of Uganda 2004).

NUSAF differs from most conventional development programs in Uganda by providing grant support directly to communities; community-level institutions are responsible for managing funds. Specific objectives of this approach are to stimulate community action, leadership development, and resource mobilization; strengthen ongoing reconciliation processes; and enable communities to articulate and prioritize their needs and to manage processes and outcomes. The project also has explicit governance and spillover objectives in fostering an environment for peace and development, improved transparency and accountability, and better leadership at all levels (World Bank 2002a).

The primary target groups for NUSAF interventions are the children and youth whose livelihoods and careers have been disrupted as a result of prolonged conflict; a particular focus is on those abducted and brutalized by insurgents, and combatants who have surrendered and returned their weapons in exchange for a secure livelihood. Female-headed households, orphans, widows and widowers, HIV/AIDS victims, the very poor, and others affected by conflict are the intended beneficiaries of NUSAF's income-generation and livelihoods assistance.

The NUSAF project has four main components. The first, the Community Development Initiatives (CDI) component, is the largest, accounting for 72 percent of the total NUSAF budget. According to the core design document, "The CDI component is intended to finance demand-driven community-based initiatives to construct and rehabilitate socioeconomic infrastructure guided by a subproject menu that conforms to specific sector policies" (World Bank 2002a, 7). Communities are encouraged to identify and prioritize their needs through facilitators (individuals or local organizations); local governments handle planning, implementation, and management of the subprojects. Investments that can be supported by the CDI component include construction, rehabilitation of school and health centers, drinking water and agriculture, village roads and bridges, food processing technologies, and community infrastructure (meeting halls and cultural centers). Community contributions in the form of labor, equipment, and materials are expected to amount to 20 percent of the subproject costs. Income generation is specifically excluded as it is covered by another project component. The CDI component is planned to reach about 30 percent of the population (2.5 million people) in the 18 districts of the region over a five-year period. Resources are allocated to districts in accordance with a composite indicator that reflects social development, poverty, and conflict (Republic of Uganda 2002, 9).[19]

In the original project design, a youth training scheme was to be launched before NUSAF. It would provide vocational and business training skills to unemployed youth, abducted children and former combatants, and child soldiers so that they could work on construction projects funded by NUSAF. Small companies formed by youth could compete for NUSAF construction contracts, thereby contributing to small-scale private sector development. The Japanese government committed support but considerable delays ensued because it desired a Japanese NGO to provide the training. The Northern Uganda Youth Action Fund was initiated in May 2004 and is being implemented in parallel with NUSAF by World Vision and funded through its Japanese counterpart with a budget of $2 million.

The second major component of NUSAF is Vulnerable Groups Support (VGS), which is designed to assist those most directly affected by conflict: displaced persons, children, youth, female-headed households, people living with HIV/AIDS, orphans and foster parents, the destitute, and the disabled. With the help of CBOs and NGOs, the most vulnerable groups would be identified and reached by interventions to support their livelihoods. VGS activities include rehabilitation and expansion of training facilities, vocational skills training for youth (masonry, carpentry, blacksmithing), income-generating activities, and support services to female-headed households and other disadvantaged groups. VGS is also intended to strengthen the capacities of NGOs and the private sector in helping to mainstream VGS activities. Vulnerable groups are expected to contribute 5 percent of the project costs in cash or kind. In practice, the majority of projects funded in this category are expected to be in conflict zones or places where conflict has recently ended.

The Community Reconciliation and Conflict Management (CRCM) component is a small but integral element of NUSAF. This third component for traditional and nontraditional approaches to peace building and conflict management, including reconciliation meetings and negotiations between tribes and clans, inter-tribal dialogue, traditional cleansing ceremonies for former combatants and abducted children, and provision of counseling and psychosocial support to those affected by conflict. CRCM specifically addresses the underlying causes and the consequences of violent conflict by strengthening social ties within and between war-torn communities and by facilitating tribal and interclan links within and across subregions, the building of trust and confidence in state institutions, and greater inclusiveness in the planning and implementation of development activities.[20] Communities are expected to contribute 5 percent of the subproject costs. The focus of CRCM subprojects is in the three subregions most affected by conflict: West Nile, Acholi, and Karamoja. According to a former member of the design team, the CRCM component was intended to form the launch pad for VGS activities by linking conflict mitigation to livelihood opportunities for children and youth who had been abducted by or served as combatants in rebel groups.[21]

The fourth NUSAF component is institutional development, primarily to support staffing of a small autonomous management unit, as well as capacity building, training, information and communications, and monitoring and evaluation. The NUSAF design team opted for an arms-length implementing agency under the overall direction of the OPM. The NUMU was headquartered in Gulu town. The expectation was that an office located in the region would minimize travel costs and logistical complications, signal the project's cognizance of local institutional realities, and increase accountability and transparency to local stakeholders. In addition, the location of NUMU in Gulu town would allowed NUMU to hire staff from the region who are committed to the project and who accept salaries lower than would be paid in Kampala.

Other management alternatives were considered and rejected by the design team. Government and community representatives rejected the NURP-I approach of working through central line ministries because a single line department could not manage the disparate sectoral foci of NUSAF interventions. The top-down bureaucratic culture of government line ministries was also considered antithetical to the demand-driven approach embodied in the project. A sectorwide approach was also rejected because of the challenge of reconciling the needs of central line ministries with those of communities. The decision to establish an autonomous implementing agency was informed by international best practice as a means of ensuring flexibility in implementation, maintaining high-quality technical support, instilling participatory skills, and connecting with community-level institutions (World Bank 2002a, 13).

The design team also gave careful consideration to the nature of the project's integration into the government's decentralization policy framework. The LGDP-II framework is meant to be inclusive, but its planning procedures remain deficient in this regard. The expectation of the design team is that integration could take place once the value of NUSAF's community-driven approach permeates local government. The location of the NDTOs within the district administration is designed to facilitate coordination with other development programs and integration with the district planning apparatus. Subprojects would be subject to technical appraisal by local government sector specialists and approval by technical planning committees at district and subcounty levels to ensure effective integration in local government planning process (World Bank 2002a, 13).

NUMU is headed by an executive director and staffed by technical directors responsible for each of the main project components, sector specialists, auditors, and other professionals. NDTOs and accounts officers are appointed by NUMU in each of the 18 districts to facilitate interaction between communities and district-level sectoral offices in the planning, appraisal, and implementation of project activities. The NUMU executive director reports to a National Steering Committee (NSC) under the Permanent Secretary of the OPM. NSC comprises line ministry officials, donors, and civil society representatives and reports to the Minister of State on Northern Uganda Rehabilitation.

NUSAF's institutional development component provides resources for sensitizing local government officials, NGOs, and politicians to the approach and philosophy of NUSAF through workshops and seminars and various media. Monitoring and evaluation will be supported through this component to track progress and environmental impacts. Mid-term and end-of-project surveys on the project's effectiveness in reaching priority groups are also planned.

A further design consideration is the flexibility of the project to adapt to changing circumstances. The project is flexible in that communities determine priorities on the basis of a wide and varied menu of options. Choices of community facilitator and contractor, CBO and NGO roles, and source of labor are left to community discretion, as is choice of intervention. The CRCM component is limited to conflict areas. The principle of self-selection underpins VGS on the assumption that the most vulnerable groups are easily identified. CDI subproject applications generally arise from more settled areas where there is scope for community supervision and management. In this way, NUSAF offers a flexible approach to project design that accommodates community preferences in the light of capacity constraints and the prevailing pattern of conflict.

Various risks are addressed in the project design. The key financial management risks relate to staff adequacy, use and approval of project funds, reliability of financial information, adequacy of counterpart funds, ignorance of rules and procedures, and identification of community needs and delivery systems. Risk mitigation measures are built into NUMU's design. Environmental risk is also anticipated through provision for environmental assessment of infrastructure projects (principally under the CDI component). The risk that attainment of project objectives would be undermined by ongoing or intensified conflict is acknowledged, but the challenge of implementation in such conditions is not addressed systematically in the design document. This oversight is surprising because part of the failure of NURP-I to achieve its objectives was due to the difficulty of recruiting staff and monitoring projects in conflict zones. NUSAF is intended to contribute to conflict mitigation by fostering development initiatives and its designers may assume that peace will ultimately prevail, but no specific contingency or mitigation plan addresses the risk of conflict escalation. In view of the spread and intensification of the conflict in some areas of the Acholi and Lango subregions since Operation Iron Fist was launched by the UPDF in 2002, this omission highlights a potential source of vulnerability for implementation.

NUSAF is predicated on generating active public support for the project's approach and demand for project resources through an extensive outreach program using print and electronic media and more traditional forms of cultural expression. Communities visited for this study confirmed some recognition of the role played by the media (especially radio) in developing their awareness of NUSAF. A major challenge for

NUSAF was to convey the message that its approach was distinct from the much-reviled NURP-I and was not simply a centrally driven development initiative identified with southern political interests. Buy-in from local government officials and politicians was intrinsic to rapid acceptance of NUSAF's legitimacy and benign intent. It highlights the importance of early efforts to sensitize decision makers through seminars and workshops.

NUSAF is also predicated on the active involvement of NGOs and CBOs in two critical areas: sensitization of local communities to NUSAF's demand-driven approach and technical advice and facilitation in the design of subprojects. A core institutional element in the project design is the requirement that communities form community project management committees (CPMCs) comprising individuals (at least 30 percent of whom are women) elected from the locality to plan, implement, and monitor the activity for the duration of the subproject cycle. NGOs and CBOs can assist in the formation, orientation, and training of these committees, which can draw and build on existing community organizations.

In theory communities are free to appoint facilitators and to use up to 2 percent of the project budget for this purpose. The community facilitators can be locally educated youth, membership organizations, or NGOs. Not all of these facilitators have received training in the demand-driven approach. Some have demanded advance payments for their services and have acted more as brokers than as facilitators helping to translate community preferences into feasible subprojects. By contrast, the CAP West Nile program facilitators were selected by communities for each subcounty and carefully trained in the philosophy and practice of a demand-driven approach. Skilled community facilitators were critical to the success of CAP and many continue to work in local government and NGOs in the subregion.

Prolonged conflict has not been conducive to the formation of strong local NGOs and CBOS, though capacity-building efforts fostered by international NGOs and aid donors have helped to strengthen community-level organizations. In recognition of this constraint, NUSAF encourages communities to get NGOs and faith-based and traditional organizations (ethnic and cultural leaders and associations) to act as facilitators and advisors in designing and implementing subprojects. Communities are expected to approach NGOs for assistance. NGOs can play a critical role in identifying and assisting vulnerable groups, which often lack planning and organizational skills, and in sensitizing communities to NUSAF (World Bank 2002a).

Some NGOs have provided a bridge between communities and local government and have strengthened the capacity of community planning committees to manage funds responsibly. But major NGOs in Gulu and Arua indicated that the NUMU staff had not closely consulted with them and that their prospective roles are poorly specified. They are also skeptical of the commitment and capacity of local government officials to implement NUSAF in an objective and effective manner; they fear that resources could be diverted or used suboptimally. The NUMU staff and local government officials believe that NGOs dislike the notion that communities should be in the driving seat and that available resources and high administrative costs provide inadequate incentives. Some claim that the availability of NUSAF resources is encouraging unscrupulous people to form NGOs in pursuit of material gain from local communities.

Substantiating these conflicting claims without more fieldwork is difficult, but NGOs could be more actively involved in NUSAF implementation as promoters of participatory planning and strengtheners of local governments' technical capacity. In addition, NGOs could increase the capacity of local membership organizations and CBOs to assume prime responsibility for sensitization and facilitation.[22] Finally, NGOs could perform an independent monitoring role to ensure that subprojects are targeted at the most vulnerable groups, that planning is based on participatory approaches, and that community investments are designed and sited without elite capture. Local government staff and NDTOs are too overstretched to perform an effective monitoring role for individual subprojects, and formal auditing carried out under the auspices of the OPM is confined to financial management and outputs.

Development Results

NUSAF has the potential to achieve results in three key areas: poverty reduction, improved governance, and positive spillover effects through efforts to upgrade community infrastructure, improve the livelihoods of the most vulnerable communities, and mitigate conflict, respectively. The community-driven approach is considered intrinsic to the potential success of NUSAF in achieving these objectives.

The premise that communities are the best identifiers of their own needs is the foundation of NUSAF's potential to maximize allocative efficiency. The poor performance of NURP-I, which emphasized centralized identification of infrastructure priorities and top-down implementation, illustrates how ignoring community preferences undermines the quality and sustainability of infrastructure investments.

NUSAF can maximize productive efficiency through its emphasis on community involvement in identifying local private contractors and employing labor directly from communities. Such an approach ensures that the program's outputs are produced by contractors with close links to local communities and thus are in a position to provide supervision and oversight to minimize or prevent substandard work and corruption. An emphasis on local contractors points to the prospect of private sector development. Microentrepreneurs (in some cases local youth with appropriate training) could be engaged by communities to provide construction and semi-skilled labor under local supervision.[23] Under NURP-I contractors were appointed by the Kampala-based implementation agency. These contractors usually had little knowledge of local realities; therefore, opportunities for corruption and substandard work were great.

A mid-term review will investigate the quality and utility of community investments and income-generation schemes. But one indicator of the project's relevance has already emerged in the more than 3,100 subprojects submitted by communities for consideration and the number of approvals following appraisal by technical committees at the subcounty and district levels. Project approvals in some districts far exceed budgetary resources for the first two financial years.

Two features of the subprojects merit particular attention: speed of implementation and quality of assets and community investments. Construction of community assets, such as boreholes for drinking water and classroom blocks for schools, has proceeded rapidly. While hardly representative, the four communities consulted for this study confirm that work has been completed on time and compare progress favorably with similar investments under NURP-I and LGDP-II. First-tranche disbursements have already been used and accounted for; applications for second and final payments for many of the first wave of investments are pending. Field observations and feedback from sector specialists at the district level attest to the quality of the work to date.[24] The potential outcomes of these investments are evident from community feedback on reduced incidence of waterborne diseases and increased levels of school attendance.

Sustainability of community infrastructure and livelihood investments is a key concern in conditions of deep poverty, poorly functioning markets, and ongoing conflict. NUSAF's effectiveness in building capacity for management of community assets and technical support from local government is, therefore, critical. In one community, a committee with responsibility for borehole use and maintenance had replaced the community project management committee. An NGO that had helped the community design another subproject was not needed after the subproject was accepted because individuals in the community had the requisite skills.

NUSAF's potential consequences for Uganda's political leadership are already becoming apparent. NUSAF is predicated on bringing development benefits to a region plagued by political insecurity and a national leadership whose legitimacy has been eroded by its inability to stem violent conflict. It is claimed in some quarters that NUSAF is part of an effort by the governing Movement to derive political legitimacy from development largesse in a region that has been inherently hostile to what is widely perceived to be a national government dominated by southerners. There is little doubt that the Movement would wish to deepen its legitimacy in a region where it has been implicated in fomenting violence and sustaining conflict, and from which former political leaders such as Obote, Okello, and Amin drew much of their political support and military resources (Lomo and Hovil 2004).

When debated in Parliament in 2002, NUSAF was criticized both by members representing the regime and those aligned with opposition parties. Movement adherents were concerned that substantial government resources were scheduled for deployment in a region considered hostile to the regime in Kampala. Opposition Members of Parliament (MPs) were concerned that the Movement would profit from NUSAF and extend its political support base at their expense. In the event that Parliament approved the NUSAF project, then these respective political concerns would be mollified by the pragmatic realization that additional development resources for the war-torn region would ultimately produce significant benefits for communities that had suffered the corrosive effects of endemic conflict. The 2006 parliamentary and local elections will be a test of the extent to which the Movement successfully derives political capital from NUSAF, though the results will depend critically on whether a durable peace process can be established by the time the elections are held.[25]

At present, elected politicians in local governments, especially at the district level, have the most at stake in NUSAF outcomes. Councilors from all levels of local government are actively sensitizing local communities to NUSAF.[26] The availability of substantial resources for development purposes offers an attractive source of political patronage in a region long deprived of such resources and where politicians are keen to reestablish their legitimacy in anticipation of a normal democratic process of constituency-based politics. Political interest in NUSAF is not automatically tantamount to opportunities for predatory behavior; it may be motivated by benign considerations emanating from recognition that NUSAF has the potential to bring badly needed development resources to a war-ravaged region. A social fund approach has the advantage of devolving responsibility to the community and protecting those responsible for project implementation from undue political influence.

One potentially negative consequence of political interest in NUSAF at the local level is evident from the resolution of Gulu District Council to ensure that each subcounty will have at least one subproject under its jurisdiction.[27] The political imperative of ensuring a balanced spread of project benefits could undermine NUSAF's objective to give priority to the most vulnerable groups and areas, although the conditions obtaining throughout the district are so challenging that a mechanism is required to allocate the funds equitably to prevent excessive concentration in and around Gulu town. The challenge will be to ensure that political commitment is retained while respecting NUSAF's distributional objectives. This commitment could emanate from the enhanced legitimacy derived by local politicians from the successful deployment of resources for developmental ends. The principal risk in the short term is from politicians' intent to derive political capital and commandeer resources from NUSAF subproject investments.

NUSAF's intended governance outcomes include conflict mitigation, strengthened local government capacity, and community empowerment. The project design process originally focused on community reconciliation and conflict mitigation, the first governance outcome. The conflict management and VGS components were to enhance the livelihood opportunities of former combatants.[28] The economic security derived from income-generation schemes funded by NUSAF is intended to offset the opportunity cost of giving up arms, as some subprojects have demonstrated. NUSAF may provide livelihood opportunities to former combatants in areas where peace treaties have been negotiated, and more investments of this nature could contribute to peace. Success in community reconciliation and the reintegration of former combatants could bring additional benefits in terms of improved respect for human rights.

However, the expectation that NUSAF can directly contribute to enhanced security in the North by encouraging the surrender and reintegration of former combatants into their communities underplays the extent to which the conflict in Acholi is sustained by grievances that are political rather than economic in nature. Weapons provide livelihoods for the LRA by helping it violently appropriate food and livestock, but the insurgency is sustained by a complex mix of ethnic and regional grievances and a millenarian discourse that transcends simple economic solutions.

Interventions like NUSAF can bring economic relief to people in the region, but only broad-based peace initiatives can ensure peace, security, and sustainable development (Lomo and Hovil 2004; van Acker 2003). The achievement of durable peace through political means would automatically improve the prospects for human rights by removing fear and gross physical abuses and by allowing IDPs to return to their villages and resume farming and cattle rearing. This turn of events would provide a strong foundation for NUSAF initiatives to succeed in the long term.

Only 2 of 1,425 approved subprojects are aimed at conflict management, which suggests that such management has become an adjunct to development interventions rather than vice versa, as intended by the project design team (OPM 2004b). For this reason, NUSAF would not be expected to significantly reduce ethnic conflict and tensions. But one subproject in an area of Gulu town has been successful in reintegrating abducted youth into the community through a traditional cleansing ceremony and in mobilizing resources for cattle rearing and poultry raising in which the former abductees would be the prime beneficiaries. This subproject is a rare example of an integrated intervention of the type anticipated in the project design.

The second type of governance outcome is strengthening the capacity and resource base of local governments, especially at district and sub-county levels. All subprojects have to be reviewed by district government officials on technical grounds and to determine how they complement district planning priorities and budgetary allocations. Once appraisal is complete, the applications are submitted to elected councilors on the District Executive Committee for ratification, which forms the basis for a recommendation to NUMU for release of funds into the community bank account.

During the design phase, bilateral donors expressed concern that demand-driven processes would skew district planning priorities at the community level and that NUSAF resources would bypass district budget processes. These concerns appear unwarranted. District officials in the two districts visited for this study are closely involved in the appraisal and monitoring of NUSAF subprojects, and they regard the funds as an infusion to the limited resources at their disposal from regular budgetary transfers. The problem is not so much that NUSAF bypasses local government but that officials—overwhelmed by community demands—cannot effectively appraise and monitor subprojects.

The main incentive for local government staff to perform these functions is additional resources, which lessen the pressure on the regular development budget. However, the absence of fuel and subsistence allowances is a disincentive, because it means staff incur expenses in taking on these tasks.

Nonintegration of NUSAF resources into the development budgets of district local governments is problematic and is attributed to the difficulty of anticipating and aggregating community preferences. However, indicative figures are available for each district. These figures could be included in budget projections, alongside resources from the consolidated grant, to provide a more comprehensive picture of total resource availability and to produce a more comprehensive overview for planning purposes. Sectoral allocations could be integrated in budget outturns on the basis of information from NUMU on subproject disbursements.

Subcounty governments were intended to assess how proposed subprojects complement local development plans and whether the additional investments make sense in view of existing infrastructure and market opportunities. In practice, these governments are not closely involved in project appraisal; district administrations dominate the appraisal and approval process. NUSAF's failure to engage subcounty governments in the project cycle could undermine subprojects' sustainability, because resources for maintenance of community assets would need to come from this source. Active engagement of subcounty administration in project identification, implementation, and monitoring was fundamental to CAP's success (CAP 1999).

The third type of governance outcome associated with NUSAF is strengthening of institutional capacity in local communities, primarily through creation of community project management committees that are responsible for subproject design and implementation. Members of these committees are elected by the community. All subprojects are required to furnish evidence of the committees, which are expected to meet on a regular basis during subproject implementation. The effectiveness of this institutional arrangement varies widely across communities and depends on social composition, physical location (rural or urban area, conflict or postconflict area), and prior existence of institutional capacity. In the West Nile subregion, where communities had experience with the CAP, anecdotal evidence suggests that the legacy of involvement in the design of CAP initiatives is the communities' ability to adapt quickly to NUSAF's procedural and organizational requirements. The number of NUSAF applications and approved subprojects in these communities is higher than in other communities in Arua and the other four districts that compose the subregion.

NUSAF eventually could have positive spillover effects. It could reduce internal displacement by providing resources to IDPs for resumption of economic activities once security concerns have been addressed. It could encourage the return of refugees. It could provide resources for community investments in areas inhabited by Sudanese refugees. These investments would have short-term benefits for the Sudanese and long-term benefits for neighboring communities. The extent to which NUSAF will generate positive spillover effects will only become clear as it nears completion.

Implementation Processes

Many aspects of implementation affect the timeliness, quality, and effectiveness of NUSAF's outputs. Many of these aspects are amenable to course corrections by NUMU, subject to the advice of the Office of the Prime Minister (OPM) and the World Bank. The focus here is on those dimensions of project management that affect NUSAF implementation in the short to medium term and that potentially have a bearing on the achievement of development results.

The $133.5 million resource envelope for NUSAF is considerable in that it exceeds the development budgets of local governments in the region. Sector specialists in district government view NUSAF as a valuable augmentation of their existing budgets, enabling them to significantly increase the overall number and reach of investments, especially in the education and water sectors. The challenge is to incorporate NUSAF commitments into district plans and budgets and to increase capacity for technical appraisal and monitoring of subprojects.

The design process resulted in preparation of implementation guidance manuals, including a comprehensive operational manual (Republic of Uganda 2002). These manuals were primarily intended for the benefit of the staff of the implementing agency and of the local government staff. Because none of the project design team were seconded or recruited to NUMU, there was a disjuncture between design and implementation in respect of staffing. The OPM provides some element of continuity, but this continuity is largely based on periodic reports furnished by NUMU rather than on independent field verification. World Bank sector specialists involved with the project design continue to have an input into implementation through periodic appraisals and field visits, and they share their reports with the OPM and NUMU. However, these arrangements were inadequate to tackle impediments that arose in the early stages of implementation.

A full complement of NUSAF district technical officers was not in place until 18 months after project inception. The two main directors responsible for the three development components were not appointed until August 2004.[29] Recruitment delays adversely affected the plan to sensitize communities and local government staff to NUSAF, because the small core team based in NUMU could not undertake training on a significant scale.

Another problem is slow procurement of vehicles and equipment. At the time of the study, none of the 18 NDTOs had received vehicles, and only a few had been given computers and office furniture. They are forced to rely on the goodwill of district administrations for loan of vehicles or to resort to expensive private hire arrangements for making field visits. Communications with NUMU and local governments (especially at the subcountry level) are problematic as they lack computers and Internet access and mobile telephones. The absence of this equipment hampers the approval of subprojects and frustrates communities that have faithfully followed the procedures laid down in the operational guidelines.[30]

Slow recruitment and procurement inevitably delayed implementation with the result that no disbursements were made for subproject activities until mid-2004. Pilot projects were launched in nine districts in mid-2003 to test out the viability of community planning processes. Concern on the part of the World Bank about slow disbursement generated an intensive period of subproject identification and appraisal from April to June 2004. Under the rubric of the Rapid Results Initiative, 1,425 subprojects received approval and funding commitments. As a consequence, the key challenge has shifted from a paucity of microproject investments to a surfeit of applications, which places considerable strain on the implementation capacity of NUMU and local government administrations.[31]

Financial management is a particular challenge in a demand-driven project in an environment characterized by capacity constraints and lack of established financial procedures for direct disbursement of funds to communities. Communities are required to open accounts in their local banks into which funds are directly disbursed from the NUMU account in three tranches on authorization from the District Executive Committee. Theoretically, transfers take just 24 hours, but delays between subproject approval by NUMU and actual disbursements mean they take several weeks.[32] Part of the problem is that the sheer number of subproject submissions approved by the district authorities has overwhelmed NUMU's capacity for processing payments in a timely and effective manner. However, NUMU has yet to appoint a financial head on the grounds that it has been difficult to identify someone with the requisite skills and experience. This delay has contributed to financial management problems and slowed disbursements that in turn contribute to community frustration and slower implementation. Many communities are now awaiting the second and final payments to enable them to complete construction work and investments.

At the community level one problem is limited availability of bank branches. Visits to banks necessitate travel, in some cases outside the district, which consumes time and resources and can be dangerous in areas where there is conflict and banditry. Another problem is the lack of basic numeracy and literacy skills needed for financial oversight. Some communities have found it easiest to engage local NGOs to assist them in financial management and making payments for materials, labor, and contractors. Others rely on advice and oversight by government officials, NUMU staff, and community facilitators. Whatever its merits in meeting community needs, a demand-driven approach clearly raises major challenges for financial management and highlights the need for durable procedures to ensure capacity building and effective and accountable use of funds at all levels. The OPM has commissioned an independent audit of NUMU financial procedures and disbursements to review financial management and implementation.

Many operational considerations relating to NUSAF implementation have a bearing on project outputs. The focus here is on three sets of implementation issues from which lessons arise: participation and inclusivity, policy dialogue and donor coordination, and learning and public relations.

NUSAF is intended to benefit poorer communities and vulnerable groups in them through a process of self-selection and prioritization of investments in line with objective circumstances. The VGS is premised on the principle of self-selection in that beneficiaries have to come from one or more clearly defined groups: widows, orphans, disabled, HIV/AIDS-affected people, and IDPs. Evidence that VGS subproject applications are targeted to or emanate directly from these groups is required for grant funds to be committed.

The bulk of VGS applications come from areas that continue to experience violent conflict or that have recently emerged from it. In the Acholi subregion, a disproportionate number of subprojects are for IDPs living in camps near larger towns. Investments in conflict-prone areas are either for small livestock rearing or income-generation projects that can be carried out in the confines of refugee camps and that are appropriate to the needs of the communities. In areas where conflict has abated, communities have received grant funds for cultivation—in the form of seeds, tools, oxen, and plows—to enable them to open up fields and plant crops for immediate food security and cash incomes. While communities may continue to live in camps for security reasons, they are able to farm in comparative safety. Farming is not feasible in areas of the Acholi subregion, where continuing conflict prevents farmers from venturing out into their fields, or in Karamoja subregion, where cattle restocking would attract armed rustlers. Communities can therefore adapt their preferences to local conditions and can use the flexibility built into NUSAF to design subprojects that correspond to local needs.

Available evidence might suggest that NUSAF's demand-driven approach generates subproject applications that are both well-targeted and appropriate to the security conditions in different areas. Provisions for NGO and CBO involvement in subproject design and implementation also improve the prospect of effective targeting. As with any community-driven approach, local vested interests might seek to capture resources for political or material advantage. However, widespread poverty and social deprivation in conflict-affected areas minimize the risk of elite capture or the exclusion of the most vulnerable communities. A more plausible risk is that extremely vulnerable groups such as individuals with HIV/AIDS, who live in conditions of seclusion or suffer from social stigma, might not secure access to program funds without expert help from outside the community.

Gender bias is also possible in an environment where women have suffered disproportionately from violence and have little opportunity to engage in processes of community deliberation. Women are entitled to one-third representation in community project management committees, but the extent to which they effectively participate in NUSAF decision-making processes is unknown. The absence of women in senior positions in NUMU is not conducive to effective monitoring of women's participation.

Reference has been made to the important role played in the NUSAF design process by World Bank personnel, several of whom had worked in the OPM or on CAP. The Kampala-based Bank staff can help identify bottlenecks and course corrections through dialogue with OPM counterparts and direct engagement with NUMU. Periodic oversight missions based on field visits could provide insight into implementation problems.

Donor coordination is not a significant issue in the current phase of NUSAF implementation, because the Bank is the only source of donor funding. Bilateral donors were engaged in dialogue during the design phase, but, skeptical of the NUSAF process, they have declined to provide financial support. (A representative of the donor coordination group on northern Uganda attends meetings of the NUSAF National Steering Committee, largely for information purposes, and some coordination and information sharing takes place between NUSAF and the European Commission's Acholi and Karamoja programs, which are implemented through offices located in the same compound as NUMU.) The possibility of peace returning to northern Uganda raises the prospect of major development challenges that will require the infusion of substantial donor resources. Realizing and demonstrating the benefits of a demand-driven approach that can complement rather than undermine local government in the region, therefore, constitutes an important public relations challenge for NUSAF.

However, NUMU has been slow to develop the information, education, and communications component of NUSAF. A specialist was not appointed until mid-2004, and a comprehensive strategy has yet to be developed. Efforts have been made to engage the media: radio and print journalists are encouraged to accompany NUMU staff and NDTOs on visits to subprojects. The media frequently carries stories about NUSAF, especially when the president, ministers, or MPs make visits and issue statements. The president's public criticism of NUSAF's slow implementation in September 2004 was widely reported in the national and local media, highlighting the visibility and significance of the project in national politics and in the region.[33]

Slow procurement, delayed recruitment, and uneven disbursement rates are all features of the current phase of implementation and were encountered in CAP and demand-driven approaches elsewhere. These problems can be solved with determined management intervention and improved monitoring by the steering committee convened by the OPM. Failure to address these problems could derail achievement of the project's objectives by inducing frustration among communities that have identified appropriate subprojects but are unable to access funds or to follow through on initial investments.

Conclusions

NUSAF's design and implementation reflect the lessons of previous programs in northern Uganda. The project's demand-driven approach was based on the largely positive experience of the Community Action Program in West Nile. This program demonstrated that poor communities in a postconflict environment can develop the capacity to identify, plan, and monitor social investment projects with appropriate guidance and facilitation. The involvement of district and subcounty governments was integral to the program's success by ensuring the active engagement and support of local officials. By contrast, the experience of NURP-I highlighted the limitations of a top-down and centralized approach in which local communities had no involvement in priority setting and implementation. NURP-I was plagued by a lack of community ownership or interest in maintaining local assets and by a lack of accountability that fostered corruption and poor quality implementation.

These lessons were readily absorbed by the NUSAF design team, which largely comprised Ugandan professionals in government and the World Bank, several with direct experience of CAP and NURP-I implementation. Many of the team were from the North and recognized the potential of scaling-up a tried and tested demand-driven approach. They carried out careful diagnostic work and community needs assessments to demonstrate the case for the proposed approach, and they argued with conviction for the inclusion of a special component for addressing the causes and consequences of conflict. The design of the VGS component was based on the principle of self-selection by clearly identified marginal groups whose lives had been adversely affected by conflict. In more settled areas the CDI component was more appropriate, because it required capacity for managing small-scale infrastructure investments in an environment where the threat of violence had abated. Design of NUSAF would appear appropriate to the particular circumstances of northern Uganda and has the potential to produce positive results in an environment characterized by conflict and poor governance. Explicit appreciation of the prevailing political dynamics in the region has informed project design and the assumptions underpinning the demand-driven approach adopted by NUSAF.

Preliminary evidence from the early stages of implementation attests to strong demand from communities for subprojects. The speed of implementation and the quality of work on community investments are indicative of the validity of NUSAF's approach. Vulnerable groups now have direct access to grant resources to enable them to rebuild livelihoods in conditions of economic adversity. Youth and children affected by violence as former combatants and abductees can be reintegrated into their communities by virtue of access to opportunities for productive employment. A special component of the project dealing with reconciliation and conflict mitigation has the potential to deal with some of the more immediate causes of violence in the region, but relatively few subprojects of this kind have received funding to date.

Scaling up the community-driven approach that characterized NUSAF and CAP in conflict and postconflict conditions poses enormous challenges. CAP implementation was premised on careful training of the field staff and communities and on intensive application of staff resources in the identification, execution, and monitoring of community investments. The training component under NUSAF has been less comprehensive, and the process of hiring and orienting community facilitators has been less systematic. Moreover, NUSAF has fewer dedicated project staff in the districts and the project management unit.[34] It depends on the local government staff in district and subcounty administrations for the bulk of subproject appraisal and monitoring, but the volume of work far exceeds local governments' capacity to undertake these tasks with sufficient rigor, thus highlighting the need to strengthen this capacity.

Three lessons arise from NUSAF's design and implementation that may have significance for social funds and development interventions in LICUS contexts. The first lesson is the relevance of a demand-driven approach in conflict and postconflict conditions. CAP and NUSAF demonstrate the validity of community-driven approaches when existing institutional capacity is weak and development challenges are enormous. The second lesson is that the sustainability of demand-driven projects is greater when local government administrations are involved in planning, appraisal, execution, and monitoring. Integrated implementation through local government bodies avoids the pitfalls of parallel institutions that have affected many social funds. At the same time, local governments are susceptible to local political influence and often face capacity constraints. The third lesson concerns the challenges of implementing community-based approaches in a conflict environment. The uneven performance of NURP-I was attributable in significant measure to its unfounded assumption that improved social infrastructure would contribute to poverty reduction, in turn helping to mitigate the causes of conflict.[35] NUSAF highlights the value of diagnosing the nature of the conflict and how it affects different segments of the population and of making conflict resolution a central element in program design. This focus may not be appropriate in all conflict environments, but identifying the most vulnerable groups, assessing their priorities, and strengthening the capacity of communities to plan and manage local development projects were fundamental design prerequisites for NUSAF.

A final consideration concerns the role of aid donors. The donor community in Uganda remains skeptical of the validity and potential effect of NUSAF, because it is not integrated into the regular budgetary process and it provides additional resources through local governments rather than supplementing existing programs. However, realization of NUSAF's considerable potential in addressing deep-set problems of conflict and development in northern Uganda could unlock additional resources from donors who are willing to work with the national government and local authorities to rebuild the region's devastated infrastructure and to create livelihood opportunities for a population impoverished by violent conflict.

Notes

1. Since the National Resistance Army assumed power in 1986, 14 violent insurgencies have occurred in different areas, not all of which have been confined to the North (Lomo and Hovil 2004, 10). Five of the 18 districts in northern Uganda lie in the Teso subregion in the east, but these districts are usually included within a political definition of the region as they are conflict affected. This wider categorization is used throughout this chapter.

2. The cattle population in Kitgum district is estimated to have decreased from 156,000 to just over 3,000 from 1986 to 1998, while in the same period the national cattle population increased from 3 million to 5.6 million (van Acker 2003, 22).

3. Variations among the northern districts are also significant. Some districts have poverty levels and social indicators comparable to those in other parts of the country. The worst affected districts are those where conflict continues in various forms. For details see Republic of Uganda (2003).

4. In this respect the NUSAF study complements the Sierra Leone study in Bennell (2004).

5. The other components of NURP-II are the Restocking Program (largely in Karamoja), the Acholiland Program, the School Roofings Grant, and the Capacitation of Vulnerable Youth (Republic of Uganda 2003).

6. While all major stakeholders were consulted, the limitations of the study should be acknowledged. A time-bound exercise of this nature (a total of 15 person days) cannot produce findings that are robust and generalizable across all 18 districts in which NUSAF is operational. This is the task of a more substantial mid-term review.

7. The most durable investment was upgraded sections of the highway from Kampala to Gulu that greatly improved the region's accessibility to the rest of the country.

8. Source: interviews with World Bank staff, Kampala and discussions with local communities during field visits.

9. The performance audit highlights the risks of conventional development approaches in conditions of conflict, concluding that "The NURP-I experience shows that, by itself, a development project, a core speciality of the Bank, is unlikely to capture the peace" (World Bank 2000, 9).

10. In the words of the performance audit, "From a macrosecurity perspective, common sense would suggest that the introduction of equipment, infrastructure and people into a theater of ongoing conflict would likely increase insecurity and defense expenditure, rather than reduce them as NURP-I designers had hoped" (World Bank 2000, 6).

11. Separation of financial management and control in Kampala from implementation in the North came under strong criticism because it opened up "a potentially rich arena for corrupt gains" (World Bank 2000, 3).

12. A recent government document on reconstruction in northern Uganda concludes: "Experience has shown that centralized design and implementation of projects undermines grassroots participation, priorities and a sense of ownership for sustainability. . . . A key lesson from NURP-I is the need for a bottom-up approach to program implementation ensuring adequate participation of the local people within a decentralized framework" (Republic of Uganda 2003, 32).

13. In the first phase there were 13 field officers, each covering one county, and 126 community facilitators at the subcountry level (CAP 1996b).

14. Beginning in 1996, two other initiatives were operated in parallel with CAP: the Women's Empowerment Program and the Arua District Capacity Building Project. Each indirectly contributed to the later evolution of NUSAF by highlighting the special circumstances of women and the importance of working through capable local government institutions (SNV 1999a).

15. According to the project completion report for NURP-I, "the results of this truly responsive approach are positive" and objectives of the CAP "were substantially achieved," especially with regard to capacity building (World Bank 1999, 6).

16. By April 1999, 103 primary schools, 29 secondary schools, 20 health units, 320 water sources, and 16 bridges and culverts had been constructed (CAP 1999a). The NURP-I project completion report states that 500,000 people benefited directly from the program, equivalent to one-third of the total population of the subregion (World Bank 1999, 6), whereas an internal impact evaluation gives a more conservative estimate of 200,000 (CAP 1999a, 18).

17. A recent government report states that NURP-II is "designed in such a way that it incorporates lessons learned from successful projects such as the Community Action Program (CAP) and challenges in NURP-I" (Republic of Uganda 2003, 32).

18. The principal donors included DFID, USAID, and the embassies of Austria, Ireland, Norway, and the Netherlands. They submitted briefing notes to the OPM and the World Bank and participated in design team meetings but considered their involvement neither sufficiently extensive nor timely. Consequently, a special working group was formed for consultation.

19. Per capita resource allocations are weighted so that worse-off districts receive a disproportionately higher allocation than better-off districts (Republic of Uganda 2002, 9).

20. The World Bank reportedly expressed reservations about this component because of potential political implications but was persuaded by the Ugandans on the design team that such an approach was integral to the project's success.

21. Interviews with World Bank staff in Kampala.

22. For example, CARE is helping several hundred local organizations in Arua and Yumbe districts to strengthen their implementation capacity, though not as yet with the explicit aim of providing more effective facilitation for NUSAF.

23. Evidence from CAP appears to confirm the potential of private sector development as a spillover from use of local contractors (CAP 1999).

24. Visitors' books of the Project Technical Committee confirm that government technical officers and NUSAF staff have made regular visits for monitoring purposes, and visitors' comments allude to the quality and speed of construction.

25. Movement politicians were heavily defeated in the Acholi subregion in the 1996 and 2001 elections by candidates known for their allegiance to the opposition. The Movement system does not allow candidates to contest elections on the basis of political party affiliations.

26. Written records and interviews with the community technical committees confirm that local politicians were among the first point of contact for NUSAF. The two LC5 chairmen interviewed for this study displayed active interest in and considerable knowledge of NUSAF and its potential benefits.

27. Interview with the LC5 chairman, Gulu District Local Council.

28. This lesson from NURP-I was highlighted in the World Bank's performance audit report (World Bank 2000). The Bank project appraisal document for NUSAF sets out this objective in the following manner: "The proposed NUSAF will operate within community value systems and therefore contribute to good government and security, particularly at local government and community levels. Support will be provided to children/youth formerly abducted during the civil wars, those who have surrendered and retired guns in exchange for a changed livelihood (abductees and gun-drop outs), and those whose careers have been disrupted as a result of the prolonged conflict and breakdown of traditional systems" (World Bank 2002a, 5).

29. NUMU attributes the delay to a lack of qualified staff in the region. The NUMU executive director noted that World Bank approval is required for all senior appointments in accordance with established procurement procedures. World Bank officials in Kampala say that approval can be completed in a matter of a few weeks and that procurement procedures do not explain the considerable recruitment delay.

30. Procurement delays became so problematic that the NUMU official responsible for procurement was fired at the instigation of the NUMU Permanent Secretary on the implicit grounds of corruption and nonperformance. A new procurement officer had yet to be recruited at the time of this study.

31. In Gulu district, 450 applications had been submitted by October; 85 have been approved to date. If funding had been approved for all the applications to date, it would account for the entire budget for the five-year project duration. In Arua district, 153 or 219 proposed projects have received funding.

32. In Arua district, many subprojects approved in July did not receive their first disbursement until two months later. In a few cases communities were still waiting for their first tranche payment in October.

33. *The Weekly Observer*, Kampala, September 16, 2004.

34. The CAP had 82 staff responsible for project implementation in four districts; NUMU's total staff complement is at a similar level for 18 districts.

35. The conflict intensified in the late 1990s, hampering implementation of NURP-I and posing a risk to project staff who were unable to establish an effective field presence in some areas. For details, see World Bank 1999, 2000.

Bibliography

Bennell, P. 2004. "From Emergency Recovery to Community-Driven Development: The National Commission for Social Action in Sierra Leone." Paper prepared for the World Bank study on LICUS, draft, World Bank, Washington, DC.

Bloom, G., W. Chilowa, E. Chirwa, H. Lucas, P. Mvula, A. Schou, and M. Tsoka. 2004. "Poverty Reduction during Democratic Transition: The Malawi Social Action Fund, 1996–2001." Institute of Development Studies, draft, Brighton, UK.

CDRN (Community Development Resource Network). 2001. "Do Not Run Faster Than the Ball: From Development Program to Local NGO: The CEFORD Story in Uganda." Community Development Research Network, Kampala, Uganda.

Community Action Program (CAP) West Nile. 1996a. "CAP Administrative Manual." CAP West Nile, Arua, Uganda.

———. 1996b. "Internal Evaluation: A Qualitative and Quantitative Assessment of the Performance of the Community Action Program, 1993–1995." CAP West Nile, Arua, Uganda.

————. 1999. "CAP Internal Impact Assessment, 1993–1998." CAP West Nile, Arua, Uganda.

Kreimer, A., P. Collier, C. S. Scott, and M. Arnold. 2000. "Uganda: Postconflict Reconstruction." Country Case Study, Operations Evaluation Department, World Bank, Washington, DC.

Lomo, Z., and L. Hovil. 2004. "Behind the Violence: The War in Northern Uganda." Monograph 99, Institute for Security Studies, Pretoria, South Africa.

Office of the Prime Minister (OPM). 2004a. "NUSAF Quarterly/Progress Report, April–June." Northern Uganda Social Action Fund, Kampala, Uganda.

————. 2004b. "Status Report: September/October 2004." Northern Uganda Social Action Fund, Gulu, Uganda, NUSAF Management Unit.

Republic of Uganda. 2002. "The Northern Uganda Social Action Fund (NUSAF) Project, Operational Manual." Office of the Prime Minister, Kampala, Uganda (revised April 2004).

————. 2003. "Postconflict Reconstruction: The Case of Northern Uganda." Ministry of Finance, Planning, and Economic Development, Office of the Prime Minister, Office of the President, Kampala, Uganda, April.

————. 2004. "Draft Poverty Eradication Action Plan." Ministry of Finance, Planning, and Economic Development, Kampala, Uganda, August.

SNV (Netherlands Development Organization). 1999a. "Decentralisation and Empowerment: From Rehabilitation to Growth in West Nile Region, Uganda." Report of an External Evaluation Mission, Arua/Kampala, Uganda.

————. 1999b. "Building the Capacities of Local Development Actors." Paper on the future of NEDA-financed, SNV-supported Development Program for West-Nile, SNV, Uganda, Arua.

van Acker, F. 2003. "Uganda and the Lord's Resistance Army: The New Order No One Ordered." Discussion Paper No. 6, Institute of Development Policy and Management and University of Antwerp, Antwerp, Belgium.

World Bank. 1999. "Northern Uganda Reconstruction Project: Implementation Completion Report." Report 19224, World Bank, Washington, DC.

————. 2000. "Northern Uganda Reconstruction Project: Performance Audit Report." Report 20664, Operations Evaluation Department, World Bank, Washington, DC.

————. 2002a. "Project Appraisal Document on a Proposed Credit to the Government of Uganda for a Northern Uganda Social Action Fund." Report 23885, World Bank, Washington, DC.

————. 2002b. "Social Funds: Assessing Effectiveness." Operations Evaluation Department, World Bank, Washington, DC.

Index

Boxes, figures, notes, and tables are indicated by b, f, n, and t, respectively.

TSP (Transition Support Program),
79–81
political purposes, use of donor-funded
institutions for, 22–24
Portuguese Timor, 59, 60–61
poverty reduction
Cambodia, CARERE/Seila Program,
87–88, 97–102, 116
Mozambique
Decentralized District Planning and
Finance Program, 181–82
DSS (Direct Support to Schools
Program), 150–51, 157–59
NUSAF (Northern Uganda Social
Action Fund), 271–72
Timor-Leste TSP (Transition Support
Program), 68, 70
Poverty Reduction and Growth Fund
(PRGF), 44–45
Poverty Reduction Strategy Paper (PRSP)
process, 44–46, 167n3
Poverty Reduction Support Credit
(PRSC), 45
preliminary analysis of LICUS problems,
7–8, 35n1
Afghanistan, microfinance initiatives,
237
Mozambique DSS (Direct Support to
Schools Program), 161
in TSP (Timor-Leste, Transition Support
Program), 75–76
private sector development in Timor-Leste
TSP (Transition Support Program),
68, 72
psychological effects of development
initiatives in fragile states,
22, 30
public relations issues, 54, 223
public support and involvement. See also
local-level community involvement;
ownership, encouraging
community-driven processes, importance
of, 9
in framework for assessing LICUS
initiatives, 52
stakeholder or user committees, 21
stakeholder participation, 16–17, 32,
50, 54

Q

quasi-statehood, concept of, 37, 40–41,
55n1

R

racial groups and horizontal inequality,
50–51
relief vs. development, 25–26, 41–42
replication. See scaling up
research/literature review, 38, 42–46
resource constraints in LICUS, dealing
with, 42, 53
Afghanistan, Mazar-e-Sharif community
fora (CF) process, 216–20
in TSP (Timor-Leste, Transition Support
Program), 76
results or outcomes. See outcomes or
results
Reynolds, Samantha, 203–4, 212, 216,
220, 221–22
Russian invasion of Afghanistan, 200–01,
230

S

sanitation and water projects
Afghanistan, Mazar-e-Sharif community
fora (CF) process, 209–10b
Mozambique, Decentralized
District Planning and Finance
Program, 184
scale of approach, 10–11
scaling up or replication, xv, 18–19, 44
of Afghanistan, Mazar-e-Sharif
community fora (CF) process to
other cities, 210–11, 212f
of Mozambique DDS (Direct Support
to Schools Program) across country,
159–60
of Mozambique, Decentralized District
Planning and Finance Program to
other districts and provinces, 190–91,
190t, 193n3, 193n5
of NUSAF (Northern Uganda Social
Action Fund), 282
of TSP (Timor-Leste, Transition
Support Program) to other
LICUS, 81–82
security
as major LICUS problem, 40
in Timor Leste
current situation, 79–80, 141
TSP (Transition Support Program)
police force initiative, 71
Seila program. See Cambodia,
CARERE/Seila Program

ECO-AUDIT
Environmental Benefits Statement

The World Bank is committed to preserving endangered forests and natural resources. The Office of the Publisher has chosen to print *Aid That Works* on 30% post-consumer chlorine-free recycled fiber paper in accordance with the recommended standards for paper usage set by the Green Press Initiative— a nonprofit program supporting publishers in using fiber that is not sourced from endangered forests. For more information, visit www.greenpressinitiative.org.

Saved:
- 10 trees
- 489 lbs. of solid waste
- 3,806 gallons of water
- 917 lbs. of net greenhouse gases
- 7 million BTUs of total energy

green
press
INITIATIVE